To Jerry
Best Wishes
3/9/13

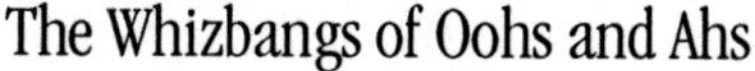

The Whizbangs of Oohs and Ahs

The Whizbangs of Oohs and Ahs

America's Salesmen: Their Lore, Lives and Laughs

RONALD SOLBERG

The Whizbangs of Oohs and Ahs: America's Salesmen: Their Lore, Lives, and Laughs
by Ronald Solberg

SEABOARD PRESS

is an imprint of JAMES A. ROCK & CO., PUBLISHERS

Address comments and inquiries to:
SEABOARD PRESS
9710 Traville Gateway Drive, #305
Rockville, MD 20850

E-mail:
jrock@rockpublishing.com lrock@rockpublishing.com
Internet URL: www.rockpublishing.com

Trade Paperback ISBN: 978-1-59663-545-6

Library of Congress Control Number: 2007927321

Printed in the United States of America

First Edition: 2008

To my father

the Fuller Brush Man

who epitomizes the legions of incorrigibly honest

and persevering men and women who,

since the beginning, traveled our trails,

paths, sidewalks, roads, and

airwaves, promoting their

ideas and selling

their wares

ACKNOWLEDGMENTS

Support thoughtfully given ... thankfully received.

I gratefully acknowledge the assistance of the Newberry Library staff and specifically Tobias Higbie, former Director of the Newberry Library's Dr. William M. Scholl Center for Family and Community History, for their support as I began my research. It was through their encouragement and on-going guidance that made this work possible. Additionally, the archives of the Chicago History Museum, Washington D.C.'s Library of Congress and the Smithsonian and their reference staffs have also proven invaluable. The Johnny Appleseed Museum at the University of Urbana in Urbana, OH, provided a wealth of information on the "real" story behind the "Appleseed Legend" and the museum's director, Joe Besecker, was especially helpful. A visit to the Weems-Botts Museum and home in Dumfries, VA, provided some very important background on early book salesman Parson Weems. (Benjamin Botts was an early lawyer who later owned the Weems home and successfully defended early American political figure Aaron Burr against treason charges in 1807.)

My wife and I visited northernwestern Alabama's Winston County to retrace the steps of late 19th century Bible salesman, A.M. Jones, the central character of my play in Chapter 7. Our Oden House Bed & Breakfast hosts (Hartselle, AL), Ann and Ray Hill, were wonderful and gracious guides, pointing us in the right directions, referring us to local historian David Burleson and to important sites. Double Springs historian Darryal Jackson was especially generous with his information and time, taking us on a tour of the County. Assistant to the Director of the Cullman County Museum, Ms. Gay Voss, provided us with some insight as to the political and cultural subtleties of past and current Alabama. Fred and Mike Wise's Crooked Creek Civil War Museum & Park was a real delight and a source of pictures of reconstructed rural residences of the 1890s.

My Science and Arts Academy parents and students have been very helpful in unexpected ways. Because I shared the fact with many of them that I was writing this book, several have come forward with information and picture opportunities. For example, student Katie Oosterbaan recalled, from a classroom reading assignment, that a reference to Winston County, AL appears in Harper Lee's *To Kill a Mockingbird.* This was important information as it helped me connect the dots as to the significance of Winston County as the home of Looney's Tavern and the local movement against secession. Additionally, parent (and voracious reader) Paul Sabaj has referred me to many a book that expanded my bibliography significantly. What wonderful exchanges we have had, both before and after school, discussing America's salesmen. Another parent, Jolana Kakavas, graciously shared some items from her personal antique collection of traveling salesman sample miniatures that would become subjects of pictures for this book.

Student Atul Kumar alerted me to the fact that Wrigley's chewing gum was the first product to use the bar code on its packaging (http:inventors.about.com/inventors). Furthermore, parent Dawn Werner shared with me the fact that she remembers, while growing up in Indiana's LaPorte County, "Going to the Scholl's Dairy for ice cream as a kid during the 1960s." Dr. Scholl was born in 1882 on his family's dairy farm near LaPorte.

A travelogue news spot that I just happened upon, while listening to a local "all-news" radio station, alerted me to "the town that patent medicine built," Marshall, MI, a community located just a couple hundred miles from Chicago. My wife and I decided to visit this historical and picturesque community where turn-of-the century patent medicine salesmen plied their wares. We are very appreciative to our hosts at the National House Inn, Michigan's oldest bed and breakfast, who shared with us information about the community .

Finally, thanks and appreciation to my wife Norma, who also happens to be a librarian extraordinaire (and proofreader/editor), and who has been of inestimable help throughout; to my father, the Fuller Brushman (and teacher) who, early on, showed me the way; to my sons Barry and Jerry, both salesmen, who personify the modern-day salesman *par excellence*; and to my mother, who was never officially a salesman, but who personified the considerable optimism inherent in that calling.

Contents

Illustrations and Photos

Prior to his Fuller Brush days, the author's father began his traveling salesman career selling this "canning and preserving" hardware (Photo by Ronald Solberg from his personal collection), page xvi.

Early 20th century country peddler makes his rounds in Woodstock, VT (Farm Security Administration, Office of War Information Photography Collection, Library of Congress, Washington, DC), page xviii.

1868 *Harper's Weekly* engraving of the peddler and, his wagon (*Harper's Weekly*, v. 12., no. 599, 1868 June 20, p. 393, Library of Congress Prints and Photographs Division, Washington, DC), page xxi.

An 1884 composite cartoon by W.H. McDougal of humorous scenes of a traveling salesman (Library of Congress Prints and Photographs Division, Washington, DC), page xxii

Looney's Tavern (Photo by Ronald Solberg), page xxv.

1870 Currier & Ives print as the "local" serenades the Arkansas Traveler (Library of Congress Prints and Photographs Division, Washington, DC), page 3.

Barbed wire fences make good clotheslines in Taos County, NM (Farm Security Administration, Office of War Information Photograph Collection, Library of Congress, Washington, DC), page 4.

1895 advertising print shows the "Home for indigent traveling salesmen of the U.S. ..." (Library of Congress Prints and Photographs Division, Washington, DC), page 7.

Poster of George H. Jessop minor comedy-drama, *Sam'L of Posen The Commercial Drummer* (The National Museum of American History, Smithsonian Institution, Washington, D.C.), page 10.

"Carry the 'Ideal' Waterman pen," 1919 French poster (Library of Congress Prints and Photographs Division, Washington, DC), page 12.

Waterman Fountain Pen ad, *c.* 1900's, page 13.

Fuller Brush products, (Photo by Ronald Solberg), page 14.

1884 poster of Louden & Co.'s "Indian Expectorant" (Library of Congress Prints and Photographs Division, Washington, DC), page 20.

Marshall, MI building showing Brooks Rupture Appliances (Photo by Ronald Solberg.), page 24.

"Medicine show," 1935, Huntingdon, TN (United States, Office of War Information, Overseas Picture Division, Washington Division, 1944. Library of Congress Prints and Photographs Division, Washington, DC), page 27.

Earl Mitchell created the MoonPie® in 1917 (Photo by Ronald Solberg), page 28.

1898 poster of mountebank and his acrobats (Library of Congress Prints and Photographs Division, Washington, DC), page 30.

Dr. Henry Sharpsteen produced the very popular "Vegetable Hindoo Oil" (Photo by Ronald Solberg), page 32.

Miniature replica of the 1918-1924 John Deere Waterloo Boy tractor (Photo by author of miniature on display at the National Farm Toy Museum, Dyersville, IA), page 36.

Miniature replica of late 19th century woodburning stove (Miniature from Jolana Kakavas antique collection), page 37.

Subscription books: Mark Twain's 1871 *Roughing It* (Canvassing book from Carol Doty Collection, Photo by Ronald Solberg), page 40.

"Traditional" 19th century Yankee peddler (Library of Congress Prints and Photographs Division, Washington, DC), page 45.

Santa Anna introduced chicle to America which was later used by Thomas Adams as a critical ingredient for his "chicklets" chewing gum (Library of Congress Prints and Photographs Division, Washington, DC), page 48.

Benedict Arnold, peddler of wool coats and caps (Library of Congress Prints and Photographs Division, Washington, DC), page 50.

P.T. Barnum (Library of Congress Prints and Photographs Division, Washington, DC), page 51.

General Motors founder William C. Durant (Library of Congress Prints and Photographs Division, George Grantham Bain Collection), page 59

Thomas Gallaudet, founder of first permanent U.S. school for deaf children (The Brady-Handy Photography Collection, Library of Congress), page 62.

1911 funeral of John Warne Gates, founder of Texaco (Library of Congress Prints and Photographs Division, George Grantham Bain Collection), page 63.

King Camp Gillette early razor model (Photo by Ronald Solberg from his personal collection), page 64.

Collis Huntington made a fortune in the hardware business (Library of Congress Prints and Photographs Division, Washington, DC), page 70.

John Chapman/Johnny Appleseed on the cover of a Classics "comic book" (The Johnny Appleseed Museum, Urbana, OH), page 72.

1940's auctioneer in Derby, CT (U.S. office of War Information, Overseas Picture Division. Library of Congress Prints and Photographs Division, Washington, DC), page 73.

Raymond Kroc's first McDonald's Hamburger Stand (1955) in Des Plaines, IL (Photo by Ronald Solberg), page 76.

Bascom Lunsford and two musicians who were visiting his Mountain Music Festival, Ashville, NC (Lomax collection, Library of Congress Prints and Photographs Division, Washington, DC), page 77.

Cereal magnate C.W. Post is buried at the Battle Creek, MI Oak Hill Cemetery (Photo by Ronald Solberg), page 83.

Foreword

Traveling salesman. So many different images readily come to my mind with those two words: a peddler with a sack slung over his back; a wry teller of tales with a farmer-city slicker story; a door-to-door salesman with a vacuum cleaner under his arm; a patent-medicine huckster with a wagon filled with ointments and elixirs; and my father dressed in a suit, white shirt and tie, carrying a sample case.

Remembering those Fuller Brush days

My personal journey into the world of the traveling salesman started in the late 1950's when I began selling Fuller Brushes door-to-door for my father. During summers between college semesters, I took my brushes on the road to small communities and farms in southern Minnesota. It was hard, but lucrative work—frequently discouraging, at other times, exhilarating. When my sales were down, Father, who was then a field manager for the Fuller Brush Company, would accompany me on my rounds. He would deftly demonstrate his method of making quick sales without lingering too long with any particular customer. It was the same thing he would do for the other more than a dozen men, for whom he was responsible.

Father and Fuller Brushes offered a simple formula for success that proscribed a specific number of contacts an hour. The contact number was less for farms than in-town customers for the obvious reason that it took longer to get from one location to another. Typically, farmers also gave the salesman larger orders. The big sales goal for the day was $100 dollars-worth of products, which included everything from brushes to cosmetics, bug spray and floor wax.

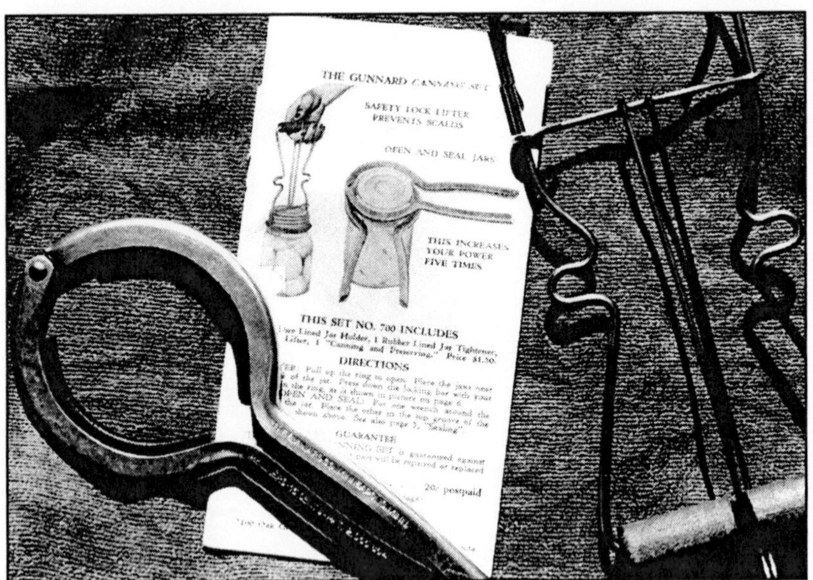

Prior to his Fuller Brush days, the author's father began his traveling salesman career selling this "canning and preserving" hardware door to door in the early 1940s. (Photo by Ronald Solberg)

Movin' on

The days of selling brushes door-to-door are long past, both for me and for the business. I moved on to teaching and then into public relations and advertising and then back to teaching. Along the way I was introduced to some of the finest and most successful salespeople in the world when I served as communications director for the Million Dollar Round Table. MDRT is an international association of salespeople who qualify for membership by selling an annual minimum volume (now much more than a "million"-dollar's-worth) of life insurance.

Coincidentally, Father reversed the process by moving from teaching to Fuller Brushes, and never looked back. Initially he, too, sold brushes during the summer months. He soon discovered that he was making more money selling brushes door-to-door in three months than he did teaching high school science in nine months. Though, in a way, he did return to teaching and education in his later years. Retiring from the brush business, Father sold classroom maps to

Arizona teachers for the Cram Map Company for several years. Fuller Brushes are still sold today, but by individual entrepreneurs and most frequently through the Internet and flea markets.

I would eventually return to Fuller Brushes and sales in quite a different way. As a history teacher I was awarded a grant by Chicago's Newberry Library to research and write lesson plans on some aspect of the turn-of-the 20th century labor activity or on the work of the "common person." Too often, it is felt, that we teach history "top-down." We tell our students about leaders, wars, and the big events but neglect the contributions and activities of the average worker and lay person.

It's all in the family

While choosing my topic, I recalled my days as a salesman. Moving forward to the current day I realized that one of my sons is doing quite well as a traveling salesman and representative for a point-of-purchase display firm. My other son is also in sales, as he is a representative for a major financial and insurance company. Seven decades of salesmen—all in one family. But, then, that probably isn't all that unusual, as I would soon discover. For these reasons and because Chicago and Illinois have historically been the centers of American retail and merchandising activity, I ultimately chose the "traveling salesman" as my research and lesson-plan topic. And what a fascinating "travel" adventure it came to be!

As I was spending hours looking through dusty tomes, I was mentioning my research work to others. Invariably, people would respond with stories about salesmen they knew or they, themselves, had been. Mother told me about peddlers that used to stop by her parents' early 1900's farm, selling fruit, vegetables, and other items. A public relations acquaintance told me about his son's very successful sales experience. A high school student volunteered that his Jewish grandfather was an early clothing salesman in Chicago. Another friend suggested that cash register, copier and calculator salesmen were very important and influential trend-setting contributors to business activity. Most recently, a *Chicago Tribune* story headlined "A Return of the Salesman," reporting that "office suppliers are revisiting the notion of direct sales and putting troops on the streets."[1] In yet another story, a local candidate campaigning for a senatorial post was touting his early experience as a Fuller Brush Man, expecting, I suppose, that this would demonstrate that he was accustomed to working hard and that he had risen from humble beginnings.

An indefatigable role in delivering product and service

This lesson-plan project evolved into something much more as I was finalizing my hypothesis about salesmen, past and present—commercial traveler, peddler, packman, chapman, monger, drummer, vendor, snake oil huckster, patent medicine hawker, colporteur. I concluded that the traveling salesman has been given little credit, and, in fact, frequently defamed and derided for his/her contributions to our society. Through distortions and visualizations in jokes, cartoons, movies, plays, and books, the traveling salesman has been demeaned and his substantial optimism and indefatigable role in delivering product and service to the population has been all but overlooked and discounted. (Though, the ultimate irony is that the salesmen frequently told these degrading jokes about themselves.)

An early 20th century country peddler makes his rounds selling hardware and groceries in Woodstock, VT. (Library of Congress)

The traveling salesman has, in fact, been very much responsible for developing the modes of persuasion that we now associate with modern merchandising, marketing, public relations, and advertising. In addition, because the traveling salesman has had to be ever responsive to the changing needs of his customers, he has been instrumental in creating and developing new products and services to meet those needs.

Truman Moore in his 1972 book *The Traveling Man* writes, "The traveling salesman has often been called a civilizing influence because he carried the latest products and newest inventions to the far reaches of the world. The benefits to civilization from tinware may not have been great, but in the hands of the peddlers, tinware appeared on the tables of the remotest cabin, and no trail was left untrod."[2]

Triumph of the everywhere community

Timothy Spears, in a 1995 doctoral work that eventually became his well-documented book *100 Years on the Road,* wrote, "By examining the traveling salesman's role in American culture between the 1830s and the 1930s, I argue that the triumph of the everywhere community cannot be understood without knowing the history of face-to-face commercial relations. The great irony of the story I tell—an historian's version of 'the death of the salesman'—is that commercial travelers paved the way for a modern mass market only to see their own relative economic importance decline." And Spears adds, " … the salesman always had to contend with his diminished value in the eyes of society. Indeed it is this sense of struggle, illuminated in texts by and about salesmen, that accounts for the traveling salesman's special status in American cultural history."[3]

In late 2004 Walter A. Friedman masterfully chronicled the evolution of America's sales techniques over the years in his book *Birth of a Salesman.* Though Spears, Moore, and more recently Friedman, are crediting salesmen through the ages for their significant contributions to society, very few other historians give much mention, if any mention is given at all, to the tens of thousands, more certainly, millions, who have worked the ways and byways of this and other countries.

America's earliest traveling salesmen

The earliest traveling salesmen in America were 18th and 19th century peddlers, mostly from New England, Connecticut especially. There were the general peddlers who sold a variety of "Yankee notions"—pins, needles, hooks and eyes, scissors, razors, combs, coat and vest buttons, spoons, small hardware, children's books, cotton goods, lace and perfume. However, there were also the specialized itinerant dealers—tin peddler, clock peddler, chair-peddler, peddlers of spices, essences, dyes, woodenware, pottery, brooms, books and many other items.[4]

It is interesting to note that peddlers were quite rare in Europe because craft guilds provided local artisans with monopolies in their territories. No such monopolies existed in America as there was a shortage of craftsman in the new world and, therefore, few guilds outside of the major towns.[5] On the other hand, A commercial traveler was far more common in England as he was regularly sent out to represent a manufacturer's line of products to various retail establishments.[6]

Some are less than reputable

There were a number of scoundrels mixed in with the hard-working and honest troops of salesmen who have populated America. As one of these, William Avery Rockefeller, 19th century salesman and father of oil baron John D., comes to mind. He is quoted as saying: "I cheat my sons every chance I get" in order to "make 'em sharp."[7]

In fact, America's "Yankee Peddlers," wrote a British observer in 1833 "are proverbial for dishonesty. They go forth annually in the thousands to lie, cog, cheat, swindle, in short to get possession of their neighbor's property ..."[8] Frankly, this characterization isn't entirely fair. Other stories and anecdotes tend to portray him a bit differently, making him a kind of prankster, similar to two legendary figures: the European Til Eulenspiegel and the South's Sut Lovingood. They were clever tricksters who were just "getting even," rather than deliberately cheating the customer. In some instances, the customer would actually challenge the "Yankee" to pull a fast one.

As depicted by this 1868 Harper's Weekly *engraving, the peddler and his wagon were a moveable feast of commodities for America's pioneer families.*

At the other extreme from Rockefeller we find John Chapman, better known as the legendary Johnny Appleseed, who crisscrossed the land, selling and planting his apple trees. Somewhere, in between, there's the fictional Professor Harold Hill, of *Music Man* fame. The "Professor" is part cheat and part do-gooder as he successfully sells a small town on starting up a boys band and in the process, though unintentionally, generates a new community spirit and pride.

Who are these "whizbangs of oohs and ahs?"

As I was researching and writing I came to understand that I was revealing something that I had believed for many years about the traveling salesman but hadn't consciously acknowledged or articulated—that America's spirit of industry and optimism may be best exemplified, and, yes, perhaps even engendered by its traveling salesman. Contrary to such renderings of the "traveling man" as the classic tragic figure by Arthur Miller in his play *Death of a Salesman*, I began to understand that there was much more to our salesman. Thus, our *Whizbangs of Oohs and Ahs*.

A DRUMMER'S EXPERIENCE IN A COUNTRY VILLAGE.

An 1884 composite cartoon by W.H. McDougal of humorous scenes of a traveling salesman in a country village: his arrival; sleeping in a crude hotel; bad manners at a boarding-house breakfast; political discussion in a barber shop; and finally, leaving town without paying his bill. (Library of Congress)

Why "Whizbangs?" My initial idea was to call this "work" the "Wizards of Ahs." An early salesman and marketing innovator whom we all know for something other than his salesmanship—L. Frank Baum—was the author of *The Wizard of Oz.* To my dismay I discovered that others were using "The Wizard of Ahs" for such things as names for their performance companies and theaters.

Further research revealed that Chicago's Marshall Field used the word "whizbangs" to refer to his late 19th century salesmen, "who like the drummers of an earlier time, knew all the jokes and sayings of the day—and could sell thousands of handkerchiefs in a two-day stay in Detroit or hundreds in a few hours in a Nebraska town."[9]

"Whizbangs" offered another couple of interesting, though admittedly, indirect, connections to the traveling salesmen. Meredith Willson in his 1957 musical *Music Man* has Professor Hill rap: "Is your son memorizing jokes out of *Captain Billy's Whiz Bang*?" as he tries to convince the town's people that they should invest in band instruments to distract their "wayward" sons. An American humor magazine by that name, featuring many salesmen jokes and anecdotes, was actually published in the early 20th century. Publisher Captain Billy Fawcett, a WWI veteran, came up with the "whiz bang" name, recalling the sound that artillery shells made as they "whizzed" through the air and "banged" into the ground.

Whizbangs' form follows function

What form should *Whizbangs* take? A series of lesson plans? A chronological study? A personal narrative? An encyclopedic listing? A novel? A play? An article? As I soon discovered, there was too much here for any one format. A personal narrative wouldn't do justice to the broader topic I was addressing. A play provided an interesting possibility. I did, in fact, write a play—*The Quaint Characters of A.M. Jones, Colporteur*—of several scenes based on the real-life journal of a late 19th century Alabama Bible salesman. The play is included as a chapter in *Whizbangs*. However, there is much more here that needed to be divided into categories that could be read in periodic sips and swallows, rather than devoured in long gulps. Therefore, *Whizbangs* has taken the form of a kind of almanac, interspersed with articles that describe the important characters (real and imagined), terms, advice, trends, organizations, achievements and accomplishments from salesman origins on into modern and future face-to-face sales forms.

Retracing a salesman's steps

One could easily represent any one of our most notable and successful salesmen as the "ultimate storied traveler" — one who told stories and about one whom stories were told. After all, the early traveling salesmen, filled with stories, were looked eagerly upon as spreaders of fact and fancy about themselves and others as they crisscrossed the land. Nowhere is that better exemplified than in the travels and tales surrounding salesmen like Mason "Parson" Weems, Johnny "Appleseed" Chapman and in the person of Bible salesman A.M. Jones. I was especially taken by one of Jones' stories — the fanciful "Looney's Tavern." The story was most unusual because nearly all of the other Jones' stories come across as factual renderings of what Jones was seeing and doing. But, Looney's Tavern? A tree becoming known as a tavern because one hunter Bill Looney climbed up into its branches to avoid a couple of panthers? His alibi to his wife the next day for staying out the night was that he was with the guys at the tavern. Yeh, right! That Jones took pains to spend an entire chapter of his journal on this tree as tavern is a mystery when the real truth about Looney and his tavern is stranger (and more interesting) than the fiction.

My wife and I traveled to northern Alabama to track down A.M. and his trail to see what he had witnessed more than 100 years earlier. As we followed up on A.M.'s now-cold trail we discovered the true and unusual story behind Looney and his tavern. Bill Looney, according to a local historian, was a legend in his own time. He remained a thorn in the side of the Confederate South, a kind of rebel against the rebels, choosing to side with the Union throughout the Civil War years. Winston County, AL, where A.M. spent much of his time, is the home of the real Looney's Tavern. The Tavern was the scene where Winston County residents met to vote against secession. Later, Alabama Confederate vigilantes would take out their resentments against the citizens of Winston by plundering and burning their lands. The people of Winston were poor hill farmers who had little in common with the wealthy plantation owners and slave holders of southern Alabama. Up until a couple of years ago, the "events at Looney's Tavern" were recreated annually through a play presented in an outdoor "Looney's Tavern" amphitheater.

As a historian I found it ironic that the process was reversed with the introduction of fact into fiction with the reference of Winston

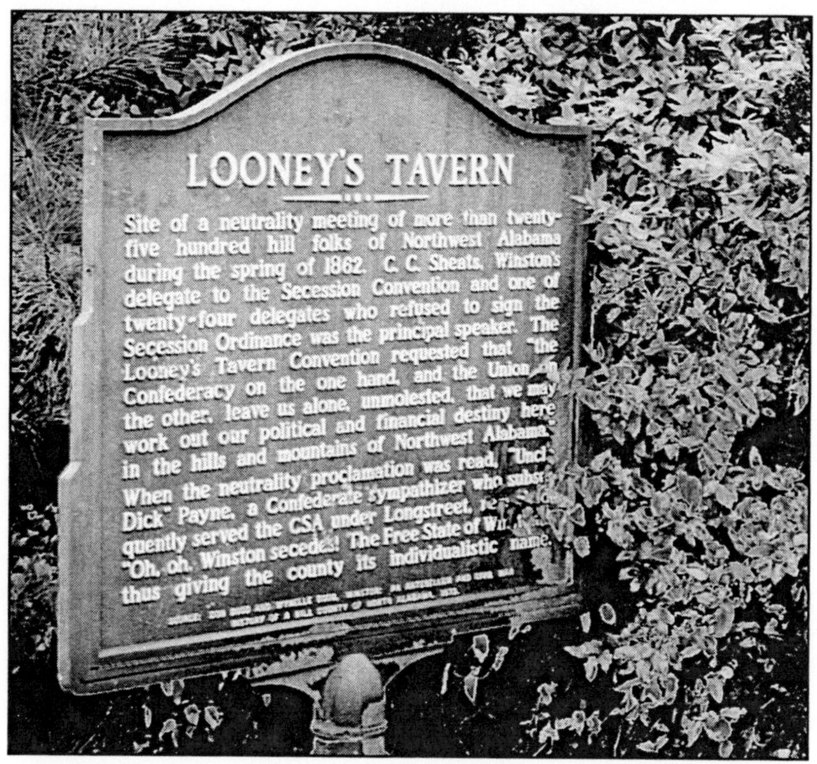

LOONEY'S TAVERN
Site of a neutrality meeting of more than twenty-
five hundred hill folks of Northwest Alabama
during the spring of 1862. C. C. Sheats, Winston's
delegate to the Secession Convention and one of
twenty-four delegates who refused to sign the
Secession Ordinance was the principal speaker. The
Looney's Tavern Convention requested that "the
Confederacy on the one hand, and the Union
the other, leave us alone, unmolested, that we may
work out our political and financial destiny here
in the hills and mountains of Northwest Alabama."
When the neutrality proclamation was read, "Uncl
Dick" Payne, a Confederate sympathizer who subs
quently served the CSA under Longstreet,
"Oh, oh, Winston secedes! The Free State of
thus giving the county its individualistic name.

There is much more to the Looney's Tavern story than what A.M. was telling us. It turns out that Bill Looney was the proprietor of the tavern where the people of Winston County voted against secession. As the historic plaque, marking the tavern's location indicates, a Confederate sympathizer present at the meeting is reported to have said, "Oh, oh, Winston secedes? The Free State of Winston!" Today, Alabamians still refer to Winston as "That Free State."

County in Harper Lee's 1960 novel *To Kill a Mockingbird.* Alabama native Lee describes a teacher Miss Caroline in the very early pages of the novel, who introduces herself to her students by telling them: "'I am from North Alabama, from Winston County.' The class murmured apprehensively, should she prove to harbor her share of the peculiarities indigenous to that region. (When Alabama seceded from the Union on January 11, 1861, Winston County seceded from Alabama, and every child in Maycomb County knew it.) North Alabama was full of Liquor Interests, Big Mules, steel companies, Republicans, professors, and other persons of no background." [10]

Are we all not knights and ladies of the road?
For all the world's our territory.
We have our exits and entrances,
Experiencing both rejection and acceptance;
And each in his time
Must joust with one
To advance to t'other.

—R.S. (with apologies to Shakespeare)

CHAPTER 1

Beginnings: Definitions and Origins

Now let's be "Getting down to brass tacks."

agent: This term is commonly used to refer to 19th and 20th century salesmen, especially the book agents and insurance and real estate salesmen. The Fuller Brush Company adopted the term for its 20th century salesmen.[1]

American Bible Society: Established in New York City in 1816, the organization employed a large sales force beginning in 1820.[2] Another notable and early Bible sales organization, the American Tract Society, was established in 1825.[3]

Spawned by English sales organizations, the societies fielded impressive forces of hundreds of colporteurs, Christian literature salesmen, who traveled the highways and byways of early America. The American Bible Society, in particular, boasts of several prominent political figures who became president of the organization. John Jay, the first Chief Justice of the U.S. Supreme Court, was elected ABS president in 1821; former New York City Mayor Richard Varick was elected president in 1828; and US. Senator Theodore Frelinghuysen was president in 1846.[4]

Furthermore, Asa Griggs Candler, who spearheaded Coca-Cola's sales activities at the turn of the 20th century with a kind of evangelical zeal, had been a vice president of the Society.[5]

Applying the book-selling techniques introduced and used by the societies, *(see also "subscription publishing")* author and humorist Mark Twain mounted a huge and very successful 1880's campaign to sell Ulysses S. Grant's memoirs.[6] A.M. Jones, late 19th century Alabama colporteur, portrayed elsewhere in *Whizbangs* in the play *A.M. Jones: Colporteur*, worked for the American Bible Society. Both societies continue their work today.

Arkansas Traveler: Traveling Salesman Sandford C. Faulkner of Little Rock, AR, is considered the first of the Arkansas Travelers, according to tradition. The story goes that in 1840 Faulkner got lost in the area's mountains. Approaching a log cabin, Faulkner met up with a squatter to ask for directions. Stubbornly ignoring Faulkner's initial questions, the squatter eventually acquiesced when the lost traveler asked to play a tune on the squatter's violin. Afterwards Faulkner was welcomed as a friend. Amiable contacts between reclusive locals and the gregarious travelers continued, following this classic "Arkansas Traveler" pattern.[7]

auction: The word "auction" comes from the Latin word "augere," meaning to increase. The Romans used the auction, as we do today, to receive bids on items, raising the respective item's price until there were no more bids. At that point, the person making the highest bid has acquired the item.[8] Vendues, "collective street sales," were an early form of the auction practiced by pre-Revolutionary-day peddlers. While goods were sold inexpensively in the vendue, (from the Latin word, *vendere*, meaning to sell) Pennsylvania's merchant peddlers were frequently passing around rum to help "lubricate the transaction."[9] *(For auction and auctioneering anecdotes, see J.P. Johnson in Chapters 2 and 5.)*

Avon Products: *(See David H. McConnell, Chapter 2)*

barbed wire: Considered an influential aid to settlement in the West, this uniquely American invention played a major role in bringing the region to agricultural pre-eminence. The product was invented by Illinois farmer Joseph Glidden in 1874. However, it was the on-

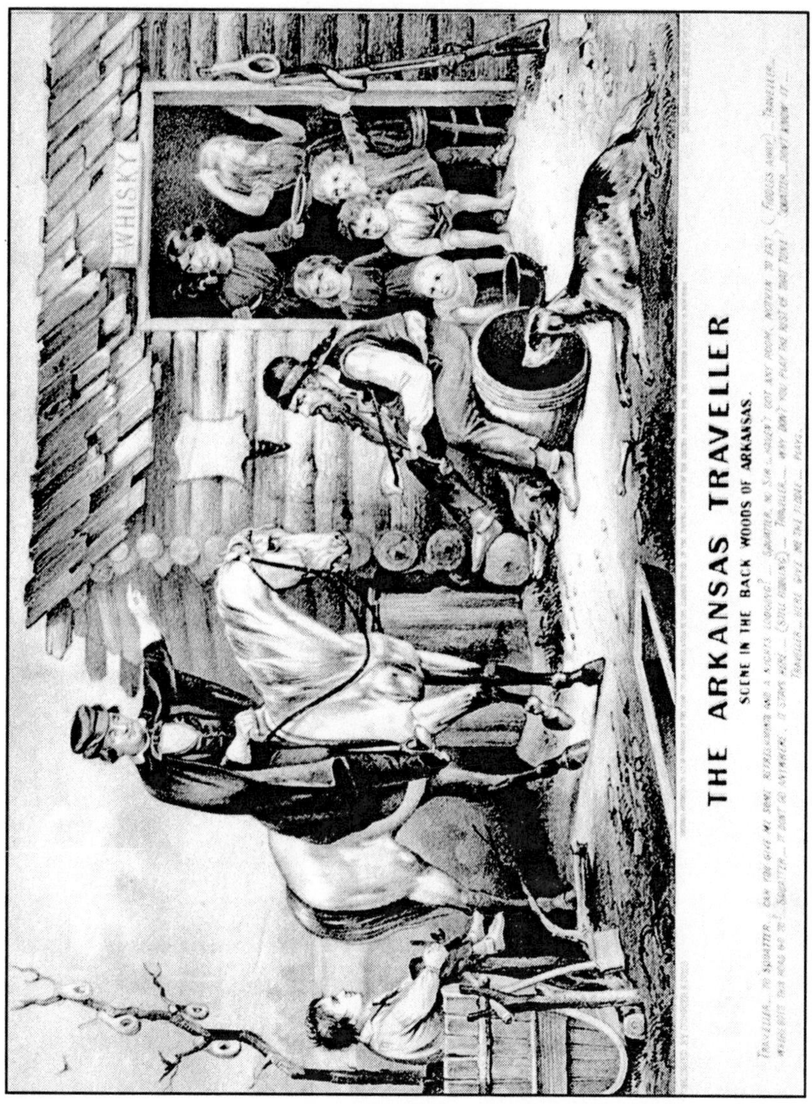

The tables are turned in this 1870 Currier & Ives print as the "local" serenades the Arkansas Traveler. However, in a companion Currier & Ives piece the traveler does serenade the family with his violin, as is the tradition. (Library of Congress)

the-road work of salesman John W. Gates *(see John Warne Gates, Chapter 2)* who arranged for an onsite demonstration of the product's usefulness that introduced barbed wire to the cattlemen of the West.[10]

Barbed wire fences make good clotheslines in Taos County, NM, according to this 1944 photograph. Barbed wire is considered one of the very important factors in making America's West suitable for settlement. (Library of Congress)

The fortunes generated by barbed wire pioneers Joseph Glidden, Isaac Ellwood, Jacob Haish (and salesman Gates) helped settle and develop DeKalb, IL, and its college, Northern Illinois University.[11]

brass tacks, getting down to: This expression probably originated with early dry-goods salesmen who used "brass tacks" set in the counter to measure off a yard of cloth. Thus, "let's get down to brass tacks" meant let's measure off your yard or two of cloth.[12]

canvasser: The word today usually refers to the solicitation of political support or opinions. In late 19th century America it was synonymous with the salesman or agent, though the role carried less prestige than that of a traveling salesman. A young 1874 canvasser decided to quit the lightning rod business in favor of becoming a commercial traveler, writing "I am going from house to house selling something that I can never sell again. I tell them good-bye and never see them again. I want a business that will enable me to sell *(and resell)* to a customer something that he will continue to use as long as he lives."[13]

catalog: The first catalogs appeared just as printing itself was getting off the ground. In 1749, England's first printer William Caxton was distributing handbills, essentially one-page catalogs, to promote his publications. Itinerant salesmen would travel the countryside posting these handbills, inviting customers to meet with the salesmen to purchase the products. However, the very first catalog, offering multiple titles that could be acquired off-site, was probably produced in 1498 by Venetian printer Aldus Manutius. English gardener William Lucas was one of the first non-printers to offer his goods through a 1667 catalog. Other European horticulturists soon followed suit. Tiffany & Company of New York was one of the first in the United States to produce a catalog. The catalog of "Useful and Fancy Articles" was published in 1846. The greatest impetus for the "Great American" catalog came with the introduction of Aaron Montgomery's mail order business in 1872. Though it would be former watch salesman Richard Sears and partner Alva Curtis Roebuck who would become synonymous with the mail order business when they introduced their catalog in 1897.[14]

chapman: An early American name for peddler, chapman is derived from the Old English word *ceapman,* "ceap" trade + "man." Coincidentally, the legendary Johnny Appleseed's given name was John Chapman.

charlatan: Actually this word has its origins with patent medicine and, more specifically, mountebank types. It can be traced to the Italian *ciarlatano*, for a "quack," but an infamous quack dentist may have helped it along the way. A.M. Latan, supposedly, was a 19th century Frenchman "who dressed in a long-robed exotic costume and often toured Paris in a magnificent dispensary car, a horn player heralding his approach. Spectators could be heard crying out '*Voila le char de Latan.*' [There is Latan's car.]" Thus, the words *le char de latan* popularized "charlatan." Though the word had been used in English since the early 17th century, undoubtedly, the Frenchman popularized its use.[15]

chewing gum *(See Thomas Adams, Chapter 2)*

colporteur The term *colporteur* is of early 16th century French origin, from *col*, "the neck," and *porter*, "to carry," and has been, historically, applied to the bearer of religious books from house to house. Even centuries before the Reformation traveling merchants carried their wares, manuscript chapters, and sometimes entire copies of the Scriptures in satchels hung around their necks or slung over their shoulders. The American Tract Society, under whose auspices the system of colportage was introduced to the American scene, was established in 1825.[16] 1880's Bible Salesman A.M Jones, who criss-crossed Alabama's 21 counties, documented his travels in a journal entitled *Quaint Characters or Colportage Sketches*. Dramatic sketches, adapted from Jones' journal, appear in the play *A.M. Jones: Colporteur* Chapter.

commercial traveller (or traveler): This agent or representative of a manufacturer, importer, or other wholesaler generates and transmits orders for goods to his employer, in quantity, by exhibiting his samples and generating sales. He was not a peddler, since he carried no goods, made no direct sales, and did business only with retailers and dealers, never with their customers.[17]

confidence man: A swindler who exploits the "confidence" of his victim. The confidence man's earliest known usage, according to Johannes Deitrich Bergmann, in his 1969 essay *The Original Confidence Man*, appeared in the July 7, 1848, *New York Herald*. The newspaper story reported the arrest of a William Thompson. "For the last few months a man has been traveling the city, known as the 'Confidence Man;' that is, he would go up to a perfect stranger in the street, and being a man of genteel appearance, would easily command an interview. Upon his interview he would say, after some little conversation, 'have you confidence in me to trust me with your watch until tomorrow?' The stranger, at this novel request, supposing him to be some old acquaintance, not at the moment recollected, allows him to take the watch, thus placing 'confidence' in the honesty of the stranger, who walks off laughing, and the other, supposing it to be a joke, allows him to do so. In this way many have been duped."

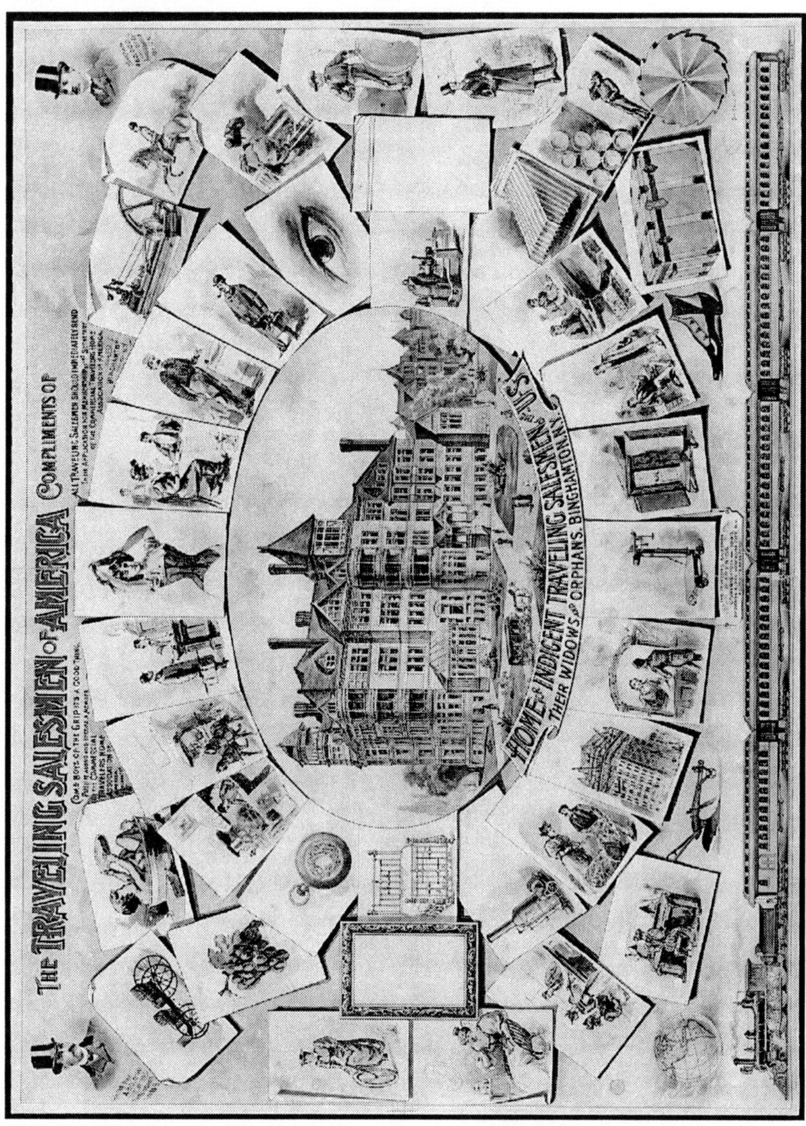

This 1895 advertising print shows the "Home for indigent traveling salesmen of the U.S., their widows and orphans, Binghamton, N.Y." to attract membership in the Commercial Travelers Home Association of America, an early professional organization for salesmen of the time. (Library of Congress)

Another popular and early reference to "The Confidence Man" appears in Herman Melville's 1857 allegorical novel, *The Confidence Man: His Masquerade*. Melville's "confidence man," a mid-nineteenth century peddler of ideas, tries to win over not-quite-so-innocent victims with his charms and false promises. Urging each to trust in the universe and even human nature, he offers healing medicines and appreciating stocks while pleading poverty. Melville's confidence man was playing a kind of metaphysical "cosmic con game."[18]

cough drops: *(See William and Andrew Smith, Chapter 2)*

credit services: *(See "dun")*

Dartnell Corporation: A Chicago-based sales management publishing firm, founded in 1917 by John Cameron Aspley, Dartnell conducts surveys of sales managers on a wide range of topics including popular convention themes and ideas about quotas. The company's main contribution is the use of statistics and other data to make the art of selling more predictable, and, thus, manageable. Today, Dartnell has teamed up with LRF Publications, expanding offerings into several areas including education, employment law, hospitality, and banking and bankruptcy.[19]

debit agents: These salesmen sold *industrial* policies, a type of life insurance made available in the late 19th century to low-income workers and their families. Primarily a low-cost burial insurance, sellers of the insurance were assigned districts, called *debits*, where they called on policyholders and collected small weekly installments of the premiums, for as little as three cents a week for insuring babies.[20]

Inspired by Britain's Prudential Company, John Dryden is credited in 1873 with "democratizing" life insurance in America by introducing the debit system and selling insurance to the poor. Dryden invested heavily in typewriters and mechanical tabulating machines to manage the massive number of "pennies" that were flowing into his company, the Prudential of America. Becoming the first commercial customer of Herman Hollerith, whose company would become the backbone of IBM, Prudential played a leading role in the evolution of information technology. By the end of the 19th century, Prudential was insuring 17 percent of the U.S. population.[21]

Dr. Scholl's Foot Products: *(See William Scholl, Chapter 2)*

drummer: Also referred to as *borers*, these peddlers sold their items wholesale to local merchants, a role that evolved in early- to mid-19th century America. *(See Henry W. Carter and Merit Welton, Chapter 2.)* The Society of Commercial Travelers said the term *drummer* came into vogue around 1854, when the business of those who traveled for commercial firms was confined to soliciting a continuance of previous orders, and making collections and new acquaintances within an extremely narrow area of trade.[22]

The traveling drummers, according to census figures, increased from 7,000 in 1870 to 60,000 in 1890.[23] However, the drummer's role and numbers declined thereafter as industries began selling goods directly to retailers and consumers. Furthermore, the rise of the mail-order houses like Montgomery Ward and Sears & Roebuck would contribute significantly to the demise of the drummer as middleman.[24]

dun: Creditors would say "Send the Dun after him" when a person was slow to pay his debts. According to an old story, the expression referred to Joe Dun, a London bailiff during the reign of Henry VIII who had proved himself particularly efficient in collecting from defrauding debtors. Some authorities trace *dun* to various words meaning din or thundering noise, sometimes connecting this with the drum that town criers pounded when they shouted out the names of debtors.[25]

Coincidentally, the word *dun* also appears in the name of an early 19th century American organization, R.G. Dun and Company, that provided credit information to subscribers. In 1933 Dun merged with Bradstreet, a former competitor. Dun & Bradstreet today is probably best known for its D-U-N-S (Dun & Bradstreet Universal Numbering System) identifiers assigned to over 2.7 million U.S. companies.[26]

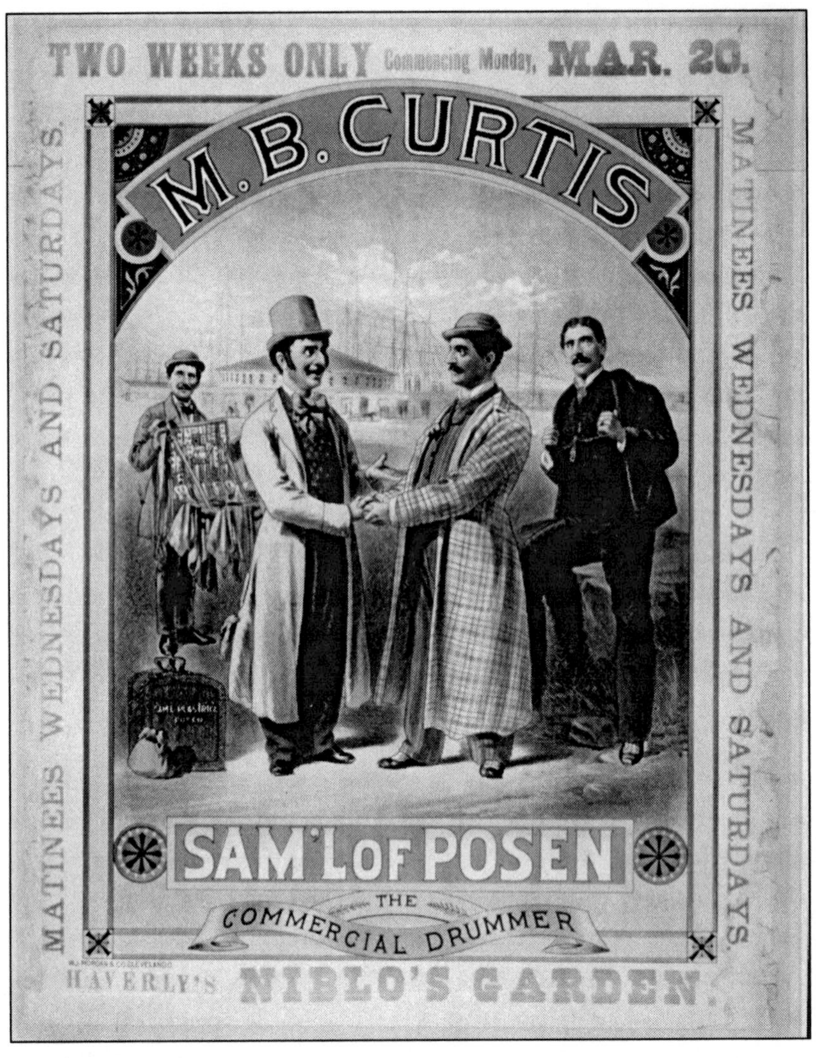

In 1881, Irish-born playwright George H. Jessop wrote this minor comedy-drama, "Sam'L of Posen The Commercial Drummer," *whose lead character is a shrewd Jewish peddler with a heart of gold. Maurice B. Curtis, an actor of note at the time, played the title role for over a dozen years, according to the Oxford University Press* American Theater Guide. *(Smithsonian Institution)*

Encyclopaedia Britannica: *(See Elkan Harrison Powell, William Benton, Chapter 2)*

first money-back guarantee: *(See J.R. Watkins, Chapter 2)*

fountain pen: This writing instrument was patented in 1884 by Insurance salesman Lewis Edison Waterman. Waterman's breakthrough was to add an air hole in the point of the pen and three grooves in the feed mechanism which provided for a smooth, even flow of the ink.[27]

Legend has it that in 1883 Waterman loaned a "new reservoir pen" to a client to sign a policy. Unfortunately, the pen didn't work and instead blotted the contract. The client, seeing this as a bad sign, declined the contract, giving it to a rival agent. In disgust, Waterman retired to his brother's upstate New York farm to design a pen that would work. The story goes that Waterman developed an ink feed which he fitted to a pen made from a wagon wheel spoke by his brother. We may never know the real details of how the first fountain pen was invented, other than the fact that an early enterprising traveling salesman was responsible for the innovation. Waterman died in 1901. Waterman pens reached a worldwide market in the 1920's with subsidiaries in Canada, France, and the U.K. Today, its Patrician model, "one of the rarest and most avidly-sought of vintage U.S. pens" can bring in $1,500 or more. U.S. Waterman, pretty much in name only, was eventually sold to the French-based company Bic in 1959 when other types of pens had gained center stage. Today, Waterman is under American ownership of the toiletries giant Gillette.

Coincidentally, another American insurance salesman would play a significant role in the development of the early fountain pen, according to Jim Gaston's "Fountain Pen Site," (http://www.jimgaston.com/parker.htm). George Safford Parker, a school teacher from Janesville, WI in 1891 formed a partnership with insurance man W.E. Palmer to manufacture Parker's own variation of the fountain pen. In 1921, Parker decided to use Chicago as a testing ground for the company's new over-sized, orange-colored Parker Duofold pen. Parker contracted with the *Chicago Tribune* to advertise its bold new pen. Supported by an innovative and aggressive newspaper advertising program, Parker sent out a force of ten traveling salesmen to demonstrate the product to retailers. This unified advertising-sales campaign was so successful that in one week the

"Carry the 'Ideal' Waterman pen, the weapon of peace" proclaims this 1919 French poster, promoting the fountain pen invented by insurance salesman Lewis Edison Waterman. (Library of Congress)

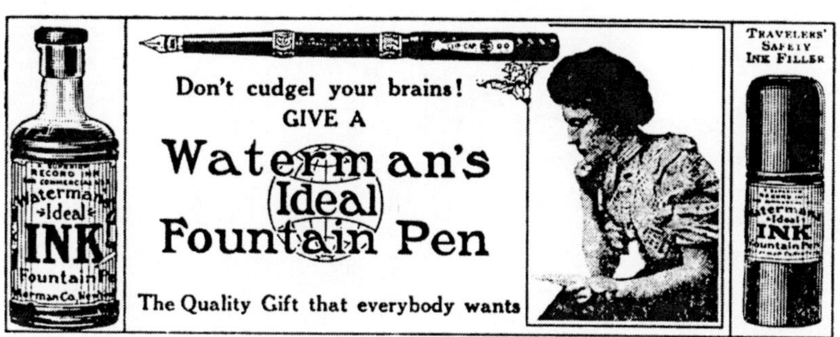

Waterman Fountain Pen ad, c. 1900's.

gross sales of the pens exceeded the gross cost of the three-month advertising campaign to which Parker had committed itself. Within four years, sales had quadrupled and, by 1926, the Duofold had made Parker the leader in the high-priced pen field. Today, Parker continues to play a prominent role in the sale of pens and mechanical pencils in over 120 countries.

free home trial: *(See Eli Terry, Chapter 2)*

Frito-Lay Potato Chips: *(See Herman Lay, Chapter 2)*

Fuller Brush Man: Alfred C. Fuller, the 1906 founder of the Fuller Brush Company, liked to quote the boosterisms "American terminates in 'I can';" and "Dough begins with 'Do,'" which he may have invented. Fuller, who built his door-to-door business into a $130 million enterprise, died in 1973, age 88. At one point his Fuller Brush Men and Fullerettes (female salesmen) called on 85 of every 100 American homes *(see "The Real-Life Death of a Salesman" in Chapter 5)*. The Fuller Brush man and woman were portrayed in such films as Disney's big bad wolf in the *Three Little Pigs* who disguises himself as a Fuller Brush Man. Red Skelton played the lead in the movie *The Fuller Brush Man (1948)* and Lucille Ball starred in *The Fuller Brush Girl (1950)*.[28]

By the early 1970s, when the Fuller Brush Company was bought out by Consolidated Foods, there were twenty-five thousand Fuller Brush persons traveling the streets and walking the sidewalks of America. Over the years it was estimated that twenty-five million *handy brushes* had been given away. Fuller Brushes and Stanley Home Prod-

In days past Fuller Brush men and women used these classic door openers, the vegetable and pastry brushes, to gain entrance into the customer's home. Today, most of Fuller's and Stanley's products are sold via the mails, Internet, and open-air markets. (Photo by Ronald Solberg)

ucts, which was a day-to-day competitor, are now sold jointly by individual entrepreneurs under the auspices of the CPAC Company.[29] *(See Stanley Home Products and Alfred C. Fuller, Chapter 2.)*

Gideons: This oldest Christian business and professional men's association in the U.S. places *Bibles* in hotel room nightstand drawers and distributes them to members of the military, hospitals, nursing homes, and to students. The Gideons was founded on July 1, 1899, by traveling salesmen John H. Nicholson, Samuel E. Hill, and William J. Knights in Janesville, WI. The hotel where Nicholson and Hill first met in 1898 in Boscobel, WI, is listed on the National Historical Register, and Room 19, where the idea of the Gideons was conceived, is marked with a special plaque. The original purpose of the Gideons, according to an early *Gideon Quarterly,* "will be to recognize the Christian traveling men of the world with cordial fellowship, to encourage one another in the *Master's* work and to improve every opportunity for the betterment of the lives of our fellow-travelers, business men and others, with whom we may come in contact; scattering the seeds all along the pathway for Christ." Today the association counts more than 130,000 members in more than 170 countries. Some properties have begun offering other religious books in their hotel rooms, such as The *Book of Mormon* in Marriott properties or Buddhist religious texts in Nikko properties.[30]

Greatest Salesman in the World, The: This novelette written by Og Mandino was originally published in 1968. The book tells the story of a man who discovers and applies the "ancient" secrets for being "the greatest salesman." *(See Og Mandino, Chapter 2.)*

grip: This term, currently out of fashion, is a traveling salesman's sample or display case. That salesmen of the past (and probably the present, as well) held strong sentiments for their "grips" is supported by the following 1889 ode:

The Drummer to his Grip

"Full many a wary mile, old Grip,
We've travelled o'er together,
Both in sunshine and the storm-
In every kind of weather.

How many hours you've waited, Grip,
alone in some hotel,
While I was selling piles of goods,
Or 'getting scooped' like—well.

I never was profane, old Grip,
You never heard me swear—
Not even when that bottle broke,
And I'd no shirt to wear.

How often you've 'held down the seat,'
you darling, dear old Grip,
When I went to the smoking car
With friends to take a sn______smoke.

I've trusted you with secrets,
Grip, in fact, you hold some now,
Which, were they known to folks at home,
Would raise an awful row.

You've kept my secrets well, old Grip,
At home and 'on the road,'
Though scores and scores of times, old friend,
You've carried a 'heavy load.'

You've seen me shed sad tears, old Grip,
When no one else was nigh,
and often tried to comfort me
With drinks of good old rye.

We've seen some hard times, too, old Grip;—
Like me, you've stood abuse;
Sometimes, like me, you've empty been,
And sometimes, 'fuller'n a goose.'

Yet, I never saw the time, Grip,
When you were really drunk,
Though oftentimes I had to 'preach'
To our old 'sample trunk.'

We're gray-haired rusty chaps, old Grip,
And don't look very fine;
The ladies never notice us,
As when we used to shine.

You know the reason too, old Grip—
They know the world we've seen;
So they 'catch on' to newer grips
And traveling men in green.

Oh, well, we've seen the time, Grip,
Whene'er we left the train,
It was to leave some gentle heart
Just fluttering with pain.

And you could tell of letters, Grip,
And faces, sweet and fair,
Which I have left, day after day
In your most sacred care.

Well, we are aged now, old Grip—
I'm forty-nine, you're seven;
Soon you'll be laid upon the shelf,
I—sailing off toward heaven.

But we will stick together, Grip,
The longest that we can,
For, next to wife, there is no friend
Like Grip to a travelling man.[31]

guides and gazetteers: Several late 19th century organizations published railway and hotel guides "translating this geography of speed and efficiency and assimilated it to the salesman's needs." One such guide, *The Pocket Companion* (1871) of the Claremont Manufacturing Company helped the commercial traveler by telling him "at a glance not only how to get to any town, but whether it will pay to go there." Brockett's *Commercial Traveller's Guide Book* provided "a kind of cultural map," identifying the best hotels and money order and express offices. It even included a list of the leading book publishers, addressing the audience's reading tastes.[32]

Another such guide, Breyfold's 1881 *The Commercial Traveler Hotel Guide and Gazetteer*, featured a key indicating hotels heated by steam, livery connected with the house, passenger elevator, sample (display) rooms, street cars pass house, and distance from depot.[33]

Today, the expression, "Recommended by Duncan Hines," is

frequently heard, referring to a quality restaurant or hotel. Duncan Hines was in fact an early 20th century traveling salesman who sold creative printing ideas. After several years on the road, Hines began publishing a list of superior eating places for friends. Receiving hundreds of requests for his "guide," Hines compiled a book *Adventures in Good Eating*. Because of his considerable success with his first book, Hines quit his job as a salesman and published a second book *Lodging for a Night*.[34]

Other guides and books soon followed. Though these guides were certainly used by traveling salesmen, they were really directed to the general traveling and vacationing public. Initially the guides were created by non-salesmen for the commercial traveler. Reversing a 50-year tradition, salesman Hines created guides for the non-salesman! *(For more about Duncan Hines, see Chapter 2.)*

hallmark: Contrary to popular belief, this word for quality didn't originate with Hallmark, the greeting card company. The official stamp of the Goldsmith's Company of London was ordered by Edward I in 1300 to mark all gold and silver to indicate their purity. The stamping was done at Goldsmith's "Hall" in London.[35] Joyce C. Hall, founder of the Kansas City-based Hallmark Company, began his foray into the card business as an 18-year-old picture-postcard peddlar.

hawker, huckster: Both words are derived from the German words *hoken, hoker* meaning to peddle. Today, the English word "huckster" tends to refer to one who produces advertisements, (perhaps a bit derogatorily), for the electronic media.

Author Richardson Wright in his 1927 book, *Hawkers & Walkers in Early America* classifies the early peddling trade into various branches—general peddlers "who hawked an assortment of useful 'Yankee notions'—pins, needles, hooks and eyes, scissors, razors, combs, buttons, etc." Wright identifies a second branch that he refers to as "specialized itinerant dealers—tin peddlers, clock peddlers, chair peddlers ... peddlers of spices, essences, dyes, pottery, brooms, books." Another branch, says Wright, was those peddlers on the canals and rivers and the wholesale itinerant merchants.

Wright makes a further distinction between peddlers who served a local clientele only and others who traveled great distances. "Trunk peddlers" were probably among this latter group, as they tended to carry their small wares in one or two oblong, tin trunks "slung on the back by a webbing harness or a leather strap."[36]

humbug: The origins of this word, meaning a fraud or hoax, are unclear. Charles Dickens popularized the word with Scrooge's "Bah, humbug" in his1843 *A Christmas Carol.* Some authorities point to the Irish expression "uim bog," meaning "soft copper," a debased money with which James II flooded England from the Dublin mint. Others suggest that because the original meaning of bug is "bogey," a "humbug" originally referred to a bug that harmlessly hums but yet frightens. The word seems to have entered the American vernacular in connection with promoters like P.T. Barnum who wrote the 1866 book, *The Humbugs of the World: An Account of Humbugs, Delusions, Impositions, Quackeries, Deceits, and Deceivers, Generally in All Ages*. Barnum was himself called "The Prince of Humbug."[37]

L. Frank Baum uses "humbug" several times in his 1900 *The Wonderful Wizard of Oz* to describe the exposed "wizard" as nothing more than a "little old man, with a bald head and a wrinkled face" who was originally a circus barker.[38]

Indian giver: This term is indirectly connected to the early selling or exchanges of products and services in that 19th century patent medicines with healing qualities were frequently portrayed as "gifts" to white people from the Indians. How those offering gifts, then taking them back, however, came to be labeled pejoratively as "Indian givers" is uncertain. Author Robert Hendrickson suggests that its origins come from the fact that traditionally "American Indians took back their gifts when they didn't get ones of equal value in return." Further, he says that the "Indian was once widely used as a synonym for bogus or false." He goes on to repudiate this characterization, however, indicating that "500 terms prefixed with 'Indian' unfairly

An 1884 poster uses the image of the Native American to fortify the curative powers of Louden & Co.'s "Indian Expectorant" for "complaints of all kinds." (Library of Congress)

impugn the Indian's honesty or intelligence."[39]

I much prefer anthropologist Lewis Hyde's more subtle explanation for the term's origins. He indicates it was a cultural misunderstanding of the words and the Indian practice of gift giving. American Indians did offer gifts, but they expected that the gifts would remain in circulation and the gifts, or their equal, would be returned. As was their way, European settlers kept the gifts, selling them or even sending them on to museums, thus taking them out of circulation. Just as the Native Americans couldn't understand the concept of the Europeans' claim to and ownership of "New World" land, they didn't understand how gifts could be taken "out of a social spiritual economy where relationships were built on reciprocity."[40]

Jewel Tea Company: *(See Frank Vernon Skiff, Chapter 2)*

Jewish peddler: This is more than just an early stereotype as 19th century Jewish Germans were forbidden to own land, limiting them to trades like peddling. A few former Jewish peddlers—Benjamin Altman, Adam Gimbel, and Meyer Guggenheim—became American tycoons.[41] *(For a brief piece on Adam Gimbel, see Chapter 2.)*

jobber: This was, and is, a wholesaler who operates on a small scale and sells only to retailers and institutions. Early in American history, they traveled primarily through the larger cities of the East Coast. Following the Civil War they began to work the interior cities—Chicago, St. Louis, Cincinnati. Newer modes of transportation and communication permitted wider distribution of goods and services.[42]

Kickapoo Joy Juice: Kickapoo, first and foremost, referenced a cheap liquor, although kickapoo undoubtedly refers back to the Algonquin Kickapoo Indian Tribe, originally resident in Pennsylvania, Ohio, and Wisconsin. Today about 800 members of the tribe live in Oklahoma. Ironically, the Kickapoo have never been known as notorious drinkers.

"Kickapoo Joy Juice" was first popularized in the 20th Century by Al Capp in his "Li'l Abner" comic strip. The term initially appeared before the Civil War in "kickapoo ranger," meaning a violent pro-slaver in Kansas. The sales connection goes back to 1881 when Dr. N. T. Oliver *(see Nevada Ned, Chapter 2, for more details)* established the Kickapoo Indian Medicine Company which was selling the patent medicine, "Kickapoo Indian Sagwa." The name "Kickapoo" was likely chosen for its "alliterative" sound.[43]

Probably made of aloes and stale beer, the "Juice" was hyped during medicine shows with the aid of half a dozen Indians and as many white performers. Author James Young describes the medicine show scene as follows:

"The show opened with the Indians sitting stoically in a half-circle, in front of a backdrop painted to reveal an Indian scene, the more realistic because of torchlight illumination. Nevada Ned, or some other 'scout' wearing long hair and buckskins, introduced the Indians one by one, briefly describing their past heroism. Five of the redskins acknowledged their introduction with a mere grunt, but the sixth delivered an impassioned oration in his native tongue. As interpreted by the scout, the tale described the dramatic origin of the remedy which had saved countless Indian lives and which was about to be offered, after great sacrifice, to the white members of the audience. When the sales pitch was finished, half the Indian and white members of the company went out among the crowd to sell, while the remaining whites played musical instruments and the Indians beat their tom-toms and broke into wild war whoops. In such a noisy atmosphere, medicine and money changed hands."[44]

knight errant: Author L. P. Brockett in his 1871 book, *The Commercial Traveller's Guide Book,* refers to England's 1780s commercial traveler as *knight errant,* "what Irving" (American author Washington Irving) "playfully calls him thirty or forty years later. Mounted on his trusty steed, and not seldom carrying cutlass, dirk, or horse-pistol to protect himself from the highwaymen who were prowling along the roads, he dismounted at the principal inn of the town, well bespattered with mud or gray with dust, and called about him with that lordly air which drivers of the mail-coach so carefully imitated some years later. His samples, few in number, were only such as could be carried in his holsters, or as we should call them saddlebags, and goods ordered were sent forward, some weeks later, by van."[45]

knockers (also knock-offs): John H. Patterson, founder of NCR, used this marketing strategy to counter the sales of competing less expensive cash register machines. NCR created look-alike copies of the competing machines, making just enough changes to avoid patent infringements. The *knockers* were then priced below that of the competition. Patterson indicated that there was no intention of selling the *knockers,* but, rather, to prevent the sale of the competitions' machines. If the prospect was not inclined to purchase NCR's other more expensive machines, then the *knocker* would be sold. This and other questionable NCR marketing practices contributed to antitrust charges against the company in 1893, 1911 and 1912. Patterson and other NCR officials were found guilty of the 1912 charges, but the charges were eventually reversed through appeal.[46] *(More about Patterson in Chapter 2.)*

life insurance: Modern life insurance probably began in 1762 when the Society for Equitable Assurance on Lives and Survivorships in London was founded. Not actively interested in selling its policies, the Society offered simple insurance, charging a large, level premium and restricted promotions to advertising and "the private enthusiasm of its members." England's Westminster Society, organized in 1792, developed the first agency selling staff. The Society paid its agents through a 5% commission on each annual premium for judging the risks presented to them for appraisal. This established a basic compensation pattern that has remained essentially unaltered through to the modern day. The first American life insurance salesman was probably Israel Whelen who in 1807 had been appointed agent of the ten-year-old Pelican Life Insurance Company of London. Life insurance sales was revolutionized in 1847 when seven mutual life insurance companies were established. Insurance products that shared surplus earnings with policyholders were now being aggressively sold person-to-person.[47] *(See Richard Martin, Chapter 2, for "first life insurance.")*

linemen: These late 19th century general and specialty salesmen, each had their own specific territories and customers. For Marshall Fields, both groups carried swatches of fabrics and materials and all manner of samples, going as far as the Pacific coast by 1890.[48]

market research study: *(See Charles Parlin, Chapter 2)*

Marshall, MI: (Founded in 1831) This Midwestern community, "the patent medicine town," should really appear in the "Personalities" (Chapter 2) section of this book. In the late 1800's and early 1900's the community boasted more than 50 different patent medicine and appliance companies with an equal number of "interesting" patent medicine personalities.[49]

Probably one of the most famous of these personalities was Verne Sharpsteen, son of patent medicine company founder Henry

Sharpsteen. With his background as a showman, comic, straight man, singer, actor, magician, and musician, Verne Sharpsteen was the right man to take the Sharpsteen show on the road. One of his more memorable presentations related to the Sharpsteen remedy, Hindoo Oil, curing everything from the common cold to tapeworms. It was the tapeworm cure, though, that caught the attention of the medicine show attendees. Sharpsteen received tapeworms from satisfied customers and displayed them in jars of formaldehyde. Each tapeworm had been measured and its length recorded on the jar's label. The record breaker was a 160-foot-long tapeworm from a Michigan farmer.[50]

Today, the community of 7,300 remains of interest because of the well-preserved and unique architecture of its historic turn-of-the-century homes and community buildings. Though there is little to remind visitors that this town was at one time a center of patent medicine activity, several of Marshall's buildings and structures (in-

The old and new reside side-by-side on this Marshall, MI, building. Though Brooks Rupture Appliances grew up along side the community's late 19th century patent medicine businesses, Brooks "appliances" were no "worthless nostrum" as they rescued many a customer from unnecessary pain. However, the Brooks family is probably better known in Marshall for its philanthropy, donating monies for the construction of the community's landmark illuminated fountain, a church that eventually became a civic center, and an airfield. (Photo by Ronald Solberg.)

cluding an impressive lighted fountain) were made possible by money made from the early medicine business.

matchbooks: The first matches, sulfur tipped splints marketed as *congreves*, were created in 1827 by English druggist John Walker. Joshua Pusey, a Philadelphia lawyer and patent attorney, is credited with creating the first "primitive" matchbook in 1889 (or according to other sources, 1892). In any case, Pusey eventually sold his invention to the Diamond Match Company. At this point, the book match might have become just another sold commodity and the millions who carry them in their pockets and purses might have had to pay for them if not for the innovations offered up by Diamond salesman Henry C. Traute. Traute suggested refinements to the matchbook, reducing the original Pusey design from a potentially explosive contrivance to a practical device for lighting. In addition, Traute insisted that the phrase "close cover before striking" be printed on the front flap.

However, it was Traute's marketing saavy that made the matchbook what it is today—a popular promotional medium. Traute got an Akron, OH, lithographer to print ads on several covers and went on the road to sell the service. He started in Milwaukee with the Pabst Brewery, receiving an order for 10 million matchbooks advertising "Blue Ribbon Beer." Next, he received an order of thirty million matchbooks from the Duke tobacco people. That was followed up by an order of one billion matchbooks from Wrigley, promoting his chewing gum. Eventually Traute's matchbook innovations took yet another turn, further popularizing the product. He envisioned that companies producing the matchbooks would sell advertising space, rather than dedicated promotional matchbooks, to various companies. This would make matchbook companies responsible for handling distribution around the country. A recent survey, according to the American Matchcover Collecting Club, shows that 98 per cent of smokers carry book matches, suggesting that as many as three people out of eight can name off-hand the advertiser on the match book in their pockets.[51]

McDonald's Corporation: *(See Raymond Kroc, Chapter 2)*

MDRT: The Million Dollar Round Table, a worldwide organization, headquartered in Park Ridge, IL, honors life insurance agents who produce a minimum volume of business. Originally, agents or salesmen needed to sell $1 million worth of business annually to qualify for the organization. Today, that volume requirement is somewhat higher to account for inflation. MDRT was established in 1927 at the Peabody Hotel in Memphis, TN, by a group of 32 salesmen, each of whom had sold at least $1 million of life insurance that year. The organization reported a 2007 membership of 35,781 in 76 countries and territories, representing 475 companies.[52] *(See Ben Feldman and Charles Ives, Chapter 2.)*

MDRT is an affiliate of the National Association of Insurance and Financial Advisors, headquartered in Falls Church, VA. Founded in 1890 as the National Association of Life Underwriters, NALU voted in 1999 to change its name to NAIFA, including financial planners in its overall membership. NAIFA represents the interests of more than 70,000 insurance and financial advisors nationwide, through its federation of over 900 state and local associations.[53]

medicine show: The medicine shows that once crisscrossed Northern America originated with the antics of Europe's mountebanks, traveling quack doctors who sold assorted notions and cures, pulled teeth, and performed magic and comedy to draw and hold a crowd. Working from small, temporary stages, mountebanks often employed assistants to help with treatments, sales pitches, and entertainment, such as singing and juggling, to attract attention.[54]

The mountebanks and traditional masked clowns and acrobats (referred to as *zanni*) who toured Italy, France, and England had counterparts in colonial America by the early eighteenth century. They became so irritating and numerous that authorities in colonies like Connecticut passed laws against the sale of "any Physick, Drugs or Medicines" by "any Mountebank." The authorities ruled that the dealing out of these medications "of unknown composition … has a practice to destroy the Health, Constitution and Lives of those who receive such Medicines." The Colony's legislature also voted to bar medicine shows themselves, declaring that such performances in-

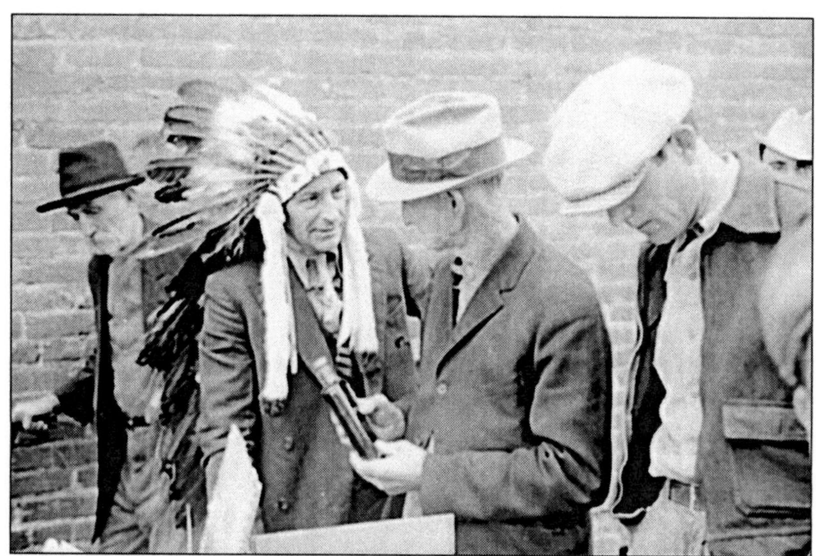

As late as 1935 this medicine show was alive and well in Huntingdon, TN. Typical of this kind of activity, white men dressed as Native Americans passed on the elixirs to customers in need of medicinal help. Despite the fact the Federal Food and Drug Act was passed in 1906 to restrict the sale of dubious cures, the "shows" were still attracting audiences and garnering sales years later. (Library of Congress)

duced "Corruption of Manners, promotion of Idleness, and the detriment of good Order and Religion."[55] *(See patent medicine, Nevada Ned, Chapter 2.)*

medicine show terms: *Al-A-Ga-Zam*, hailing sign of pitchmen; *bally act*, added attraction, like dancing girls, acrobats, or strongmen; *chopped grass*, herbal medicine; *coconuts*, money; *flea powder*, powdered herbs; *fuzz*, a policeman; *keister*, satchel that opened into a display case, mounted on a tripod; *lot lice*, show patrons who hung on without buying anything; *velvet*, profit.[56]

Merry-andrew: According to Dr. Robley Dunglison's 1844 *Dictionary of Medical Science,* the merry-andrew was an itinerant quack who offers his nostrums for sale at fairs and markets. They were named after a Dr. Andrew Boorde, who lived in the reigns of Henry VIII, Edward VI and Queen Mary, and who was in the habit of frequenting fairs and markets at which he harangued the populace.

The 1877 *W&R Chamber's Etymological English Dictionary* defined merry-andrew as "a buffoon—one who attends a mountebank or quack doctor."

monger: In the Latin dialect spoken by Roman soldiers in western Europe, *mangones* were conniving dealers or traders in anything. This word passed into English as *monger* and was used for many compound words, including fishmonger.[57]

MoonPie®: A graham cookie-marshmallow-chocolate confection created by Chattanooga Bakery salesman Earl Mitchell, Sr. in 1917 is another example of an enterprising salesman listening to the interests of his customer and creating a product in response to those interests.

Mitchell, a traveling salesman for the Chattanooga Bakery, a subsidiary of the Mountain City Flour Mill in Chattanooga, TN, while servicing his territory, visited a coal mine's company store. Inquiring of the miners what they would enjoy as a tasty snack, they indicated the need for a luncheon item that was hard and had a filling and was about "as big as that rising moon." Noting that the miners were currently enjoying a personal concoction of graham cookies dipped into marshmallow cream and hardened by the sun's rays, Mitchell returned to the bakery, requesting a similar creation—but, with one addition—chocolate.

Chattanooga salesman Earl Mitchell created the popular MoonPie® in 1917. Originally offered as a chocolate confection only, today it comes in banana, vanilla, and strawberry flavors as well.

Mitchell went back to the miners with the layered creation. The response was so enthusiastic that the MoonPie® became a regular item for the bakery and eventually the bakery's only item since it didn't have the resources to produce anything else. Today, the Chatanooga Bakery produces a wide variety of flavored MoonPies® along with related memorabilia.[58]

mountebank: Quacks frequently sold their medications at medieval fairs by mounting a bench and giving their pitches—so often that they were given the name *mountebanks*, from the Italian *montambanco*, "mount on bench;" it was also used by Shakespeare to mean a boastful pretender, as in playing the mountebank.[59]

The following is a picturesque account of an early mountebank from the 1723 *A Journey through England*:

"I cannot leave Winchester without telling you of a pleasant incident that happened there. As I was sitting at the George Inn, I saw a coach with six bay horses, a calash and four, and a chaise and four enter the inn, in a yellow livery turned up with red; four gentlemen on horseback, in blue trimmed with silver; and as yellow is the colour given by the dukes in England, I went out to see what duke it was; but there was no coronet on the coach, only a plain coat-of-arms on each with this motto, *Argento laborat Faber.*

"Upon inquiry, I found this great equipage belonged to a mountebank; and that his name being Smith, the motto was a pun upon his name. The footmen in yellow are his tumblers and trumpeters, and those in blue his *merry-andrew*, his apothecary, and spokesman. He was dressed in black velvet, and had in his coach a woman that danced on the ropes. He cures all diseases, and sells his packets for sixpence apiece. He erected stages in all the market-towns twenty miles round; and it is a prodigy how so wise a people as the English are gulled by such pickpockets. But his amusements on the stage are worth the sixpence, without the pills. In the morning he is dressed up in a fine brocade night-gown, for his chamber practice, where he gives advice, and gets large fees."[60]

multilevel marketing: This marketing strategy places emphasis on the generation of sales forces by rewarding sales people who recruit others to sell a particular line of products or services. These others, then, are encouraged to recruit still other sales persons to sell the products, who are in turn rewarded for enlisting even more sales people.

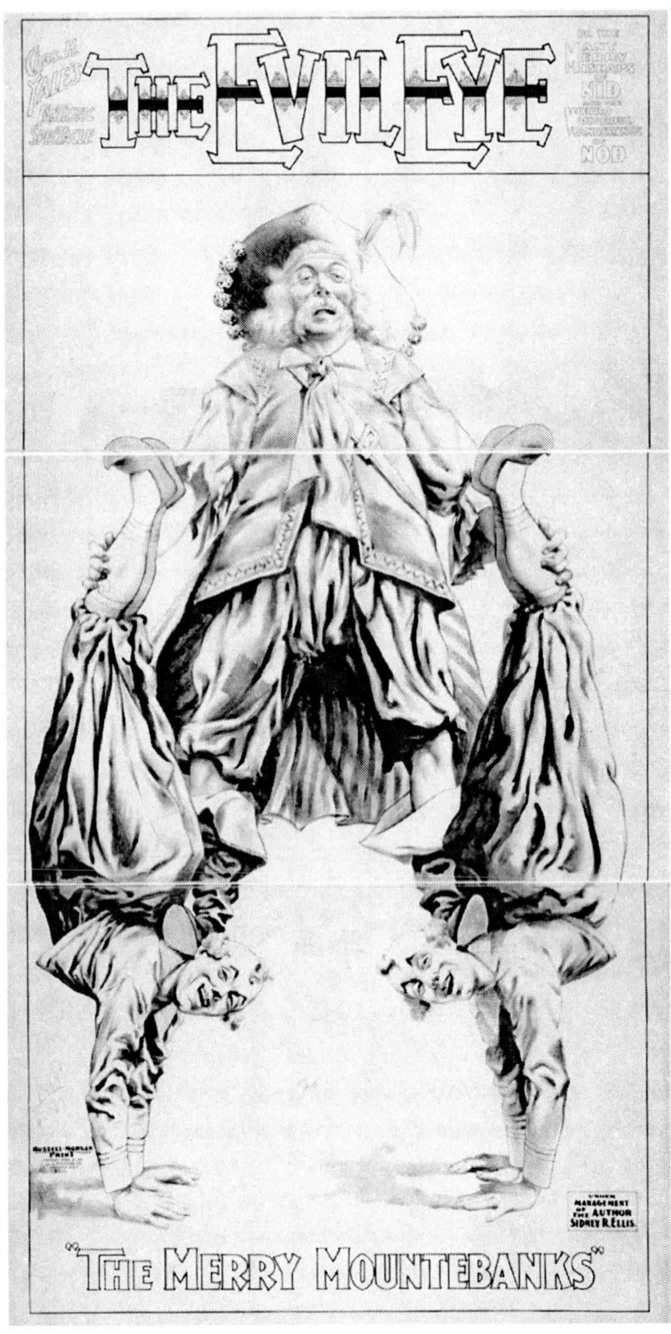

A poster's mountebank and his acrobats promote a 1898 fantastic theatrical spectacle, "The evil eye, or the many mishaps of Nid and the weird, wonderful wonderings of Nod." (Library of Congress)

The system has come under attack when organizations have emphasized the recruiting process over the sales process, thus becoming a kind of pyramid scheme, where the last to become recruited can lose out significantly. In these instances, each person recruited must make some investment in the inventory and sample items. In effect, the ever-expanding sales force becomes the real market for the products.

The Florida Attorney General cautions potential multilevel marketing participants to "find out what safeguards the company has in place to buy back unsold merchandise from you and whether you are obligated to establish a certain volume of retail sales before being able to move up the network of distribution. If the multilevel marketing plan focuses primarily on the recruitment of new members, it may be in reality an illegal pyramid scheme which should be avoided."[61]

National Association of Realtors®: Headquartered in Chicago, IL, NAR is the professional association for real estate salesmen and agents. It was originally founded as the National Association of Real Estate Exchanges on May 12, 1908 at the YMCA Auditorium in Chicago. As of Dec. 31, 2006, the Association reported a membership of 1,367,732.[62]

packman: A peddler.

patent medicine: Pennsylvanians Thomas and Sybilla Masters applied for a patent (the first ever granted to American subjects by the Crown) from the English king on a device for refining corn in 1715. However, the Masters had more in mind than pounding maize to feed their neighbors. For as their petition read, "the said Corn so refined is also an Excellent Medicine in Consumptions & other Distempers." Known as Tuscarora Rice, the Masters' ground maize holds the distinction of being America's first patent medicine. Unlike Tuscarora Rice, most American patent medicines were not actually patented, a term held over from the days when European royalty granted patents to their favorite medicine makers. Legally, *patent*

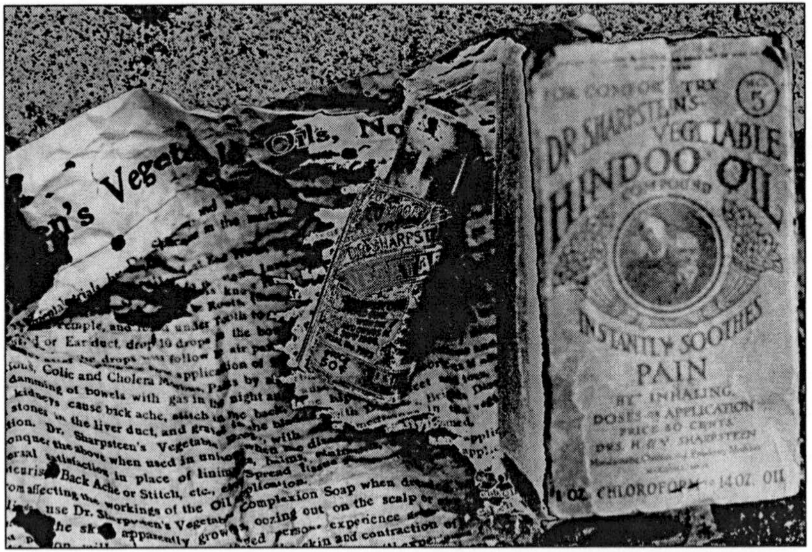

Marshall, MI, Dr. Henry Sharpsteen produced the very popular late 19th century patent medicine "Vegetable Hindoo Oil." As the flier suggests, much of Sharpsteen's "medicines" were promoted and distributed via the mails. That the "oil" contains significant amounts of chloroform (10%), does indicate that the medicine did indeed"instantly sooth pain." (Photo by Ronald Solberg)

medicines were in fact *proprietary* drugs. For the medicine men and women were far more interested in protecting, through copyright, their trademarks—the unique shapes and colors of the bottles, along with the label designs and printed matter—than their formulas. Some of the most popular medicines of the nineteenth and early twentieth centuries contained considerable alcohol, opium, and cocaine, which probably encouraged many an unsuspecting customer to continue the treatment.[63] The Federal Food and Drug Act of 1906 effectively curbed the worst of the patent-medicine trade, though enforcement by the U.S. Postal Service contributed significantly to the decline of patent medicine sales via the mails.[64]

In an 1896 *Harper's Weekly* advertisement Anheuser-Busch billed its "Malt-Nutrine" as a doctor-recommended food drink that "is a wonderful vitalizer and flesh builder—recognized and recommended as such by the medical profession in general."[65] Other well-known items of the time included Lydia E. Pinkham's Vegetable Compound,

Bliss Cough Syrup, Merchant's Gargling Oil, and Herrick's Sugar Coated Pills. In 1859, the patent-medicine business was valued at $3.5 million ($75 million by today's standards) and by 1904 it increased to more than 20 times that amount.[66]

Pearl Street: From 1820 to 1850, more than a couple hundred dry-goods jobbers and wholesale grocers along with a half-dozen hotels were located along this "long-winding way" in Lower Manhattan. The custom of drumming and the related physical display of goods to attract potential retailers likely began in the boarding houses and hotels found there.[67]

peddler (also spelled earlier, pedlar): Peddler derives from the Old English word, "ped," a pack in which articles were stored to be hawked about the streets. Historian Walter A. Friedman cites three different types of early peddlers—those who traveled independently, purchasing items for resale; those who worked for a storekeeper or independent supplier and received a salary or commission; and a third type who were hired by an organization that distributed manufacturer's or merchants' goods.[68] *(See the term "hawker" for another historian's view on the different types of the early American peddler.)*

pitch, the: Today, the pitch is often understood as a high-pressure sales talk. However, the origin of the word *pitch* was explained somewhat differently by Dr. N.T. Oliver, a 70-year-old ex-medicine-show star who published his memoirs in the *Saturday Evening Post* in 1929. Wrote Oliver: "The word 'pitch' and its derivative, 'pitchman,' come either from the pitch-pine torch under which he once worked by night, before the coming of the gasoline flame and the electric light, or from the verb, as 'to pitch a tent'."[69]

pitch's "six points": 1) Attract an audience and hold 'em.; 2) Make the product sound indispensable; 3) Repeat important points; 4) Don't be afraid to use superlatives; 5) Get the audience to react; and 6) Don't reveal the price until the end.[70] *(See also "turn.")*

ponzi scheme: A money-making scam named after the early 20th century Carlo "Charles" Ponzi who popularized it in the United States. As a variation of the pyramid scheme Ponzi encouraged people to make investments in his promissory notes, promising extraordinary short-term returns (50% in ninety days). Initially Ponzi did, in fact, return the investments at the rate promised—but he was doing so with the money that he was receiving from new investors. Eventually, it all caught-up with him (and his investors) when the money he was having to pay out exceeded the money he was receiving in new investments.

An estimated 40,000 people invested approximately fifteen million dollars (about $140 million by current standards) with Ponzi. However, his total assets came to about $1.5 million or $13.5 short of paying off his investors. Ponzi was sentenced to five years in federal prison for mail fraud. Eventually, he was freed but re-sentenced for other offenses. While out on bail he disappeared—only to reappear in Florida where he was involved in a new pyramid scheme. He was purchasing land at $16 an acre, subdividing each acre into 23 lots and selling each lot for $10, promising that the $10 investment would translate into a substantial return. Unfortunately, much of the land was under water and virtually worthless. He was again sentenced to jail and eventually deported to his native Italy in 1934.

Dictator Mussolini eventually appointed Ponzi as a Rio de Janeiro branch manager for Italy's new airline. As the Second World War brought the demise of the airline, Ponzi was forced to wander from job to job. Ponzi died in 1949 at the age of 67 in the charity ward of a Rio de Janeiro hospital with only $75 to his name—just enough money to cover the cost of his burial.[71] *(See "multilevel marketing" for cautionary note by the Florida Attorney General on the hazards of the pyramid scheme.)*

potato chip: This popular snack food was created "on the fly" by a New York State chef in response to a complaint by a "distinguished" guest. George Crum at the Moon Lake Lodge Resort in Saratoga Springs, NY, in 1853, received Cornelius Vanderbilt's complaint, indicating that Crum's fried potatoes were too thick. Crum returned a thinner deep-fried chip to Vanderbilt, much to the diner's delight. Thus, was the potato chip born, becoming known originally as the Saratoga Chip, a favorite of the resort's patrons. However, it wasn't until the 1920's that the potato chip became more than a regional curiosity. It was then that traveling salesman Herman Lay *(see Herman Lay, Chapter 2)* popularized the item to the point that the name "Lay" became synonymous with the all-American snack.[72]

quack: An abbreviation of the 16th century word *quacksalver*, it meant an ignorant charlatan who peddled nostrums and cure-all medicines in the street. The word is derived from the "quack" sound a duck makes and the "salve," a medicine or ointment. In America, quacks were called medicine men, after the Indian medicine men, as early as 1830.[73]

rebating: This is a questionable sales practice in which a salesman, especially an insurance agent, offers to share part of his commission with the prospect as an inducement to buy. A 1905 New York legislative investigation into this and other such insurance practices (interlocking directorates, creation of subsidiary financial institutions to avoid restrictions, etc.) led to them being declared illegal.[74]

samples, salesman's (miniatures): The salesman frequently carried with him scaled-down or miniaturized versions of the real-life product to assist him in making the sale. The use of the "Lilliputian" article was especially prevalent among the farm implement salesmen who sold plows, grist mills, windmills, loaders, and other heavy equipment. Many of the samples, though 1/6 to 1/8 scale, were working models. According to one collector of such samples, the salesmen would haul the highly-detailed samples from town to town and farm to farm, showing people how the piece of equipment actually worked. "It was a cost-effective way for the machinery companies to do business, instead of loading the reaper or other machine on a train and sending it around for people to see." The models were used mostly around the turn of the century up to the early 1940's. Interestingly, some samples were larger than life: a ten-penny nail two feet long and size 24 shoes. Another grouping of salesman's samples were given out as favors, promotions, or Christmas gifts, to remind a customer of a company or product. They may have come in the form of ash-trays, lighters, paper weights or even as toys. In many instances, it is difficult, if not impossible, to distinguish a sample intended to demonstrate a particular piece of machinery from a toy model.[75]

Carl Holliday in his book *Woman's Life in Colonial Days*, Dover Publications, 1999, cites a somewhat different and earlier application of the salesman miniature or sample. "There were, of course, no fashion plates in that day, nor were there any living 'models' to strut back and forth before keen-eyed customers; but fully dressed dolls were imported from France and England, and sent from town to town as examples of properly attired ladies." One of the ladies of the day is quoted as saying to a friend after seeing the dolls in her shopping expeditions: "Caroline and I went a-shopping yesterday, and 'tis a fact that the little white satin Quaker bonnets, cap-crowns, are

This miniature replica of the 1918-1924 John Deere Waterloo Boy tractor, though now considered a "toy," would have been considered a realistic replica/sample of the full-sized version, one used by early 20th century farm implement salesmen. The Water Boy, John Deere's first mass-produced tractor, had a water cooled, two cylinder engine that burned kerosene, a cheaper fuel for farmers to purchase. (National Farm Toy Museum, Dyersville, IA)

Salesman's Woodburning Stove Sample. This late 19th century cast-iron woodburning stove salesman's sample is little more than a foot high and yet resembles the real-life model in the smallest detail. All parts work – openable doors, removable stove lids and functional pots and pans. (Miniature from Jolana Kakavas' antique collection)

the most fashionable that are worn—lined with pink or blue or white—but I'll not have one, for if any of my old acquaintances should meet me in the street, they would laugh."

Seth Thomas Clocks: *(See Eli Terry, Chapter 2)*

shill: A swindler's assistant or booster, acting as a decoy, the word may have originated from the name of American humorist Benjamin Penhallow Shillaber (1814-1890) who came into some disrepute when accused of "borrowing" material from the writings of an English author.[76]

snake oil: Snake oil, or something passing for it, was taken very seriously by patrons of nineteenth century medicine shows. Any kind of snake oil lent mystery and magic to a medicine, but rattlesnake oil was especially prized, given that rattlers presumably didn't happily donate the oil. Actually, rattlesnake oil didn't come from slithering reptiles, but rather from drug laboratories. White gasoline and wintergreen oil was a popular 'snake oil' substitute.

Snake oil originally came from China where it was used to alleviate inflammation and pain in rheumatoid arthritis, bursitis and similar conditions. Chinese laborers on section gangs doing the grunt work in building the railroad track to link North America coast to coast gave it to Europeans who suffered with joint pain. When rubbed on the skin above the pain, snake oil brought relief, or so it is said.[77]

In 1989 nutrition-oriented doctor Richard Kunin from California decided to find out what snake oil, acquired from San Francisco's Chinatown, contained. His findings: 75% unidentified carrier material (probably to emulsify the snake oil and help transport it through the skin), and camphor. The remaining 25% was oil from Chinese water snakes, containing an elevated 20% EPA (Eicosapentaenoic) a polyunsaturated fatty acid and a precursor to the anti-inflammatory prostaglandin series 3. Salmon oil, the next best source of EPA, contains a maximum of only 18% EPA. Other fish oils contain less. Rattlesnake oil contains only 8.5% EPA. According to this analysis, the snake oil (the Chinese water snake variety) salesman may, after all, be vindicated.[78]

Society of Commercial Travelers: This New York-based organization as well as the Chicago-based Merchants and Commercial Travellers Association were first formed in 1869 to fight the growing number of state and community licensing laws and fees that were being enacted to protect local merchants against competition offered by the traveling salesman. These and several other such organizations eventually broadened their functions, providing insurance, social activities, and professional support and prestige to the expanding cadre of salesmen and saleswomen.[79]

S.O.S Pads: *(See Edwin W. Cox, Chapter 2)*

spiel: From the German, *spielen*, meaning to play a musical instrument, this has become an Americanism frequently used to reference "sales talk" or "line," especially from a carnival barker or salesman.[80] Author and curator Tim Samuelson in his description of a *sales pitch*, as used by TV salesman Ron Popeil, entitled his Chicago exhibit, "Isn't That Amazing: The Irresistible Appeal and *Spiel* of Ronco and Popeil."

Stanley Home Products: Founded in 1931 by Frank Stanley Beveridge and Catherine O'Brien in Westfield, MA, it was envisioned as an opportunity for people to start their own businesses with a small investment, selling products that people use everyday. This "vision" became Stanley Home Products, a direct selling company offering household cleaners, brushes, and mops. Today, Stanley is a division of The Fuller Brush Co., a CPAC company. Both companies and their products are promoted together and separately on the Internet by independent entrepreneurs.[81] *(See also "Fuller Brush Man.")*

subscription publishing: This became an accepted method of publishing and promotion in 17th century England and eventually in 19th century America. Sometimes called a "canvassing book," the sales dummy was really an elegantly bound prospectus of sample pages from a soon-to-be published book. The prospectus was placed in the hands of an agent to sell directly to the consumer. During its heyday in the late 19th century, tens of thousands of the book agents were going door-to-door across America. Many of the agents were, in fact, women *(see Harriet Wasson, Chapter 2).* Frequently the prospectus featured illustrations prominently to enhance the sale. The point of the subscription system was to sell a book before it was published. Mark Twain, in particular, sold many of his well-known books, using the subscription system. The success of his *Innocents Abroad* made him a staunch advocate of the system, saying, "Anything but subscription publications is printed for private circulation."

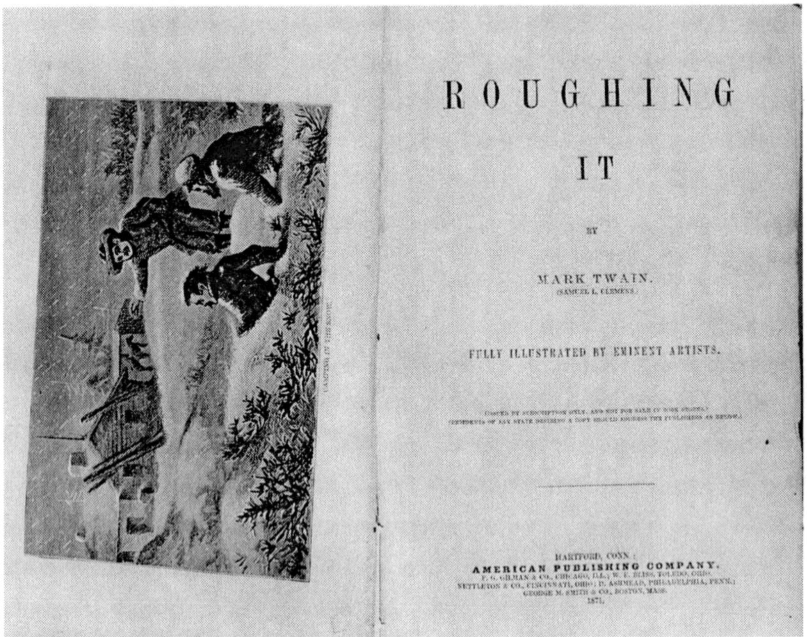

Subscription publishers promoted their books prior to publication by putting abridged samples of the book, like Mark Twain's 1871 "Roughing It," in the hands of their canvassers. Customers who wished to purchase the book would affix their signatures in a space provided at the end of the book, thus consummating the deal (and endorsing the acquisition for others). (Carol Doty Collection, photo by Ronald Solberg)

He later wrote, "When a subscription book of mine sells 60,000, I always think I know whither 50,000 of them went. They went to people who don't visit bookstores."[82]

tontine: This type of life insurance policy, popular in the late 19th century, is named after a seventeenth-century Italian banker who suggested the "scheme" to Louis XIV to raise money for the state. All who bought into a tontine policy forfeit their share of the dividends earned upon death or default. Forfeited accumulated dividends would go to the surviving policyholder(s) for an agreed-upon period or upon the death of all but one. Equitable Founder Henry B. Hyde, in particular, popularized the tontine-related insurance product, calling it "a new discovery in life insurance" and "the greatest reform thus far promulgated by any life insurance company." The tontine-style policy eventually fell in disfavor in 1905 when the government banned its sale.[83] *(See Henry B. Hyde, Chapter 2 for more details.)*

Traveling Salesman Problem (TSP): This mathematical problem that consists of establishing a "route" or tour between cities just once for the least cost (distance or time) while returning to a starting point began as a chess-board puzzle. It most likely originated with German mathematician Leonhard Euler who in 1759 investigated the problem of moving a knight to every position on a chess board once. However, the problem may have gained some of its original fame (and thus it's name) when German salesman B.F. Voigt in 1832, writing on how to be a successful traveling salesman, indicated that covering as many locations as possible without visiting any location twice is most important when scheduling a tour. 19th Century Mathematician Sir William Rowan Hamilton followed that up with the creation of the Icosian Game that requires players to complete tours through 20 points by using only the specified connections. *(Ed. note: an icosahedron is a polyhedron having 20 faces).* A growing number of mathematicians since the 1920's have recognized the important principles of the problem and its possible applications and solutions to non-salesman activity such as constructing school bus routes, drilling holes in circuit boards, optimizing a NASA imaging sequence for celestial objects when repositioning satellites, genome sequencing, and for minimizing energy when determining the most favorable disposition of atoms in a glossy material such as glass.[84]

That in 2007 Google reported more than one million "hits" in a search for TSP websites suggests the extent of the popularity and interest generated by the problem.

TSP has experienced a role reversal, it seems. Computer scientist Weixiong Zhang of Washington University has developed a TSP algorithm for electronic agents, small pieces of software that traverse the Internet seeking out information or performing tasks on behalf of people or larger computer systems.[85] Originally used by people to help human agents service their customers, TSP solutions are now being used by computers to help electronic agents service computers!

trade marks: *(See William and Andrew Smith, Chapter 2)*

turn, the: The art of revealing the price and asking for the money, after "the pitch." Six steps: 1) Break the suspense. 2) Reveal a high "suggested retail" price. 3) Suggest a "special" discounted price. 4) End with a low irregular "dollars and cents" price. 5) "But, wait, there's more!" 6) The money-back guarantee.[86]

Tuscarora Rice: Made from ground corn, America's first patent medicine. *(See also "patent medicine.")*

twisting: This is an unethical procedure by an unscrupulous insurance salesman to pressure a policyholder to switch existing policies from competing companies. The insuree is frequently induced to use accumulated cash values in his/her current policy to purchase a policy from another company.[87]

vacuum cleaner: Few products have been so linked to the traveling salesman as has the vacuum cleaner. In 1938, for example, about 70% of all vacuum cleaners were being sold door-to-door—the Hoovers, the Electrolux, the Kirbys. [88] It is probable that one of the earliest developers of the motorized (gasoline-powered!) vacuum cleaner, American John S. Thurman, was also the inspiration for the direct-to-the-customer marketing of the device. After inventing his "pneumatic carpet renovator," in 1899 Thurman went door-to-door in a horse-drawn cart providing a carpet vacuuming service in St. Louis, MO. Later, Hoover launched a national advertising campaign in the 1908 *Saturday Evening Post,* offering a free ten-day trial. Each such vacuum cleaner came with its own salesman, delivered by the local dealership, who would demonstrate the machine to the prospective customer.[89]

In more modern times, when door-to-door vacuum cleaner sales was no longer in vogue, David Oreck was taking his light-weight "commercial-grade" upright to the air-waves, where he, like Ron Popeil, traveled by television to viewers' living rooms to sell his product.

Vaseline Petroleum Jelly: *(See Robert Augustus Chesbrough, Chapter 2)*

vending machine: The term vending machine seems to have been introduced either by the Adam's Gum Company in the 1880s to describe the machine the company used to sell tutti-fruitti gumballs on New York City elevated train platforms, or at about the same time by the Fran H. Fleer Gum Company. Fleer's founder had agreed to an experiment proposed by a young vending machine salesman. The salesman argued that vending machines were so great a sales gimmick that people would actually drop a penny in them for nothing. Frank Fleer agreed to buy several machines if the young man's pitch proved true. The experiment was conducted at New York's Flatiron Building. The salesman set up a vending machine there with printed instructions to "drop a penny in the slot and listen to the wind blow." He got Fleer's order when hundreds of people contributed their pennies and continued to do so until "New York's Finest" hauled the machine away.[90]

vendor: One who vends or sells, especially such as a hawker or peddler from the Latin word *vendere,* to sell.

vendue: A public sale or auction.

whizbangs: Late 19th century term for those, who like "the drummers of an earlier time, knew all the jokes and sayings of the day—and could sell thousands of handkerchiefs in a two-day stay in Detroit or hundreds in a few hours in a Nebraska town," according to Lloyd Wendt and Harry Kogan who chronicle the creation and growth of Marshall Fields in their 1952 book, *Give the Lady What She Wants.* "They were gay, energetic, and smooth, these new drummers. They told their rollicking stories and, when they were finished, they whisked out their sales books and asked offhand, 'Now, Mr. Smith, how many dozen of these you gonna need this season, eh'?"[91]

The word "whizbang" has also been used in other ways. For example, "whizbang" referenced the sound that WWI artillery shells made as they "whizzed" through the air and exploded with a "bang." One of the other meanings of the word goes back to the 1920's and 1930's humor magazine, *Captain Billy's Whiz Bang*, "now considered the great-grandfather of the *National Lampoon* and other humor magazines."[92]

Coincidentally, *Captain Billy's Whiz Bang* is referenced in Meredith Willson's 1957 musical *Music Man* by Professor (and traveling salesman) Harold Hill: "Is your son memorizing jokes out of *Captain Billy's Whiz Bang*?" as he tries to convince the town's people that they should invest in band instruments to distract their "wayward" sons. This is actually an unintentional anachronism since *Whiz Bang* would be published later, some years after Professor Harold Hill and the *Music Man* era. *(See Meredith Willson, Chapter 6.)*

wooden nickel (don't take any): First recorded in 1915, it means don't be duped by someone offering you something of value that is virtually worthless. The expression has interesting origins with Yankee peddlers of the early 19th century who were allegedly selling wooden nutmegs, which cost manufacturers a quarter-of-a-cent apiece, mixed in with real nutmegs, worth four cents each.[93] However, an 1830 anecdote relates how "the Kentucky nation have commenced a rivalship with the Yankee land, in the manufacture of wooden eatables" when a merchant purchases what he thinks are juicy Kentucky hams "from the boats passing down the Mississippi." Instead, "the hams, when opened, proved to be wood, neatly turned in the shape of a hog's hind leg; and the Kentuckian shewed that he was 'up to a trick or two'."[94]

yankee peddler: "The whole race of Yankee Peddlers," wrote a British observer of American character in 1833, "are proverbial for dishonesty. They go forth annually in the thousands to lie, cog, cheat, swindle, in short to get possession of their neighbor's property in any manner it can be done with impunity." Though, it is undoubtedly unfair to generalize, as this Englishman did, about this early type of traveling salesman, who most certainly originated from "staid-old Boston in the late seventeenth century," carrying with him an "amazing assortment of little (but, very important) things," such as needles, pins, buttons and combs, table knives and spoons. The actual origin of the word "Yankee" is unclear but it's first usage seems to have appeared in a letter written by British General James Wolfe who was referring to the Americans contemptuously as "Yankees" during the French and Indian War of 1758. The most likely origin of the word is *Yan Kees*, a disdainful Flemish and German nickname for the Dutch that the English first applied to the Dutch in the New World.[95]

A crowd of young and old surrounds this "traditional" 19th century Yankee peddler with something for everyone. (Library of Congress)

CHAPTER 2

Personalities: "A to Z"

"Hey, who mixed chewing gum with my baking powder?"

Adams, Thomas (1818-1905)

Adams, a New York City entrepreneur and "inventor," in a chance meeting was introduced to chicle by former Mexican president Santa Anna (conqueror of Alamo) who was in exile in the United States in the 1850s. Anna suggested that it might have "industrial" applications. Adams experimented with chicle, attempting to blend it with rubber for carriage tires, but to no avail.

Eventually, he suggested to his son Tom, Jr. that chicle might make for a kind of chewing gum. Tom, Jr., who was a salesman in wholesale tailor's trimmings and traveled as far west as the Mississippi, offered to take a few boxes of the chicle-based gum out on one of his trips. They decided on the name of Adams New York No. 1. It was made of pure chicle gum without any flavor and was wrapped in little penny sticks of various colors of tissue paper. Tom, Jr. concluded that he would be unsuccessful in selling the gum through the drug trade after visiting his regular customers in the tailors' trimming business. On his next sales trip Tom, Jr. determined that he would leave it on consignment with the druggists if they would display it prominently on their counters.

GENERAL D. ANTONIO LOPEZ DE SANTA-ANNA.

Though Santa "the Alamo" Anna may be credited with introducing chicle to America, he wasn't recommending it as a chewing gum base. He was thinking more of it as an additive for carriage tires. While that didn't work out, the rest is history as Thomas Adams eventually used chicle as a critical ingredient for his "chicklets" chewing gum. (Library of Congress)

Before his return to New York, reorders for the chewing gum, totaling approximately 300 boxes, came in to his father.. This response eventually prompted Tom, Jr. to leave his job and devote full time to building up the promising chewing gum business.

The chewing gum evolved through the years as it was enhanced with the addition of some flavor by Louisville, KY, drugstore owner John Colgan in 1879. Ohio Doctor Edward E. Beeman, in the early 1880s, added pepsin powder to the gum to aid in digestion.

However, it was popcorn salesman William J. White who, at about the same time, discovered how to add the "put-and-keep-flavor" of peppermint to the gum, thus making it more attractive to the customer. His gum, eventually named "Yucatan," became a smash hit. In 1899 the leading gum manufacturers organized themselves into the American Chicle Company. William White became president and Thomas Adams, Jr., was chairman of the board of directors—both, former traveling salesmen.

Soap and baking powder salesman and Chicagoan William Wrigley, Jr. introduced modern processing, packaging, and advertising to popularize chewing gum. While his first two brands, "Lotta Gum" and "Vassar" were soon forgotten, in 1892 Wrigley introduced Wrigley's Spearmint and followed the next year by "Juicy Fruit," both of which became America's top sellers at the turn of the century. He continued to popularize his products with aggressive and creative merchandising. In 1915, Wrigley sent out free sticks of gum to the 1.5 million listed telephone subscribers. He would do so again four years later to more than seven million subscribers nationwide.[1]

Alcott, Amos Bronson (1799-1888)

Father of Louisa May (author of *Little Women*) early in life disdained entry into Yale in favor of becoming a trunk-peddler, hawking tin ware and almanacs door to door. Later he convinced his brother Chatfield to join him, making anywhere from 33 to 200 per cent profit—sufficient inducement to keep them following the road for several years, not only in the South but in New Jersey, as well.

As he made contact with various people and organizations, including a Quaker community, Alcott realized that his real interest was in education and teaching. After teaching at several schools, he was invited in 1828 to take over classes offered by the Boston Infant School Society. In 1834 Bronson started up his own school, the Temple School of Boston, using the educational philosophy of inductive reasoning and Socratic dialogue. A friend of transcendentalists Henry David Thoreau and Ralph Waldo Emerson, Alcott eventually became superintendent of schools for Concord, MA.[2]

Anderson, Sherwood (1876-1941)

This early 20th century American author of *Winesburg Ohio,* a collection of short stories, predicted in 1904: "About the best thing that can be said about the old dyed-in-the-wool, six-months-twice-a-year traveling man is that he is passing. Winds of time will sweep the old boys into the past, and there will be no new ones in their places, and that's fine." When Anderson wrote this, he was working on the "mass marketing" side of merchandising and sales.[3]

Both hero and traitor, Benedict Arnold is a duplicitous Revolutionary War historical figure who started out as a peddler of wool coats and caps, working for his father. (Library of Congress)

Arnold, Benedict (1741-1801)

Before becoming the American Revolutionary War general and eventually traitor, Arnold was a peddler of wool coats and caps.[4]

Ash, Mary Kay (1915-2001)

Founder of Mary Kay Cosmetics, one of the largest beauty product firms in the U.S. today. Mary Kay's force of 300,000 sales people worldwide has sold more than $1 billion worth of cosmetics.[5] (*See also Stanley Home Products in Chapter 1 and more about Ash, "A bumblebee who could fly," in Chapter 3.)*

Barnum, P.T. (1810-1891)

Although never officially what one might term a traveling salesman, Barnum did travel and certainly used "salesmanship" techniques, though frequently for questionable ventures—promoting "a 161-year-old black woman who 'supposedly' once nursed George Washington;" the "Fejee Mermaid," believed to be a preserved mermaid obtained from Japanese sailors; the two-foot-tall General Tom Thumb "from England;" and the not so strange, but talented singer, Jenny Lind, "the Swedish Nightingale." In 1873 he spent a fortune promoting "Barnum's Traveling World Fair, the Greatest Show on Earth."

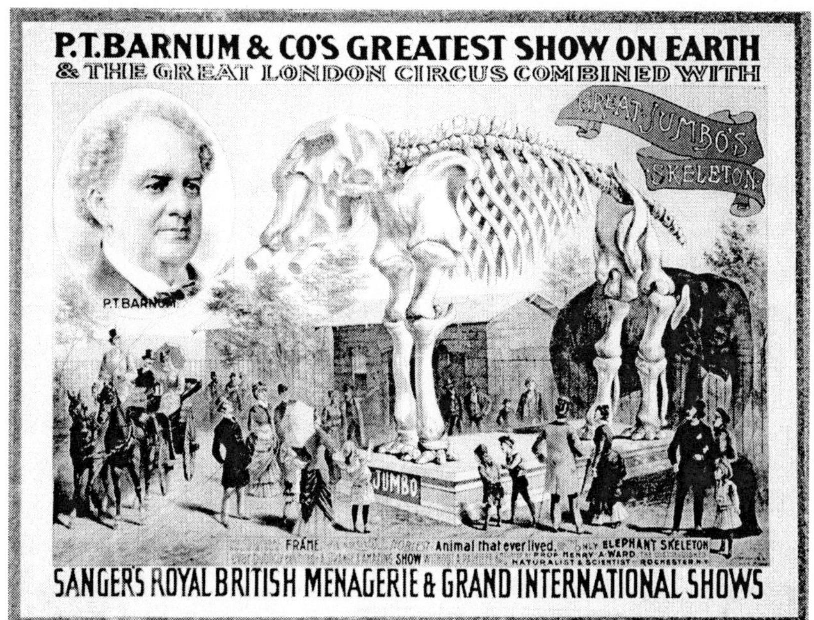

Today we know P.T. Barnum as a name appearing in the "Barnum and Bailey Circus" banners and signs. During his lifetime, especially during the late 19th century, he was seen in many different lights. Showman, promoter, schemer, exposer of frauds, and medicine man "par excellence." Some have even suggested that Barnum is the model for Baum's "Wizard." (Library of Congress)

Near the end of his life, he became partners with Bailey, who assumed the duties of the circus. Ironically, Barnum was also the author of the 1866 book, *The Humbugs of the World: An Account of Humbugs, Delusions, Impositions, Quackeries, Deceits, and Deceivers, Generally in All Ages.*[6]

Baum, L. Frank (1856-1919)

Better known as the 1900 author of *The Wonderful Wizard of Oz,* Baum was earlier a successful traveling salesman, founding his own business, Baum's Castorine Company, which made axel grease out of crude oil. Later he became the top traveling salesman for a Chicago crock and glassware wholesaler, Pitkin and Brooks.

Baum was also a window display pioneer, founding in 1898 the National Association of Window Trimmers, a first-of-its-kind trade organization whose object was "the uplifting of mercantile decorating to the level of a profession." A year earlier he published the first issue of *The Show Window,* a medium-sized monthly journal of decorative art. He continued editing the publication until 1902 when it was sold.

In addition to his writing, sales, and window dressing activities, Baum was a man of many interests and talents including the theater (both actor and playwright), radio play production, and, after moving to California, a grower and exhibitor of prize dahlias and chrysanthemums.[7] "His blooms won so many awards in strong competition in that land of flowers that he was often described as the champion amateur horticulturist of Southern California."[8]

Baum's *Wizard* is probably a many-layered literary work. 20th Century historians have hypothesized that *The Wonderful Wizard of Oz* is much more than a children's story—that it is a clever and insightful socio-political allegory about the life and times of the people of the late 19th century. Specifically, *Oz*, according to the historians, addresses William Jennings Bryant's populist movement that supported the silver standard over the gold standard for U.S. currency.

Becher, Barry and Edward Valenti

Very much in the mold of Ron Popeil, Becher and Valenti traveled TV's airwaves, promoting their Miracle Painter, Armourcote cookware, and the Ginsu knife. They were joint authors of the 2005 book *The Wisdom of Ginsu: Carve Yourself a Piece of the American Dream.*

Benton, William (1900-1973)

Labeled a "supersalesman" in Edwin P. Hoyt's 1962 book, *The Supersalesmen*, Benton clearly excelled at many different careers, most which required the gifts and talents of good salesmanship.

Upon graduation from Yale in 1921 Benton went to work for the National Cash Register Company, an organization known for the quality of its salesmanship and leadership of its president, John H. Patterson. After a successful couple of years working as a salesman for NCR, Benton moved into advertising.

In 1929 he co-founded the advertising agency Benton and Bowles with Chester Bowles. Benton's first account was General Foods, eventually garnering half of the company's business. Soon Benton and Bowles had all of the Colgate-Palmolive business and was billing two million dollars a year for Bristol-Meyers. Retiring from the advertising business in 1935, Benton went on to acquire Muzak, creating the idea of "subscription radio," the forerunner to today's "pay television."

Benton became a part-time vice president of the University of Chicago, 1937-1945. While at Chicago he provided for the University's acquisition of *Encyclopaedia Britannica* from Sears, Roebuck Company, becoming the *Encyclopaedia's* chairman of the board and publisher.

In 1945 Benton accepted an appointment as U.S. Assistant Secretary of State for Public Affairs, during which time he helped organize the United Nations. Benton spearheaded the publication and promotion of Mortimer Adler's *The Great Books* and *Syntopicon* with considerable success. *The Great Books* were eventually selling at the rate of nearly $30 million annually, or ten times the Britannica Company's total volume when Benton took it over.

Still a resident of Connecticut, Benton was appointed to fill the unexpired term of the state's resigning U.S. Senator Raymond E. Baldwin in 1949. Benton was subsequently elected to the post in 1950, serving until 1953. In 1950 Benton, in fact, was the first politician to promote his candidacy via television commercials.

During his later years, Benton devoted his energies to his philanthropic and business life, serving on nineteen philanthropic boards, including the boards of five universities.[9]

Beveridge, Frank Stanley

(See "Stanley Home Products" in Chapter 1)

Birdseye, Clarence (1886-1956)

In 1912, at the age of twenty-six, Birdseye was working as a fur trader in Labrador when he became interested in the way Eskimos preserved their foods. Developing a "quick freeze" method of preserving foods, Birdseye invested everything he owned in Birdseye Seafoods, Inc. in 1923. The Postum Company bought the rights to his patents and plants for $22 million in 1929. *(See C. W. Post)* Postum was later named General Foods. By 1934 Birdseye accounted for 80 percent of the frozen food business in the country.[10]

Breedlove, Sarah

(See Sarah Breedlove Walker)

Candler, Asa Griggs (1851-1929)

Candler became a very successful marketer for early Coca-Cola when he hired a troop of traveling salesmen who promoted the soft drink to soda fountains, hotels, restaurants, delicatessens, and grocers. With an evangelistic zeal matching that of the Bible-selling colporteurs, (Candler had been a vice president of the American Bible Society), Candler urged on his salesmen by providing them with giveaways for customers such as clocks, glasses, trays, and, in the early days, even Coca Cola stock.[11]

Carey, Mathew (1760-1839)

Making the transition from printer to publisher in the 1790s, Carey was one of the first American publishers to secure a national market for his books. He competed successfully with English imports through his network of book dealers and traveling salesmen. Hiring legendary book salesman Mason Locke "Parson" Weems, Carey created one of the most dynamic partnerships in the history of publishing.[12] (*See more about Weems in Chapter 3.*)

Carter, Henry W. (1822- ?)

Because of his regal-like bearing, Carter was called the "merchant prince" of wholesale peddlers in mid-19th century New England. Headquartered in Lebanon, NH, Carter had five teams of four horses each, and one of six magnificent, well-matched horses with a silver-mounted harness. The huge wagons were brilliantly painted, some with scenes on the sides, and always kept highly varnished. "They made an impressive sight as they dashed up the main street of a country town and drew rein before the general store or the local hotel. In winter the wagons were put on runners. These wagons were rolling, wholesale jobbing establishments, carrying a complete stock equal in variety to the large whole stores of the cities. Each load was worth several thousand dollars." He soon took over the sales for overalls (work pants) from manufacturer Converse Cole of Meriden, NH. Eventually his two sons were admitted as partners and the company became known as H.W. Carter & Sons which survives to this day as a maker of work clothes, overalls and children's clothing.[13]

Although Carter was not a patent medicine salesman per se, his public persona emulated that of the early 18th century English mountebank: "I saw a coach with six bay horses, a calash and four, and a chaise and four enter the inn in a yellow livery turned up with red." (*See "mountebank" in Chapter 1 for further description.*)

Chapman, John

(See Johnny Appleseed)

Chesebrough, Robert Augustus (1837-1933)

In 1859, Brooklyn Chemist Chesebrough visited the Titusville, PA, oil field and was intrigued by the pasty paraffin-like residue that stuck annoyingly to drilling rods, gumming them into inactivity. However, workers also reported the gooey stuff hastened healing of their burns and wounds. After months of work on the "stuff" to purify its essential ingredients, Chesebrough developed a clear, smooth substance he called "petroleum jelly." The eventual name "Vaseline" probably came from compounding the word from the German *wasser*, "water," and the Greek *elaion*, "olive oil."

In a horse and buggy, he traveled the roads of upper New York State, dispensing free samples of Vaseline to anyone who promised to try it on a cut or burn. The public's response was so favorable that within half a year Chesebrough was employing twelve horse-and-buggy salesmen, offering the jelly for a penny an ounce. Consumers found many uses for Vaseline including a stain remover for wood furniture, a second life to dried leather goods, rust prevention for outdoor machinery and corrosion prevention for battery terminals. Chesebrough, himself, never missed a daily spoonful of the jelly. He lived into his late 90s.[14]

Christoforo

Early model for the "quack doctors," Christoforo worked Florence's grand piazza before the Ducal Palace in the 1840s and 1850s. He hawked potions for a patent-medicine manufacturer and then sold his own panacea during breaks in the well-attended magic act.[15]

Clark, David (1864-1939)

Arriving in America in 1872 from Ireland when he was eight years old, David Clark entered the candy business in the 1880s, working as a traveling salesman for three years. Eventually he bought a peddling wagon, horses, and merchandise and went into business for himself. Clark founded the D.L. Clark Company in 1886 when he started manufacturing candy in two back rooms of a small house in Allegheny, PA, now Pittsburgh's North Side.

During Clark's lifetime, the D.L. Clark Company became a leading candy manufacturer as the Clark Bar emerged as one of the nation's favorite treats. The company experimented with a variety of ingredients that had never before been used in candy, introducing confections filled with coconut, mint and peanut butter. Three of its best creations were the Clark, Zagnut, and Clark Coconut Crunch bars. Further, the company scored an important marketing success when it introduced the five-cent-sized Clark bar. Initially, the bar was individually wrapped to facilitate shipment of candy to American troops during WWI.

The Clark Company was acquired and reacquired over the years. Most recently in 1999 it was acquired and its products manufactured and distributed by the New England Confectionery Company (NECCO).[16]

Colt, Samuel (1814-1862)

Inventor of the revolving-cylinder pistol, Colt was also an entertainer, pitchman and salesman. To finance his gun research and development, Colt embarked on a novel four-year career as a showman. As a kind of patent medicine huckster, he billed himself as "Dr. Coult of Calcutta," giving lectures on laughing gas in towns and cities throughout the United States and Canada.

An advertisement he wrote for a newspaper in Portland, ME, in October 1832 informed the readers that laughing gas "produced the most astonishing effects upon the nervous system; that some individuals were disposed to laugh, sing, and dance; others to recitations and declamations, and that the great number had an irresistible propensity to muscular exertion, such as wrestling, boxing and with innumerable fantastic feats." Profits were largely passed on to gunsmiths in Hartford, Albany, and Baltimore, who meticulously handcrafted prototypes of about nine rifles.

The "laughing-gas years" served not only for fund raising, but launched Colt's celebrated career as a pioneer Madison Avenue-style pitchman. Colt's advertising, public speaking, and public relations skills were so successful that he was pressed into service to cure an apparent cholera epidemic on board a Mississippi river boat.[17]

Cox, Edwin W.

A 1917 San Francisco door-to-door salesman, Cox sold the new, highly-touted aluminum cookware. However, because it was difficult to get into the kitchens to demonstrate his products, he found sales were mediocre. He needed a gimmick, a free introductory gift, allowing him to display his line.

Experimenting with small, square steel-wool pads hand-dipped into a soap solution, Cox discovered that the yet-unnamed pads opened doors and boosted sales. Within a few months, demand for the pads out-grew Cox's ability to dip and dry them in his kitchen. He stopped selling pots and pans and went into the business of manufacturing soap pads. Turning to his wife for a name, Mrs. Cox responded with "S.O.S Pads," meaning, "Save Our Saucepans." The product had a name that stuck![18]

Davey, John and sons Wellington and Martin

This trio created Davey Tree Expert Company and its nationwide network of salesmen to keep tree surgery business busy and profitable.

John Davey, born and trained in England in horticulture and landscape gardening, moved to America in 1873, eventually living in Kent,

OH. Davey wrote the book, *The Tree Doctor* in 1901, a milestone in his career, landing him speaking engagements and clinics.

Incorporating in 1904, John and his sons established several different schools and institutes for tree science and surgery.

Davey began a long association with the Federal government with the treatment of trees at the White House, the Washington elm in Washington D.C., and a horse chestnut planted by the first president in Fredericksburg, VA. Davey also performed work on trees on the Parliament Grounds in Ottawa, Canada. The NBC "Davey Radio Hour," which included an eight-minute talk by Martin Davey on tree care, was on the air for 26 weeks in 1930. The Davey family sold the company in the late 1900s.[19]

DeVos, Sr., Richard

(See Jay Van Andel)

Durant, William C. (1861-1947)

Founder of General Motors in 1908, Durant was described by Fred Smith of GM's Olds Division as "The strongest and most courageous individual then in the business and the master salesman of all time. No man ever lived who could sell such a variety of commodities in so short a space of time: cigars, buggies, automobiles, ideas, and himself, believing wholeheartedly in his wares and in the last item especially."[20]

As a boy, young Durant stacked lumber at a mill. For another $3 a week, he became a nighttime seller of patent medicine made by a local drugstore. He quit the sawmill job when he found a second selling job—this time as a traveling cigar salesman. His employer, George T. Warren, was skeptical when young Durant asked for $2 a day in travel expenses. After a two-day swing to Port Huron, MI, Durant came back with orders for 22,000 cigars. Flabbergasted, Warren asked for an explanation. "Easy," explained Durant. He convinced Port Huron storekeepers to bypass the local wholesaler and order directly from Warren's Flint factory. For a time he worked for Warren, earning $25 a week, replacing three other salesmen while doing so.

Termed "the strongest and most courageous individual then in the business and master salesman of all time," General Motors founder William C. Durant began work as a patent medicine salesman before moving on to cigars, real estate, fire insurance, and, of course, automobiles. Durant pictured here with his wife. (Library of Congress)

Next he sold real estate, then worked as a bookkeeper for the local water company where he graduated to the service department, handling complaints and winning new customers. Selling fire insurance would come next. Witnessing the large number of fires consuming the hastily constructed wood structures of the era, Durant set up a fire insurance agency with a school chum. Successive acquisitions eventually moved him into the fledgling automobile industry and the creation of General Motors.[21]

Salesman Durant's rise to influence and power in General Motors is not particularly surprising when one understands that others—Norval Hawkins (Ford) and Richard H. Grant (Chevrolet) with strong salesmanship backgrounds—also ascended the industrial ranks of power. In fact, almost one-quarter of the chief executives of the top two hundred companies in 1917 had spent part or much of their careers in sales.[22]

Feldman, Ben (1912-1993)

Feldman, a late 20th century salesman of East Liverpool, OH, is generally considered the finest life insurance salesman of all time and one of the nation's all-time great salesmen in any field. Among his accomplishments were a lifetime sales volume of more than $1 billion, an average of more than $20 million a year, a $100 million year, and single-day sale of more than $20 million of life insurance products. Feldman perfected a series of techniques for selling life insurance that earned him a place in the *Guinness Book of World Records* as the most outstanding salesman in history.[23]

Feldman created the concept of "key-person insurance" where the owner or top official of a business is insured so as to protect the company's interests should the "key" person die prematurely. A film, *The Man from East Liverpool*, documents Feldman's techniques and success. Ben Feldman, an agent for New York Life, was a long-standing member of the Million Dollar Round Table.[24]

Field, Marshall (1834-1906)

Founder of the giant retailer Marshall Field & Company, Field began his sales work in the 1840's as a commercial traveler for the Chicago dry goods business Cooley, Farwell, & Co. Later, when Field had established his own business with partner Levi Leiter, he would send out a large force of jobbers and drummers to compete with Eastern wholesalers. The substantial force helped Field survive the financial "panic" of the 1870's and the "Great Chicago Fire" of 1871 that decimated Field's flagship building on State Street.[25]

Field came to employ two types of traveling salesmen—the general lineman who sold a variety of items within a specific territory and the specialty salesman who sold specific and higher quality goods that included linen and lace.[26]

When Field acquired Potter Palmer's dry-goods business in 1865, Field continued Palmer's courteous consumer policies, such as the money-back guarantee. The policy, "unprecedented in contemporary Chicago," helped distinguish Field from other retailers doing business in the Midwest.[27]

Ford, Luther

(See Al Stewart)

Fuller, Alfred C. (1885-1973)

A native of Nova Scotia, Fuller established the Fuller Brush Company in 1906 in Hartford, CT. Although the company began with a line of brushes, it eventually offered, through an agent force of many thousands of door-to-door salesmen, a wide range of products including waxes, insecticides, cleaners, polishes, soaps and even cosmetics. Fuller organized his agency force into divisions, districts, branches, fields and territories. The field manager was the lowest level administrator and generally hired and supervised 15-20 salesmen and saleswomen who traveled their respective territories.[28]

The 1950's Fuller Brush Man was armed with tried and true strategies that led to the reachable "$100-Day." At a 40% commission, a successful dealer could earn a reasonable salary for the time. Agents acquired premiums from the company—pastry and vegetable brushes and perfume and hand cream samples—that opened doors, giving them entrance to the households. (Successful use of such premiums gave other entrepreneurs ideas for new product lines—S.O.S Pads, Avon Cosmetics, and Wrigley Chewing Gum).

In addition to the premiums each dealer was armed with a "grip" or case, filled with samples and "leave-behinds" that included fliers and catalogs. Another strategy, not always easily followed, was that agents were encouraged to make a set number of door-to-door stops each hour. Too many or too few stops meant that an agent was spending too little or too much time with individual customers. Meeting the hourly "stop-goal" was a reliable predictor of success. Today, Fuller Brushes are sold primarily by individual entrepreneurs via the Internet.[29] (*For more about Alfred Fuller and his son, Howard, see the story "The real-life death of a salesman" in Chapter 5.*)

Gallaudet, Thomas Hopkins (1787- 1851)

Born in Philadelphia, Thomas Hopkins Gallaudet, for whom Gallaudet University, a college for the deaf was named, worked as a traveling salesman and itinerant minister following graduation from

A traveling salesman and itinerant minister, Thomas Gallaudet founded the first permanent school for deaf children in the United States after becoming interested in the educational plight of the deaf student. (Library of Congress)

Yale in 1810. However, when he became acquainted with the 9-year-old deaf daughter, Alice Cogswell, of a minister friend, Galaudet became consumed with learning more about the proper education for the deaf. After studying in Europe with the premier deaf educators of the day, he returned to the U.S. to raise private and public funds to found a school for deaf students in Hartford, CT, which later became the American School for the Deaf, the first permanent school for deaf children in the United States. Gallaudet served as principal of the school from 1817 to 1830.

Gallaudet resigned his position on April 6, 1830, to devote his time to writing children's books and to the ministry. In 1857, the Columbia Institution for the Instruction of the Deaf and Dumb and Blind, located in Washington DC, incorporated and hired Edward Miner Gallaudet, son of Thomas Hopkins Gallaudet, as the school's first superintendent. Gallaudet's deaf mother, Sophia Fowler Gallaudet, who was the widow of Thomas Hopkins Gallaudet, became the school's matron. Columbia was later named Gallaudet University in honor of the Gallaudet family legacy.[30]

Gates, John Warne (1855-1911)

"Bet-a-Million" Gates was a barbed wire salesman, steel company owner, oilman, and philanthropist. Born in Winfield, IL, Gates attended college briefly at Northwest College in Naperville, IL. After minimal success in the hardware business, Gates began work as a barbed wire salesman in Texas. Eventually finding himself in San Antonio, Gates made a wager, betting that his new wire would hold

People and cars line up outside New York City's Plaza Hotel for the 1911 funeral of John Warne Gates, founder of Texaco. Gates began his career as a very successful barbed wire salesman. (Library of Congress)

a herd of the "toughest" longhorn cattle. A corral of the wire was built and 25 head of wild longhorn cattle were driven into it by excited, whooping cowboys. The longhorns charged the fence, but it held. A second attempt also held. By nightfall, Gates had more orders for the wire than he could fill. Production of the wire went from 10,000 lbs. in 1874 to more than 120 million lbs. in 1881.

Because Gates was refused a partnership in his Illinois-based Washburn-Moen company, Gates quit and established his own wire company in St. Louis, the Southern Wire Company, "the largest manufacturer and distributor of unlicensed 'moonshine/non-patented' barbed wire."

With his substantial financial resources, Gates' later achievements included ownership or control of several steel companies, including the Republic Steel Company. Perhaps his most notable accomplishment was the establishment of the Texas Company, later to become Texaco. Because of his notorious gambling (and successful) ways with the stock market, poker, and horses, Gates became known as "Bet-A-Million" Gates.

Several Port Arthur, TX, institutions were the benefactors of Gates' wealth—Gates memorial Hospital, St. Charles Home for Boys, the Port Arthur Business College and Lamar University at Port Arthur.[31]

Gerrish, Perley G.

Gerrish is credited as the discoverer of market testing. He was a drummer for Squirrel Brand assorted nuts and had made, on his own, a peanut bar which none of his customers would buy. Undeterred, Gerrish loaded a wagon and drove from Boston to Providence, market testing his peanut bar, handing out free samples to school children. When he covered the territory next time, he found merchants softened by the children's crusade, eager to stock the peanut bars. Gerrish along with another employee purchased the Squirrel Brand Company in 1905. One of the Company's first combination bars with multiple ingredients was the Goo Goo Cluster, made of caramel, marshmallo, peanuts, coconut, and milk chocolate. The Goo Goo Cluster is still sold today as is another bar from 1912, the Nut Goodie, one of the pioneer nut rolls. Eventually Squirrel Brand candies would be acquired by the New England Confectionery Company (NECCO).[32]

Gillette, King Camp (1855-1932)

A traveling salesman, Gillette was seeking a product that would make his fortune. He was given advice by William Painter, inventor

Following the advice of a fellow entrepreneur/inventor who suggested that the most profitable product is one with built-in obsolescence, traveling salesman King Camp Gillette introduced a safety razor that used pressed-metal disposable blades. This is one of Gillette's early razor models that came in its very own felt-lined travel case. (Photo by Ronald Solberg)

of the disposable crimped beer bottle cap. The most profitable product, Painter pointed out, was one with built-in obsolescence—something that consumers would willingly purchase over and over again.

Gillette hit upon the perfect product while shaving one morning—a razor blade that was simply disposed of and replaced, instead of being constantly re-sharpened. "I stood before that mirror in a trance of joy," he later wrote. Gillette realized that his disposable blades would have to be cheap but one of high quality if they were to succeed. But in 1895 the technology to make steel blades cheap, thin, hard, and sharp was unavailable. He was turned away or discouraged by one expert after another, until, in 1901, Massachusetts Institute of Technology professor William Nickerson agreed to collaborate on the project.

Razor blades of the time were forged, but Nickerson and Gillette devised a method of pressing the blades out of thin sheets of steel. They also designed a safety razor to hold them, increasing the convenience and value of the product. In 1903 the first batch of 51 razors and 168 blades was ready—Gillette gave most of them away to help publicize the product by word of mouth. His marketing ability soon began to yield results. By 1904 he had sold 90,000 razors and 123,000 blades. By 1906 he was selling 300,000 razors a year. Perhaps his greatest marketing coup was securing a contract to supply the U.S. Army during World War I.[33]

Gimbel, Adam (1815-1896)

Adam Gimble was the founder of Gimbels Department Stores with the first such store being in Vincennes, IN. After expanding the business considerably over 40 years, he sold his business to his sons Jacob and Isaac, who opened up Gimbels stores in Milwaukee, Philadelphia, and New York City. Other businesses were acquired, including Saks and Company in 1923 with branch stores opened in several other cities. The company was absorbed in 1973 by the Brown and Williamson Tobacco Corporation and later by B.A.T. Industries PLC. The last Gimbels store closed in 1987. Born in Bavaria, Adam Gimble emigrated to the U.S. in 1835. He began as a peddler of notions, traveling up and down the Mississippi River.[34]

Girard, Joe (1928-)

Although not a traveling salesman, Michigan automobile salesman Joe Girard is listed here because of his substantial accomplishments, innovative techniques, and contributions to the business of selling.

Girard set an all-time record in 1973 by selling 1425 individual units. His lifetime total of one-at-a-time "belly-to-belly" selling was 13,001 sales, all retail, with a record 174 automobiles in a month, according to the 1990 *Guiness Book of Records*. In addition to being a motivational speaker, Girard is an author of best-selling sales technique books including the 1989 *How to Close Every Sale* and the more recent *How to Sell Yourself.*

Some of his sales techniques included sending out nearly 13,000 greeting cards a month celebrating everything from Halloween to Groundhog Day. He paid out thousands of dollars to a network of people who referred sales—priests, teachers, plant foremen, students and mechanics—before the practice was discouraged by the Big Three auto companies. He stocked a bar with 50 different types of liquor to soothe a customer's nerves, carried 10 brands of cigarettes, plus toys and balloons for children. If a potential customer threatened to walk, he would get down on his knees and beg for the sale. If finances were a problem, he'd call friends, relatives, and strangers out of the directory to get a co-signer for the car loan.[35]

Heinz, Henry J. (1844-1919)

Born in Pittsburgh, PA, Henry demonstrated an early salesmanship flair at the age of 12 by selling vegetables successfully from the family garden to neighbors and grocers. Following a bookkeeping stint at the nearby Duff's Business College, Henry worked for a time with his father's brick business.[36]

However, he eventually turned to his first love, raising and selling vegetables, distributing his own brand of horseradish to grocers throughout the city. At the age of 25 he joined with neighbor L. Clarence Noble in the canned vegetable business. Their first product, horseradish, was bottled in clear glass containers, so as not to mask the purity of the product. They added pickles, vinegar, and sauerkraut to their product line, selling and delivering their items by horse-drawn wagons to Pittsburgh stores. Heinz resurrected the business following the banking failure of 1875, expanding the product line to tomato ketchup, pepper sauces, olives, mincemeat, mustard, baked beans and soups.[37]

Establishing branches in cities outside of Pittsburgh, Heinz fielded a team of salesmen who visited grocers and were paid on a commission. The sales force grew from 2 in 1877 to 125 in 1893, to 952 in 1919. A very creative promoter, Heinz distributed pickle-shaped pins at the 1893 Chicago World's Columbian Exposition, allowing the public to tour his spotless factories. In fact, it is said that Heinz invented the public factory tour.[38]

In 1900 Heinz erected New York City's first electric sign. He promoted his products at the 1902 World's Fair in Buffalo and constructed a pavilion on a 900-foot pier in Atlantic City. The slogan, "fifty-seven varieties?" Heinz coined it in 1896, "simply because he liked the sound of the number."[39]

Hill, Napoleon (1883-1970)

An American author, Hill is widely recognized as the founder of the modern genre of personal success literature. His most famous work *Think and Grow Rich,* is one of the best-selling books of all time, selling over 7 million copies. At age 13 he was writing as a "mountain reporter" for small-town newspapers. After graduation from law school, he received an assignment to write a series of biographies of famous men, beginning with Andrew Carnegie, steel magnate and philanthropist. Carnegie believed that the process of success could be elaborated in a simple formula that could be duplicated by the average person. Impressed with Hill, Carnegie commissioned him to interview over 500 millionaires in order to discover and publish this formula for success. Lasting for over twenty years, the project brought Hill into contact with most of the famous people of the time.

The rags-to-riches formula by Hill and Carnegie culminated in the 1928 book *The Law of Success*. From 1919-1920 Hill was editor and publisher of the magazine *The Golden Rule*, eventually becoming advisor to such leading figures of the day as President Franklin Roosevelt. In 1952-62, Hill worked with W. Clement Stone of the Combined Insurance Company of America to teach Stone's "Philosophy of Personal Achievement" and to lecture on the "Science of Success." In 1960, Hill collaborated with Stone on the book, *Success Through a Positive Mental Attitude*. Both Hill and Stone would become famous for the "PMA" philosophy, especially as it applied to salesmanship.[40]

Hines, Duncan (1880-1959)

Born in Bowling Green, KY, Duncan Hines entered the printing and advertising business in 1905 as a traveling salesman, selling "creative printing" ideas to industrial firms. In the course of his travels Hines realized that "some eating places on the road should be avoided like the plague, while others were well worth the return visit." After a number of bad eating experiences, he and his wife began compiling a personal list of superior eating places—specialties of the house and quality of food and service. Instead of mailing traditional Christmas cards to their friends and family, they printed the lists and mailed them out. They received an unexpected enthusiastic response to Duncan's "lists," receiving hundreds of requests for copies from people they never heard of. As a result, and as a hobby, Hines compiled a book that he called *Adventures in Good Eating*.

Because of the success of the book, Hines resigned from the printing firm job to devote full time to his traveling and writing work. In 1938 he published his second book *Lodging for a Night*; in 1939, *Adventures in Good Cooking* and *The Art of Carving in the Home*; in 1948, *Duncan Hines Vacation Guide*. He published two additional books in 1955: *Duncan Hines Food Odyssey* and *Duncan Hines Dessert Book*.

Hines was approached in 1948 to lend his name to a line of packaged foods from top manufacturers. Eventually, hundreds of products including ice cream and cake mixes were sold under his name. The venture was a success and in 1956 Proctor & Gamble purchased the brand with the authority to put the Duncan Hines name on various food products, primarily on mixes. Aurora Foods, Inc. acquired the brand in 1997.

Hines not only personified the traditional traveling salesman, but he "invented" a service (the travel guide) that supported his fellow travelers and created a "brand," as well, that became an American idiom for quality.[41]

Hunter, Max (1921-1999)

Hunter is one of two American traveling salesmen who made their living as traveling salesmen but are notable for quite a different reason—collecting songs (and expressions) of the people. Bascom Lamar Lunsford is the other traveling salesman/song collector. A peddler of tools and other items, Hunter became known as one of the nation's premier collectors of traditional Ozark songs, stories and expressions. A native of Springfield, MO, Hunter's collection of 1,600 Ozark Mountain folk songs, recorded between 1956 and 1972 on 40 2-disc CD sets, and transferred to several volumes of manuscripts, is permanently housed at the Springfield-Green County Library.

Some of Hunter's more notable expressions include: "Ugly as a mud fence," "Pretty as a speckled pup," "I'm tellin' you boys, and it's God's own truth, there are people in this town who wear clean shirts over dirty underwear," and "You're spreading it faster than I can shovel it." Other tidbits that Hunter collected included ways to cure warts "by stealing your neighbor's dish rag" and warding off bad luck after a black cat crosses your path "by putting on your hat backwards and the cat won't know if you're coming or going."

For his monumental 30-year effort of collecting the "hillbilly" music and stories Missouri's State Arts Council in 1998 presented Hunter with its prestigious Missouri Arts Award.[42]

Huntington, Collis P. (1821-1900)

This founder of the Southern Pacific Railroad started out at age 15 as a peddler of clocks throughout the South and West. At age 27 Huntington joined the Gold Rush in California, but not to pan for the valuable mineral. Instead he made a small fortune by selling picks,

Beginning his sales work as a clock peddler at age fifteen, Collis Huntington moved west when he was 27-years-old to sell supplies to gold prospectors. Eventually he would make a fortune through a hardware business which provided him the money to organize a railroad company with two partners. (Library of Congress)

shovels, and other supplies to farmers and prospectors. Using the monies he earned by selling the prospecting tools, Huntington eventually started up a very successful hardware store operation in Sacramento, CA with Mark Hopkins.

At the age of 39, Huntington joined Hopkins, Charles Crocker and Leland Stanford, organizing a railroad company (the Central Pacific) that would provide a direct route to the silver mines newly opened in what is now Nevada. In 1884 the four men consolidated their railway power in the West with the establishment of the Southern Pacific.[43]

In Frank Norris' novel *The Octopus* Huntington is reviled as the villainous Shelgrim; but the historian Eugene Huddleston draws attention to the solid accomplishments at the end of the melodramas: "He left a transportation system that unified East with West from the Great American Desert to the Golden West."

Hyde, Henry B. (1834-1899)

Hyde founded the Equitable Life Assurance Society, conceiving of life insurance sales in military-style terms. Supporting his sales force with regular inspirational letters, Hyde gave special incentives to agents, such as gold watches, for developing new business. Using martial-like language, Hyde wrote: "My only solicitude is lest our matchless company of agents, like a valiant army flushed with victory, should lapse into a condition of inactivity, through the very sense of invincibility, and make no steps in advance."[44]

Hyde's success in building the Equitable was spectacular. In 1860, the company ranked ninth in sales. By 1869 it was number one in sales. By 1886 Equitable's substantial assets made it the world's largest life insurance company. There was a dark side, however, to this monumental growth—Equitable's promotion and sale of the tontine policy, one that "deferred dividends," rather than paying dividends regularly, thus making more money available to Equitable to sell even more insurance. From 1870 to 1885, two-thirds of Equitable's $613 million in new business was tontine in character. The chief defect of the tontine policy was the outlandish promises of big profits that failed to materialize, and the lack of an annual accounting of how much, or how little, each policyholder had earned. These tontine policies did tremendous damage to the reputation of life insurance and its agents when the policies failed to pay off as promised. A 1905 governmental investigation into insurance-selling practices eventually led to a ban on tontine policies.[45]

Ives, Charles (1874-1954)

Here was a traveling salesman who led a double, perhaps triple, life. Ives played piano, organ, cornet, violin and drums, but never made a living as a composer or a musician. Ives was a very successful New York Life Insurance salesman by day—earning an early award as an esteemed Million Dollar Round Table member—essentially inventing the concept of estate planning. (*See MDRT in Chapter 2, "Definitions and Origins."*)

Ives partnered up with Julian W. Myrick in 1909, forming one of the most successful insurance agencies in the history of the business. In their first year the partners collected $1,600,000 in premiums (over 18 million in 1990's dollars). In 1914, it was $7,700,000; in 1919, $22,500,000. Their advertising of the 1920s would proclaim the New York company "THE LARGEST AGENCY without exclusive territory IN THE COUNTRY."

In 1929 the last year Ives was in business, the company made $48,000,000. In their twenty-one years in business the partners would take in the unprecedented sum for any agency of $450,000,000. Of that, apparently, Ives in his first dozen or so years may have made

$1.8 million for himself. In 1990's dollars that amounts to nearly 20.5 million dollars during the first, and less prosperous, half of his career.[46]

But, there was another very important side to Ives. At night Ives would hurry home to write his compositions, considered by many to be the most innovative American composer of the 20th century. His favorite piece was his *Holiday Symphony* in which the sounds of a small-town celebration are heard with competing marching bands, political discussions, fireworks and even women unloading picnic baskets. Ives borrowed material from other sources such as old hymns, cowboy songs, Christmas carols, and spirituals. He even borrowed a theme from Beethoven's Fifth Symphony. Though, in every instance he used what he borrowed in new and interesting ways. He was famous for composing music for solo piano, orchestra, chamber music and songs for voice.

And what about that third side? Ives was a big baseball fan and participated in and played at many sports such as baseball, football, track and tennis.[47]

Johnny Appleseed (1774-1845)

In reality this legend was the very real John Chapman, born in Leominster, MA. "Johnny" was missionary, nurseryman and traveling salesman of the American frontier who helped pave the way for 19th century pioneers by supplying apple-tree nursery stock through-

Will the real Johnny Appleseed please stand? The legendary Johnny Appleseed, has become more real to us than his true-life counterpart John Chapman, as the cover of this Classics *"comic book" suggests. It's unfortunate because his bona fide exploits and contributions far outstrip those of the fictionalized character. (The Johnny Appleseed Museum)*

out the Midwest. Although the legendary figure of "Johnny Appleseed" is known chiefly through fiction, Chapman was a genuine and dedicated professional nurseryman who expected to make a profit from the sale of his seedlings. In the early 1800s, Chapman collected apple seeds and began his trek westward selling and giving away seedlings from the Alleghenies to central Ohio and beyond.[48] (*For a more extensive narrative about John Chapman, see Chapter 3 "What's in a name?"*)

Johnston, J.P.

Johnston was a triple threat as he was a late 19th century Midwestern salesman, auctioneer and author of the book, *Twenty Years of Hus'ling*, chronicling his experiences and describing his techniques.

Auctioneers are frequently enlisted by farmers and others who are selling off machinery, commodities and livestock . Here a 1940's auctioneer calls off a winner of a bid at a farm in Derby, CT. The auction probably started with the early Romans. In fact our word "auction" comes from the Latin word "augere," meaning to increase. (Library of Congress)

"My success as an auctioneer was assured from the result of my first sale. I soon learned that it required only hard study and close application to make it a profitable business. I did not give up on my furniture polish, but as soon as possible bought an extra suit of clothes, a silk hat and a wig with which to change my appearance from a polish-vender to an auctioneer. I would peddle from house to house during the day in a dark suit and derby hat, with my hair clipped close to my head, while in the evening I would appear on the auction-wagon attired in a flashy, plaid suit, a blonde wig and silk hat. In no instance was my identity ever discovered."[49] (*Read more from J.P. Johnston in Chapter 5.*)

Jonathan Slick *(Also, see Sam Slick)*

Stories about fictionalized character and peddler Jonathan Slick and his home "Down East" came from many humorous books of the 1830's, 40's and 50s. Written chiefly by Seba Smith, they told about a Yankee named Jack Downing, his family and the "sellingest people in the world," including Slick. "They could peddle anything—a ton of ice to an Eskimo or a warming pan to a South Sea Islander—at a good price, too."

Jonathan was born in Slicksville, just about the middle of Down East. Neighbor Scrooge, who owned and ran the general store, kept his eye on Jonathan from the start and soon saw that Jonathan was an up and comer.

"By the time he was seven," Scrooge told people, "he'd saved up two dollars and twelve and a half cents out of his allowance for sugar plums. At eight, he was earning fourteen cents a day for riding the horse that led the oxen in plowing over on Deacon Goodrich's farm. At nine, he was peddling molasses candy, gingerbread and cherry rum at country fairs—got good money for 'em, too. And, at ten, he was a clerk in my general store, where he could strike a better bargain than many a grown man.

"In New England, he never sold much, since he figured that Yankees were too keen for him to make the profit he could other places. Out beyond New England, though, he'd string the bells on his cart, whistle "Yankee Doodle," and keep an eye open for customers. And after a few years on the road, he could give most any man a head start and out swap him.

"Take the time he came riding into a town not far from Albany, NY, he wore a bell-shaped white hat, a light green coat, yellow nankeen britches that just came down to his calves, and a pair of boots that he'd got from a boot maker in a swap for a cobbler's awl. The sun was shining on the tin pans on his yellow and blue cart, the bells were tinkling, and Jonathan was feeling as chipper as a squirrel."[50]

There may be some confusion as to the identification and origin of this Jonathan Slick versus another Jonathan Slick and Sam Slick, referenced elsewhere. Ann Sophia Winterbotham Stephens, an early

19th century author who used the pseudonym "Jonathan Slick," was the author of melodramatic "dime novels" that have no relationship to the "Slick" peddlers appearing in other works.[51]

Kafka, Franz (1883-1924)

This early 20th century German author wrote the novella *Metamorphosis* about Gregor Samsa, a traveling salesman who wakes up one morning and finds himself changed into a bug. Kafka, himself, was very much connected to the sales business as he worked for the Workers' Accident Insurance Company of the Kingdom of Bohemia. His principle duties involved travel to industrial accident sites, assessment of workers' injuries, and determination of what, if any, compensation should be paid. Scholar Robbie Batson in his "Kafka-Samsa, Reality Through Symbolism," essay suggests that Kafka's own personal life parallels in many ways that of Samsa—chronic health problems with tuberculosis, conflict with family members, feelings of isolation, and an early death.

Other writers and poets who worked in insurance sales, according to online reviewer Robert W. Moore, were German novelist Thomas Mann, American poet Wallace Stevens, and U.S. Poet Laureate Ted Koose.

Kay, Mary

(See Mary Kay Ash)

Kroc, Raymond A.(1902-1984)

Illinoisan Ray Kroc mortgaged his Oak Park home in 1954 and invested his entire life savings to become the exclusive distributor of a five-spindled shake maker called the "Multimixer." Hearing about the McDonald's hamburger stand in California running eight Multimixers at a time, he packed up his car and headed West. Arriving at the California hamburger stand, Kroc proposed to the owners Rick and Mac McDonald that they open up several restaurants, convinced that he could sell eight of his Multimixers to each and every one. The brothers inquired as to who might open them up. Kroc volunteered to do so—and he did so in Des Plaines, IL in 1955. This "first" McDonald's is no longer a functioning restaurant but

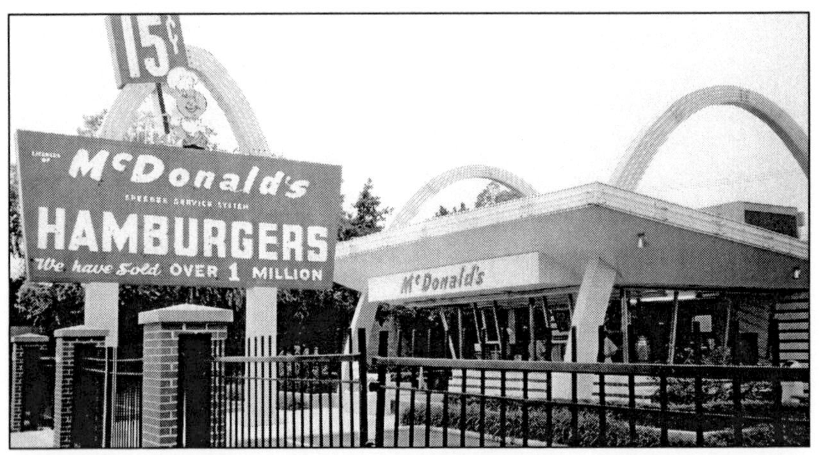

Raymond Kroc opened up his first McDonald's hamburger stand in 1955 in Des Plaines, IL. Today it stands as a museum displaying McDonald artifacts. A newer and working version of the McDonald's stand resides immediately across the street from the museum. (Photo by Ronald Solberg)

serves as a museum containing McDonald's memorabilia and artifacts, including the Multimixer! Though, there is a newer version of the McDonald's hamburger stand immediately across the street.

In 1961 Kroc bought out the McDonald brothers for $2.7 million after annual sales hit $54 million. The rest is history, of course, as Kroc revolutionized the fast-food business with a clean, efficient, and economical offering of standardized, appetizing fare, worldwide. When Kroc died in 1984 there were 7,778 restaurants and had served 45 billion hamburgers.[52]

Lauder, Esteé (1907-2004)

Born in Queens, NY, as Josephine Esther Mentzer of Jewish immigrants from Eastern Europe, Esteé went on to command a multibillion-dollar cosmetic empire.[53] (*See detailed Esteé Lauder narrative in "The Sweet Smell of Success" in Chapter 3.*)

Lay, Herman (1909-1982)

A 1920s Southern traveling salesman, Lay helped popularize the food from Atlanta to Tennessee that had been created earlier in the late 1800s, on a whim, by George Crum at the Moon Lake Lodge in

Saratoga Springs, NY. While the chips were sold locally and throughout the New England area for several decades, it wasn't until the 1920s, with the invention of the mechanical potato peeler, that the chips could become something more than a regional curiosity. Lay peddled the chip to grocers out of the trunk of his car, building a business and name that would become synonymous with the thin, salty snack. Lay's potato chips became the first successfully marketed national brand, and in 1961 Herman Lay, to increase his line of goods, merged his company with Frito, the Dallas-based producers of such snack foods as Fritos Corn Chips.[54]

Lunsford, Bascom Lamar (1882-1973)

The "other" traveling salesman/song collector. *(See Max Hunter).* Early in his life, Lunsford sold nursery stock on his "jaunts" through the Carolina hills as he collected music of the mountain folks. Though the word "sold" may be an exaggeration, as his employer once said that "Lunsford's excursions cost the company $500 on one trip for lodging and food in exchange for fruit trees." Today that area is widely known for its annual apple festival.

As one might be tempted to link Bascom to the moniker, "Appleseed," another comes to mind as he moved on as "The Traveling Beekeeper." However, Lunsford was to become much more than nurseryman and beekeeper as he was also a professor, lawyer, county solicitor, publisher, Department of Justice special agent, and father of seven. While Lunsford would eventually give up on his

Bascom Lunsford listens to two musicians who were visiting his Mountain Music Festival, Ashville, NC. Though Lunsford is noted most for his collection of over 3,000 of the native songs of the Southeast, he was selling nursery stock as he traveled the mountains of the area. (Library of Congress)

peddler ways, moving on to these other activities, it was his early experiences associating with the mountain people that would introduce him to the folk music of the region.[55]

In the end, Lunsford's real passion became the "creating, collecting, performing, and advancing the music and dance of his native western North Carolina mountains." His greatest accomplishment would be the preservation of over 3,000 folk songs and the founding of numerous folk festivals, including the prestigious Bascom Lamar Lunsford Mountain Music and Dance Festival of Mars Hills, NC. Lunsford's substantial music collection is currently housed in the Appalachian Room of the Memorial Library at Mars Hill College.[56]

Malone, Annie Turnbo (1869-1957)

Malone may lay claim to being the nation's first Black millionairess (though some would say that Malone's student and early agent, Madame C.J. Walker, should receive that credit). Born in Metropolis, IL, Malone developed hair care products which she sold door-to-door through the African American community of Lovejoy, IL (now called Brooklyn).[57]

Eventually Malone would build her cosmetic business into a $14 million empire that would include the St. Louis-based Poro College to train students as Poro agents.[58] (*See expanded article about Malone in "The Sweet Smell of Success" in Chapter 3.*)

Mandino, Og (1923-1996)

Mandino is known primarily as author of several popular sales philosophy and motivational books, including *The Greatest Salesman in the World,* one of the most popular sales-related books ever published. However, Mandino would suffer through some early setbacks before experiencing triumph.

Mandino struggled in his early years, selling insurance and barely making ends meet. Following his continuing bout with the bottle, Mandino's wife and daughter walked out on him. As he hit rock bottom, Mandino considered suicide, though he commented later that "I joke about it now and say that I was such a spineless individual at the time that I couldn't even muster enough courage to do away with myself."

Then, on a serendipitous visit to a library, Mandino discovered "PMA" in insurance salesman and executive W. Clement Stone's book *Success Through a Positive Mental Attitude.* "My life has never been the same since then."

Mandino returned to the insurance business, working for one of Stone's Combined Insurance Company of America agencies, headquartered in Boston. Eventually Mandino was promoted to sales manager "in the wide-open, and cold, territory of Northern Maine."

Mandino's ability as a word smith eventually came to the attention of Stone who needed an editor for his Chicago-based company magazine. His successful writing and editorial activities attracted the attention of a publisher who offered a book contract to Mandino. Eighteen months later, *The Greatest Salesman in the World* was published. Over two million copies of the "little" book are now in print. Though he died in 1996, Mandino's work and ideas live on in eleven other books and in his "Success System: Managing Your Six Advisors" education and consulting program.[59]

Martin, Richard

In 1583 when this Englishman made a wager with a syndicate of thirteen merchants that William Gybbons would not die before a specified time (one year) he became the father of what we now know to be life insurance.[60]

The record of this transaction has been preserved because its settlement went to court. Gybbons died in 1584, just shy of the one-year duration of the contract. The syndicate members claimed that Gybbons had survived twelve lunar months of twenty-eight days, thus fulfilling their end of bargain. Therefore, they refused to pay. However, the court ordered them to pay on the first insurance policy.—and the first insurance contract dispute![61]

McConnell, David H. (1858-1937)

One of the most successful direct-sales companies is Avon Products, and it is one of the largest cosmetic companies in the world. Avon was founded in 1886 by David H. McConnell, a door-to-door book salesman from Oswego, NY, who gave the ladies a free vial of perfume to gain entrance to the parlor where he could extol the merits of *Pilgrim's Progress* and *The American Book of Home Nursing.* The perfume was more interesting to the ladies than either of the books and McConnell decided he should be in the perfume business.[62] (*See more about McConnell in "The Sweet Smell of Success" in Chapter 3.*)

McNeal, Violet

This early 20th century "relatively rare pitchwoman" recalled in her 1947 autobiography, *Four White Horses and a Brass Band,* that she mixed her medications herself in a disinfected bathtub before bottling and labeling the goods. "Vital Sparks," her medicinal boost to male virility, were pieces of rock candy rolled in powdered aloes. "Tiger Fat," a salve with supposedly exotic ingredients, was composed of items purchased wholesale from a mainstream druggist and suspended in a Vaseline base.[63]

Miller, Arthur (1915-2005)

American playwright Miller wrote the 1949 play *Death of a Salesman,* chronicling the tragedy and eventual demise of "common man" and traveling salesman Willy Loman. Miller was awarded the Pulitzer Prize for his prolific and groundbreaking work in drama.

Ned, Nevada

The stage name of Dr. N.T. Oliver who ran American medicine shows in the 1880's and 1890's. Oliver also authored crime novels. He later wrote in 1929: "The actors, famous in legitimate pictures and vaudeville who have, in their time, passed out the Indian Prairie Flower and the Buffalo Salve are many more than the records show. Few have chosen to mention it to interviewers."

Among the "famous names" referenced by Oliver were: Harry Houdini, James Whitcomb Riley, George Burns and Gracie Allen, George M. Cohan, Minnie Pearl, Chico Marx, Carmen Miranda, Roy Acuff, and Lester Flatt (on a radio show that pitched patent medicine).

Country music great Hank Williams and his medicine show in turn were re-created in the 1964 film biography *Your Cheatin' Heart,* starring George Hamilton as Williams.[64]

Oliver in a 1929 *Saturday Evening Post* article described the colorful medicine show scene as: "Here full evenings of drama, vaudeville, musical comedy, wild west shows, minstrels, magic, burlesque, dog and pony circuses, not to mention Punch and Judy, pantomime, movies, menageries, bands, parades and pie-eating contests, have been thrown in with Ho-Ang-Nan, the great Chinese herb remedy, and med shows have played in opera houses, halls, storerooms, ball parks, show boats and tents, large and small, as well as doorways, street corners and fairs."[65]

Oliver authored a 1895 book, *Lee's Priceless Recipes*, containing "300 secrets for the home, farm, laboratory, workshop, and every department of human endeavor."

Nicholson, John H. & Samuel E. Hill

(See "Gideon Bibles" in Chapter 1.)

Palmer, E.E.

This early 20th century salesman and author of *Forty Years of Hustling* created and sold sparkling and chipped glass outdoor signs.[66]

Parlin, Charles Coolidge (1872-1942)

In 1911 drummer Charles Coolidge Parlin, compiled the first comprehensive market-research study program for the Curtis Publishing Company. His early studies of the farm implement, department store and automobile industries were complete and definitive, according to an Advertising Hall of Fame citation. However, market research did not become widespread until the late 1940s, after the buying spree that greeted the end of WWII subsided. [67]

Patterson, John H. (1844-1922)

Patterson's trend-setting traveling salesman activity really began with his 1884 acquisition of the patent for the "Incorruptible Cashier." He named his company that produced the machine, National Cash Register (NCR).

With military-like precision and regimentation, Patterson organized one of the most aggressive and tenacious sales forces in all of industry. Conducting staff rallies round the country "with the fervor of an evangelist," Patterson taught and led his salesman using his *NCR Primer: How I Sell a Cash Register*. He emphasized visual aids, saying: "Remember, the optic nerve is twenty-two times stronger than the auditory nerve!"[68]

Through his speech-making and some self-promotion, Patterson had considerable influence on salesmanship and management methodology of the day. His methods were described widely in articles and books. Well-regarded early 20th century salesmanship author St. Elmo Lewis, who had worked for both NCR and Burroughs, gave high praise to Patterson and his *NCR Primer*.

However, it is probably most significant that many notable "graduates" from Patterson's "NCR University" went on to sales and management leadership in other companies—Alvan McCauley, President of Burroughs; Charles Kettering of General Motors; Hugh Chalmers of Chalmers Motor Company; William F. Bockhoff of National Automatic Tool; Joseph E. Rodgers, Addressograph-Multigraph; Henry Theobold, Toledo Scale; William Sherman, Standard Register; and Thomas Watson, IBM.[69]

Patterson's influence continued through into the late 20th Century. It was estimated that in 1984 that as many as one-sixth of the CEO's of the period had been NCR men.[70]

Pattison, Edgar & William

As the first American tinsmiths, Scottish immigrants Edgar and William Pattison settled in Berlin, CT, in the mid-1700s. As a result, this region became the tin capital of New England, according to modern-day Massachusetts tinsmith George Monte. Tinware would become one of the most important and "civilizing" products peddled throughout the early American colonies and territories.

Popeil, Ron (1935-)

Chicago-based Popeil is a modern-day traveling salesman who personally sells (and invents) products—Veg-O-Matic, Pocket Fisherman, Pasta Machine, Ronco Power Scrubber—"traveling" the airwaves through his television infomercials. He built his business into a booming telemarketing empire grossing over $1 billion in sales. (*See longer article on Popeil in "It's Location, Location, Location" in Chapter 3.)*

Porter, Bill **(1932-)**

(See J.R. Watkins)

Post, C.W. **(1854-1914)**

An early traveling salesman for farm implements, Post eventually became a manufacturer of implements which he, himself, was inventing: seed planter, steam pump, cultivator, sulky plow, harrow, and hay stacker.

Cereal magnate C.W. Post is buried at the Battle Creek, MI, Oak Hill Cemetery. Though Post is best known for his cereal products, he began work as an Illinois farm implement salesman and inventor. Post died in 1914. The cemetery plot for fellow cereal maker William Keith Kellogg is located just a few yards away. (Photo by Ronald Solberg)

Born and raised in Springfield, IL, Post established the Illinois Agricultural Works in 1885. However, he would become better known for his development of a coffee substitute Postum and the breakfast cereals Grape Nuts and Post Toasties. The inspiration for these food products came from a chance meeting between Post and Dr. John Harvey Kellogg at his nationally known health-food and therapy clinic in Battle Creek, MI. Post had entered the clinic to recuperate from a mixture of debilitating maladies.

Post, called the "grandfather of advertising," is credited with introducing the first nationwide advertising campaign to promote his food products, becoming the largest single advertiser in the country.

In the meantime, W.K. Kellogg, a cereal competitor, was launching his own breakfast foods, but was unable to beat Post's worldwide reputation until after Post's death.

Throughout his life, Post advocated nutritional and dietary reforms that may have contributed in part to the Pure Food and Drug Act of 1906. In addition to his many other achievements, Post established the model town of Post in western Texas in 1907.[71]

Powell, Elkan Harrison (1888-1966)

Although not originally owned by Sears, the *Encyclopaedia Britannica*, was sold through the Sears, Roebuck & Company catalog beginning in 1915. Sears did eventually acquire the *Encyclopaedia*. However, following the infamous stock crash of 1929, it became increasingly difficult for Sears to sell the *Encyclopaedia* by catalog only. Sears put vice president Elkan Harrison Powell in charge of marketing the encyclopaedia. He in turn developed a direct sales methodology that increased profits and came to characterize the culture of the *Britannica* operations throughout the rest of the 20th century.

Powell organized a sales force of 400 salesmen "who knew how to leverage parental aspirations and anxieties into a sale worth between $1,500 and $2,000, depending on the choice of binding. The company was a culture of salesmen, not scholars."

The *Encyclopaedia* was acquired by the University of Chicago from Sears in 1941. Annual sales by the end of the 1980s approached $650 million. Today, with advances in computers and use of the Internet, *Britannica* is offering up its encyclopedia via online services.[72]

Although *Encyclopaedia Britannica* salesmen were not really in vogue until the 1930s, there is evidence that *Britannica* was fielding a direct-sales staff in the U.S. somewhat earlier. For example, Georgetown, Colorado's Hotel de Paris contained two salesman's rooms that were set aside especially for traveling salesmen. Many different salesmen visited the hotel, including the *Encyclopaedia Britannica* salesman, whose name appears several times, 1881-1882, in the hotel's guest registry. The hotel, now maintained by the National Society of Colonial Dames of America in Colorado, currently serves as a meeting place and museum.[73]

Many hotels have catered to traveling salesmen by offering special facilities and showrooms to do business and to display their merchandise. (*See Statler, Hines and "Pearl Street" in Chapter 1.*)

Rockefeller, William Avery (1810-1906)

Although most pitchmen are long forgotten, at least one solo pitchman is remembered today, more for his family's famous name than anything he did on the road. William Avery, an early patent medicine salesman, was the father of John D. Rockefeller, famous oil baron.

Known as "Doc" Rockefeller, William Avery traveled the Midwest after the Civil War, peddling packaged herbs and billing himself as "the Celebrated Cancer Specialist." He sold his cancer cure for the then-stupendous sum of 25 dollars and was known as a good storyteller who played a mean banjo.

Leaving his wife and soon-to-be-famous son John D. Rockefeller behind, Doc lived in a bigamous marriage in South Dakota as Dr. William Levingston. Although relations between father and son were understandably strained, John D. never entirely rejected the influence of "Doctor Bill." Indeed, the petroleum mogul took patent medicines for his health long after the family business changed from snake oil to Standard Oil.[74]

The "Doctor" put on minstrel shows featuring "Negroes in black face" to sell his wares. He once bragged, "I cheat my sons every chance I get" in order to "make 'em sharp."[75]

Sam Slick *(See also Jonathan Slick)*

Slick is a creation of early 19th century Canadian Author Thomas Chandler Haliburton. A resourceful Yankee clock peddler and cracker-barrel philosopher, Slick is noted for many sayings that have become commonplace in English idiom: "This country is going to the dogs;" "Barking up the wrong tree;" "There's many a true word said in jest."

Haliburton had Slick, who peddled cheap clocks in Canada, warn Canadians against upsetting their trade balance with tacky U.S. imports.[76]

Scholl, William (1882-1968)

Scholl demonstrated an early skill and ingenuity as the Midwestern farm family's personal cobbler for its thirteen children. At the age of sixteen his parents apprenticed him to a local shoemaker. A year later, he moved to Chicago to work his trade. Employed as a shoe salesman during the day, he worked his way through the Chicago Medical School's night course. The year he received his medical degree, 1904, the twenty-two-year-old physician patented his first arch support, "Foot-Eazer," a product that would eventually launch an industry in foot care products.

Convinced that knowledge of proper foot care was essential to selling his support pads, Scholl established a podiatric correspondence course for shoe store clerks. In an especially innovative merchandising move Scholl assembled a staff of consultant/salesmen who crisscrossed the country delivering medical and public lectures on proper foot care.

Scholl created a national surge in foot consciousness in 1916 by sponsoring the "Cinderella Foot Contest." The search for the most perfect female feet in America sent tens of thousands of women to their local shoe stores. A panel of foot specialists selected "Cinderella," and her prize-winning footprint was published in many of the country's leading newspapers and magazines. As Scholl had hoped, thousands of American women compared their own imperfect feet with the national ideal and rushed out to buy his products.[77]

The Scholl yellow-and-blue packages are a familiar part of the American scene in stores across the country. Scholl's College of Podiatric Medicine and Museum was, until 2005, headquartered in a landmark building site in downtown Chicago.

Scott, William Dill (1869-1955)

Born in the rural Illinois town of Cooksville, Scott went on to play a important role in defining the psychology of the successful salesman.

A prolific writer on the topic, Scott headed up Northwestern University's Psychology Department in 1909. In 1916 Scott became head of the Bureau of Salesmanship Research at the Carnegie Institute of Technology (now known as Carnegie Mellon), undertaking a substantial effort to identify the characteristics of successful salesmanship. The American Psychological Association elected Scott as president in 1919. In 1920 he became president of Northwestern University, a post he held until 1939.

Scott's most important contribution may have been his work on standardized personnel hiring policies that were eventually used not only by sales-related organizations but by the U.S. Army.[78]

Sears, Richard

(*See Elkan Harrison Powell and "catalog" in Chapter 1.*)

Shaklee, Dr. Forrest C. (1894-1985)

Along with his sons Forrest, Jr., and Raleigh, Shaklee founded Shaklee Products in 1956 to produce and sell nutritional products through a "network marketing" system of over 700,000 members worldwide in Canada, Japan, Malaysia, Mexico, and the U.S.[79] (*For more details on the "network marketing sales system" see Jay Van Andel.)*

Singer, Isaac (1811-1875)

Born in Pittstown, NY, Singer was an inventor, manufacturer, and innovative merchandiser/salesman of sewing machines. His innovative sales tactics included demonstrations and the installment pay plans, beginning with a down payment for as little as $5, "thus appealing to low-income-level buyers. Singer sent canvassers to cover country districts and towns, going from house to house. Singer's horse-and-buggy salesman soon became a part of the American scene." Singer's sewing machine was probably America's first home appliance.[80]

Skiff, Frank Vernon (1869-1933) & Frank P. Ross

Skiff, the son of a grocer and born in Newton, IA, was employed with the India Tea Company in Chicago in the 1890s. Skiff, however, concerned about the product's freshness, became dissatisfied

This 1892 poster touting Isaac Singer's sewing machine's international popularity suggests that the sewing machine might have been one of the earliest of America's home-grown products to generate such fame. Countries featured are Italy, Spain, Tunis, Manila, Bosnia, Japan, Norway, India, Sweden, and Portugal. (Library of Congress)

with the way coffee was being sold out of bags, bins, and large canisters. In 1899 Skiff went into business for himself with only $700 cash, a horse, wagon, and his idea to operate a business that would offer freshly roasted coffee daily directly door-to-door to the consumer.

As his coffee business increased, he was asked about other products. Skiff added teas and an assortment of spices to the list of household necessities. By 1927, Skiff was offering more than fifty foods, laundry and toilet products.

In 1901 Skiff's brother-in-law Frank P. Ross joined him as a partner. In 1902, Skiff and Ross were selling "Teas, Coffee and Spices" under the "Skiff and Ross" name. They soon named the venture "Jewel Tea Company," chosen because in those days, anything special was called a "jewel."

Primarily as a home delivery service that offered an assortment of coffee, tea, spices and premiums, the company established a few stores to show and sell their product lines. These stores, however, were more of an advertising showcase and were available only in certain areas.

Jewel reached the million-dollar mark in annual sales in 1910 and had established 400 routes. By 1915 it was recording more than $8 million in sales supported by 850 routes. In 1916 Jewel incorporated in New York, expanding into new territory and operating a total of 1,645 routes.

Skiff and Ross left the Jewel business in 1919. In 1924 Jewel's Home Service Division was launched where recipes were developed, products evaluated, pointers sold and ideas promoting more products reviewed.

A monthly publication, the *Jewel-News* and a series of cookbooks, were soon published and the most famous name in Jewel's history was adopted, "Mary Dunbar," a sort of "Betty Crocker" for the business. Throughout the years, all items, packaging, appliances and publications tested and approved by "Mary Dunbar" received her "Seal of Approval."

Jewel's future was reshaped with the onset of WWII when women replaced men in operating both service routes and stores that Jewel had acquired over the years. One-fourth of the food stores had women managers and during 1944, 700 women were route saleswomen. In 1949 catalogs were distributed free by salespeople to established customers and orders were taken bi-weekly and filled through the mail. Eventually in the early 1980s the route-serviced Jewel Home Shopping Service was eliminated in favor of the Jewel store-based business.[81]

Smith, William (1830-1913) & Andrew (1836-1894)

These brothers traveled New York's Hudson River and the Catskills, selling large jars of cough drops to country merchants. They had inherited the cough drop business from their father James in 1866. They were soon bothered with imitators who offered cough drops under the name of Schmidt Brothers, Smith and Brothers, or some such plagiarism. To identify their product, the Smith Brothers used a trademark—one of the first—of the still famous bearded portraits of the brothers. They also began to use factory-filled packages. While they were not the first to package a product commercially, they were the first to successfully capitalize on the practice.

William and Andrew acquired the lifelong nicknames of "Trade" and "Mark," for on the cough drop package the word "trademark" was divided, each half appearing under a brother's picture.[82]

Statler, E.M. (1863-1928)

As the moving genius behind the modern hotel, Statler got most of his ideas on hotel innovations by chatting with drummers in the smoking cars. His hotels were designed to please these critical travelers. In the days before Statler built his first big hotel in Buffalo in 1907 most hotels offered one bathroom to a floor. Heat and hot water were unreliable, and "no proprietor called his house really full until all the double beds were fully occupied, often by bedmates who were complete strangers."[83]

Strauss, Levi (1829-1902)

Immigrating to America in 1847, the eighteen-year-old German Jew Levi Strauss walked the streets of New York peddling cloth, yarns, needles, scissors, buttons, combs, books, shoes, blankets and kettles door-to-door, eventually traveling as far out as Pelham in Westchester County. Strauss moved on to Louisville, KY, where he tried selling his goods in the Kentucky hills.

As the Gold Rush of 1849 heated up, Strauss moved his business to San Francisco to sell his items to the California miners where he joined up with his brother-in-law David Stern in a "dry goods and clothing" wholesale business. Legend has it that a miner complained that "Should'a brought pants. Pants don't wear worth a hoot in the diggin's. Can't get a pair strong enough to last." The legend continues to tell us that Strauss then tailored a pair of pants from canvas intended for a Conestoga wagon to meet the miners' needs. Though now called "jeans," Strauss originally referred to the pants as "waist high overalls."

However, it was the tailoring efforts of another Jewish immigrant Jacob Davis that completed the "Levi's Legend." Making his pants from wagon covers and tent cloth, Davis used rivets to fasten the easily-torn pockets. He eventually added a distinctive orange seam thread to match the color of the rivets. Davis soon partnered up with Strauss, a man with superior business skills and much-needed capital. Davis sold his share of the patent to Strauss in 1873 and retired from the business. By the 1890s Strauss's company was employing over 500 workers with sales of more than $2.5 million. In 1890 the patent ran out, freeing others to copy the design.

Throughout his life, Strauss remained active in philanthropy as a trustee of the Pacific Hebrew Orphan Asylum and the Home and Eureka Benevolent Society. He established 28 perpetual scholarships to the University of California, four from each congressional district in the state.

During his later years, Strauss fraternized with such San Francisco dignitaries as *San Francisco Examiner* publisher William Randolph Hearst and the witty newspaper writer Ambrose Bierce, author of *The Devil's Dictionary*. *(See Bierce's definition of an auctioneer in Chapter 6.)*[84]

Stewart, Al

Stewart was an 1870s traveling salesman for a Chicago wholesale grocer who made and sold Mrs. Stewart's Bluing (MSB) to customers in Iowa and Minnesota. In 1883 Stewart sold the rights to MSB to wholesaler and Minneapolis resident Luther Ford.

Ford made immediate plans to extend distribution of the product across the region. Production and distribution grew slowly until 1910, when Ford's two sons put their efforts into a more aggressive sales program. By 1925, additional factories existed in Portland, San Francisco, St. Louis, Pasadena, and Winnipeg, Manitoba. Eventually, with business booming, the salesman system of distribution was replaced by the appointment of food or grocery brokers. In 1986 the business was moved from downtown Minneapolis to suburban Bloomington. Although MSB has had considerable competition from other "bluing" products over the years, MSB continues to be a popular clothing whitening agent, even to this day.

The face of the stern elderly woman appearing on each bottle's "legendary" label is not that of Stewart's wife or mother, but rather that of his mother-in-law. Both his wife and mother refused to become a label.

MSB isn't used just to whiten clothes. It has been sold to schools, scout packs, science supply houses and consumers as the foundation for a science project to make a "Salt Crystal Garden."[85]

The Wm. A. Kilian Hardware Company of Chestnut Hill, PA, (http://www.kilianhardware.com) suggests that the product may also be used for swimming pools, bird baths, white hair and pets, and for cleaning crystal and glass.

Kilian offers up the following recipe for growing the crystals: Day #1 Place damp sponge pieces in a shallow glass or plastic bowl. Over sponge, pour 2 tablespoons each of Mrs. Stewart's Bluing, salt, water, and ammonia; Day #2 Add 2 more tablespoons salt; Day #3 Add 2 tablespoons each MSB, salt, water, and ammonia. Avoid pouring on crystal growth; Repeat Day #3 as necessary to keep crystals growing. For color, add drops of food coloring or ink to each piece.

Stone, W. Clement (1902-2002)

Salesman, businessman, philanthropist, and self-help book author, Stone started his business career at age 13 when he owned his first newsstand. At age 16 he moved to Detroit to help out his mother with an insurance company she opened there. He was soon making $100 a week, selling casualty insurance.

Based on his early success in the 1920s Stone established the Combined Insurance Company of America and by 1930 had over 1000 agents selling for him across the country. The company, headquartered in Chicago, eventually would become the Aon Corporation in 1987.

In 1960, Stone teamed up with Napoleon Hill to write *Success Through a Positive Mental Attitude.* The two also founded a monthly digest, *Success Unlimited.*

Stone made substantial charitable donations of over $275 million to mental health and Christian organizations. Stone was a significant supporter of the Boys and Girls Clubs of America and served on its national board. Og Mandino, popular sales motivational writer, credits Stone and his PMA ("Whatever the mind can conceive and believe, the mind can achieve with PMA") for turning his life around.[86]

Sut Lovingood

Sut is a kind of 19th century Yankee peddler who was given to trickery, using some chicanery to achieve his ends. The subject of American humorist writer George W. Harris's stories, *The Lovingood Papers,* Sut may be a real or fictional character. It is unclear whether Sut was Harris himself, someone Harris knew, or an entirely fictional character.

Mark Twain, in 1867, wrote: "It was reported, years ago, that this writer was dead—accidentally shot in a Tennessee doggery before the war, but he has turned up again, and is a conductor on a railroad train that travels somewhere between Charleston, SC, and Memphis. His real name is George Harris. I have before me his book, just forwarded by Dick & Fitzgerald, the publishers, New York. It contains all of his early sketches that used to be so popular in the

West ... the book abounds in humor, and is said to represent the Tennessee dialect correctly. It will sell well in the West, but the Eastern people will call it coarse and possibly taboo it."[87]

Another writer, Cohen Hennig, agrees that Harris was widely known as "Sut." But he goes on to say that there was a real Sut. His name was William S. Miller. His obituary notice, found by Ben Harris McClary in the *Athens Tennessee Post* of August 28, 1858, refers to him as "Sut" and states that he was the "hero of *The Lovingood Papers.*" Sut Miller died at Ducktown, Polk County in the East Tennessee mountains where Harris had once worked as manager of a copper mine.[88]

Terry, Eli (1772-1852)

Terry was a 1790's "Connecticut Yankee" who conceived of the idea of reducing the size of a clock so that it could be set on a shelf. Up to this point, itinerant clock salesman sold only the works and the purchaser had to provide the case for the long clock, either making it himself or having the local cabinet-maker build it for him. A young mechanic, Seth Thomas, from West Haven, would later help Terry set up his business. The "Seth Thomas" clocks would become famous as Thomas acquired the original Terry factory.[89]

"The 'free home trial,' still popular with merchandisers today, is nothing more than a variation of Terry's clock peddler's tactic."[90]

Til Eulenspiegel

This early legendary European figure is a prototype for America's Yankee peddler. "Eulenspiegel" (meaning owl mirror), is a German folk hero who played pranks on fellow countrymen, exposing weaknesses and frailties—something like a Robin Hood of trickery, Til was inclined to play his pranks on the elite and wealthy.

Til received his name from one of the first tricks he is reported to have played on his fellow countrymen. When only 15, Til "erected a little tent at Damme upon four stakes and he cried out that everyone might see within, represented in a handsome frame of hay, his present and future self."[91]

"He would display his face, or sundry things, in the frame, reflecting as in a mirror, something about the people to themselves. Frequently he used his mirror to obtain valuables or monies from the naive citizenry. Upon completing his observations, Til would say 'Ik ben ulen Spiegel,' even as it is still said today in East and West Flanders. And from thence there came to him his surname of Ulenspiegel."[92]

Nineteenth century composer Richard Strauss, (1864-1949) enhanced Til's fame by writing the tone poem *Til Eulenspiegel's Merry Pranks*.

Traute, Henry C.

(*See "matchbooks," in Chapter 1*)

Tupper, Earl (1907-1983)

Reminiscent of the 18th century tin ware peddler, Earl Silas Tupper made available useful containers and utensils to households across America. However, he was to update both the product and manner in which it was sold and distributed. Describing himself as "ham inventor and Yankee trader," Tupper not only created a new product but created an innovative system of promoting and selling it to the American public.

As a farm boy in Harvard, MA, Tupper discovered he could make more money with a lot less work by buying and selling other kids' vegetables than by raising his own.

While working as a chemist for DuPont in the 1930s, Tupper founded a mail-order business to sell combinations of combs, toothbrushes, and other toiletry items. By 1937 he had made enough money to leave DuPont. On his own he set to work with polyethylene, a new synthetic polymer that produced a soft, durable plastic. Through his work he developed an especially resilient product that could be molded into a wide variety of household items.

By 1947 his company, established in 1942 as the Tupperware Corporation, reached sales of $5 million annually. He eventually discovered that Tupperware sold best through a system whereby housewives would invite friends and neighbors to their homes for parties. In 1951 Tupperware Home Parties were incorporated and retail sales were discontinued. Within three years Tupper had signed up nine thousand dealers who arranged parties and sales had topped $25 million.

In 1958 Tupper sold his company to Rexall Drugs for more than $9 million.[93]

Van Andel, Jay (1924-2004) with Richard DeVos, Sr. (1926-)

Van Andel with DeVos founded the $6 billion global direct-sales giant Amway, relying on a vast sales force to sell products and recruit others to do the same.

Creating Amway in 1959, Van Andel started with the sale of vitamins, then soap and other home care products. Amway expanded rapidly with the development of a network of distributors who were encouraged to sell and consume the company's products and to promote the virtue of direct sales to others. The Amway sales method has been continuously supported via self-help books and motivational tape recordings, binding together Amway's 3-million international troop of salespeople.

Retiring as chairman of Amway in 1995, Van Andel devoted much of his later years to philanthropic causes, including the Van Andel Institute which financed research for a range of human health topics. He also contributed millions to urban renewal projects in Grand Rapids, MI (his hometown), and was a trustee of the Heritage Foundation and the Hudson Institute.

Throughout his life, Van Andel was critical of the interfering tendencies of big government. Though the Federal Trade Commission spent six years investigating whether the company's practices were an illegal pyramid scheme, charges were eventually dropped.[94] (*See "multilevel marketing" in Chapter 1.*)

Richard DeVos, listed by the 2007 *Forbes* magazine as one of the richest men in the world with a fortune of $3.5 billion, is a heart transplant recipient and owner of pro basketball's Orlando Magic. DeVos was inspired by his successful 1997 transplant experience to write *Hope From My Heart: Ten Lessons for Life*.[95]

Voigt, B.F.

This 19th century German salesman/author wrote that the successful and efficient traveling salesman planned his itinerary so as to cover as many locations as possible without visiting any location more than once. Voigt probably contributed the name, if not principle, to the resulting mathematical "Traveling Salesman Problem" that curries considerable interest even to this day.[96] *(See "Traveling Salesman Problem" in Chapter 1 for further information.)*

Walker, Sarah Breedlove (1867-1919)

Walker was one of the first American women of any race or rank to become a millionaire through her own efforts, sharing that "title" with her early St. Louis teacher and "boss," Annie Turnbo Malone.

Madame C.J. Walker, as she would eventually become known, offered a nearly a mythic appeal to African American women through her cosmetic business, elevating sophisticated glamour to a new level. In the process her company's 20,000 agents would generate annual sales of a quarter of a million dollars.[97] *(See expanded article on Walker in "The Sweet Smell of Success" in Chapter 3.)*

Wasson, Harriet

Wasson was a California subscription book-seller in the 1870s who authored anonymously a book about her experiences as a door-to-door saleswoman. The book, *Facts, By a Woman,* was published in 1881 to counter the innuendo she experienced as a woman in the book-selling trade.

Wasson indicates that she decided to write the book upon hearing a woman, remarking to other women about a female book agent she had turned away from her door: "I cannot, for the life of me, see how any woman that has the least sort of respect for herself can engage in such an occupation. Why the very idea is enough to repel a pure-minded person."

Before becoming a book agent, Wasson tried unsuccessfully to support herself by selling something called "plaiting machines" door-to-door. That was somewhat more respectable for Wasson, it seems, since most of her customers were other women. On the other hand, selling books was less respectable since it brought her into contact with more men customers.

The first book Wasson ever peddled was Mark Twain's *Tom Sawyer.*[98] *(See "subscription publishing" in Chapter 1 for more about Wasson's profession and Mark Twain's interest in the subscription system to promote his books)*

Watkins, J.R. (1840- ?)

Twenty-eight-year-old entrepreneur Watkins founded the J.R. Watkins Medical Company in Plainview, MN, in 1868, giving birth to one of America's first natural remedies companies where traveling sales people marketed directly to consumers, door-to-door. There is some claim that Watkins originated the concept of network marketing. *(See Van Andel and Shaklee for more details.)*

In 1869 Watkins introduced America's first money-back guarantees and the "Trail-Mark" bottle which indicated how much of the product could be used and still returned for a full refund. Watkins Red Liniment, made from Asian camphor and red pepper extract, was the company's first product which is still sold today.

The company was moved to Winona, MN, in 1885 where the Watkins Museum resides to this day. One of the company's most famous products, its vanilla extract, was introduced in 1895.

Ninety percent of Watkins production capacity was dedicated to the WWII effort in 1942—products included pure dried whole eggs, dessert powder, gelatin desserts, lemon juice powder, orange beverage base powder, louse powder, and insecticide powder for body-crawling insects.

A made-for-TV 2003 TNT movie, *Door to Door*, about Watkins Associate Bill Porter won six Emmys, including best made for TV movie and best actor for William H. Macy. Despite the fact the real-life Bill Porter was born with cerebral palsy, he was honored by Watkins as "Salesman of the Year" for his outstanding sales record.[99] ABC News broadcast a short documentary on Bill Porter in a December, 1999 "20/20" segment.[100] A 2002 book *Ten Things I Learned from Bill Porter* was written by Porter's long-time assistant Shelly Brady.

Watson, Thomas J (1874-1956)

An early sales manager for John Patterson's National Cash Register Company, Watson became president of the small Computing-Tabulating-Recording Company in 1914, later to become the better known IBM in 1934.

Watson introduced the novel idea of bringing salesmen in on meetings with his engineers so that the engineers could explain technical issues with the salesmen. On the other hand, the engineers could hear about customer issues and problems from the salesmen. It was this kind of training and preparation that made the IBM salesmen the best-informed in the business.

Watson, who was fond of aphorisms, contributed the one word "THINK," a word that would soon become IBM's credo. Watson demanded his salesmen "think their way to success."[101]

Thomas Watson's son, Thomas Watson, Jr., took over the presidency of IBM in 1951, aggressively moving the company into electronics and computers. IBM became a billion-dollar company in 1957, moving it far ahead of its business-machine competitors.[102]

Weems, "Parson" (1759-1825)

Born Mason Locke Weems in Anne Arundel County, MD, the "Parson" was a 19th century American book peddler, 'the best known and most romantic of all,' who was responsible for fabricating the

Early 19th century Mason Locke Weems may have been the most successful book salesman ever. He not only sold religious materials but dispensed books that he himself had authored. One book that he wrote—a biography of George Washington—although more fiction than fact, has become something of a classic because of its "I cannot tell a lie" episode. (The Weems-Botts Museum)

George Washington cherry tree story … for thirty years there was no more familiar figure on the roads of the Southern States than this book and Bible salesman, storyteller, fiddler, and author, who, 'provided gypsy-like with horse and wagon, year-after-year' … So famously did his trade prosper that in one year he sold three-thousand copies of an expensive Bible."[103] (*See Mathew Carey. Also see extended article on Weems in "Worth More than a Thousand Trees" in Chapter 3.)*

Welton, Merit

"A button salesman for the Scovil Manufacturing Company of Waterbury, CT, made a trip through the Midwest in 1832 to sell buttons by sample … He took orders, demanded payment in cash, and deliveries were made later by freight. Mr. Welton was the first drummer, so far as we know, and this first trip was not a success."[104] He completed the circuit in ten weeks. More successful later trips were made in 1833 and 1834.[105]

White, William J.

(See Thomas Adams)

Wrigley Jr., William (1861-1932)

Born in Philadelphia, Wrigley began his sales career, selling his father's soap and other products door-to door. Wrigley first discovered chewing gum as a premium, given away to help sell baking powder, but soon people were asking for the gum and ignoring the baking powder. He quickly reversed the procedure and started giving away other premiums to persuade retailers to buy his gum. In 1892-93 Wrigley started manufacturing his own gum. Today, the Wrigley Company sells about half of America's chewing gum.

An early owner of the Chicago Cubs baseball team, Wrigley founded the All-American Girls Professional Baseball League in 1943. It was the first professional women's league in the country.[106]

Wrigley was instrumental in the establishment of the island of Catalina (off the shore of Los Angeles, CA) as a conservancy, protecting it for all generations to come. He had bought the island earlier in 1919, improving it with public utilities, new steamships, a hotel, a casino, and extensive plantings of trees, shrubs, and flowers.[107] (*See Thomas Adams for more Wrigley details.)*

Ziglar, Hilary Clinton "Zig"(1926-)

This salesman, motivational speaker, author, and born-again Christian began work as a door-to-door salesman for the Wearever Aluminum Company. Early on he struggled, however, as he freely admits: "It was really a question of survival. When our first baby was born, I had to literally go out and sell two sets of cookware in order to get her out of the hospital."

His turn-around occurred when a Wearever sales executive took him aside and told Ziglar that if he recognized his ability, he could become a "great one." Apparently that was the kind of encouragement Ziglar needed since he soon became the second highest achiever of some 7,000 Wearever salesmen.

Since 1970 Ziglar has traveled over five million miles, delivering his life improvement messages. Headquartered in Dallas, TX, Ziglar Training Systems offers public seminars, customized educational programs, workshops and keynote speakers.

Ziglar has written twenty-three books on personal growth, leadership, sales, faith, family and success including his very popular 1984 book, *See You at the Top,* which was republished as a 25th anniversary revised edition.[108]

CHAPTER 3

Personalities: "The Trailblazers"

Intimate knowledge of product, uncanny sense of territory

The Sweet Smell of Success

Several sales men and women have become very successful at creating and selling their own cosmetic lines, building their respective businesses into industry behemoths. David H. McConnell's route to that pinnacle was, perhaps, the most unusual and circuitous of the lot.

> *Sell when you can, you are not for all markets*
> —William Shakespeare

In the 1880s, McConnell was a 16-year-old door-to-door salesman, peddling books to the residents of Oswego, NY. However, he was finding it increasingly difficult to gain entrance to the parlor where he could complete his sale. To open the doors to the homes on his route he began using the tried and true technique of offering a free gift in exchange for being allowed to make a sales pitch—in this instance, a small vial of perfume. McConnell actually blended the original scent himself with some assistance from a local pharmacist.

In salesmanship, a foot in the door is worth two on the desk.
—Evan Esar

McConnell soon realized that the perfume was much more interesting to the housewives than either of his books, thus the astute salesman wisely switched to the perfume business, abandoning his books. In 1886 McConnell organized his New York-based California Perfume Company, named in honor of a friend and investor from California.

The first "Avon Lady" was Mrs. P.F.E. Albee, a widow from Winchester, NH. She began her chime-ringing career selling the company's popular Little Dot Perfume Set; eventually she recruited other women, training them as door-to-door salespeople. Taking a clue from Albee, by 1887 McConnell had hired twelve women to sell his line of eighteen fragrances.

The company was renamed Avon for the simple reason that the New York state town in which David McConnell lived, Suffern on the Ramapo, reminded him of Shakespeare's Stratford-on-Avon.[1]

Chance favors the prepared mind.
—Louis Pasteur

Despite hefty cosmetic competition, Avon currently ranks first in cosmetic sales nationwide. Avon's force of salespersons has grown from the early dozen to more than 5 million representatives worldwide. Avon's line of cosmetics has expanded from 18 perfume fragrances to products for the skin and hair, bath and body, nail, face, and eye coloring, and wellness and vitamin items. In 2004 Avon launched a line of men's care products, as well. McConnell's Avon Company. The sweet smell of success? Indeed! Also, now, achieving the very sweet feel of accomplishment.[2]

You haven't got a chance

In 1936 an American business executive arrived in France. He carried a sample case of cosmetics. The customs inspector asked incredulously, "You're bringing cosmetics to sell in France?" The businessman answered with a "Yes." The inspector said, "You haven't got a chance." "Well, you may be right," responded the young man, "but my father, Max Factor, is convinced we have something women want." (Anonymous)

A bumblebee that could fly

Mary Kay Ash began her sales activity selling child psychology books door-to-door in the late 1930s. Ash eventually became a sales representative and manager for the Stanley Home Products Company from 1939 to 1952, later she was national training director at the World Gift Company.

In 1963 with $5,000 Ash founded Mary Kay Cosmetics in a Dallas storefront. Taking a page from the McConnell-Albee book, Ash's firm sold products door-to-door using nine saleswomen called "beauty consultants."

> *Aerodynamically, the bumblebee shouldn't be able to fly, but the bumblebee doesn't know it, so it goes on flying anyway.*
> —Mary Kay Ash

The business grew steadily, helped by Ash's positive philosophy and generous use of incentives such as free pink Cadillacs and diamond jewelry for successful sales people. The firm remains a major presence in today's competitive beauty market.[3]

She never worked a day in her life

Cosmetic saleswoman Esteé Lauder used the premium, but in a somewhat different and innovative way. In the 1930s, Lauder was on the road in New York, selling a face cream brewed in a kitchen by her chemist uncle. She traveled to local beauty salons, demonstrating the product to "women marooned under hair dryers." Eventually, in 1948, Lauder was granted counter space at Saks Fifth Avenue.

> *I never worked a day in my life without selling—and selling it hard.*
> —Esteé Lauder

With only a meager advertising budget, Lauder created, what today is considered a "promotional mainstay"—a "gift" (premium?) with a purchase." She went on to introduce such products as the scented bath oil, "Youth Dew," and such brands as "Clinique" and "Prescriptions." She died at age 97 in 2004, leaving behind a company worth $10 billion.[4]

Success times two

The nation's first Black millionairess may have been cosmetic magnate Annie Turnbo Malone (1869-1957). Malone developed her own hair care products that she sold door-to-door in southern Illinois to the local African American communities.

It is said that Malone, while attending high school in Peoria, IL, learned from her chemistry lessons that harm was being done to follicles and scalp by the mixture of goose fat, meat drippings, and coarse soaps commonly used by Black women to style their hair.[5]

Malone moved her business to St. Louis in 1904, coinciding with the World's Fair there. She trained agents nationwide and began marketing her products under the name "Poro."

> *If I have a formula or rule, it can be summed up in single, too-familiar cliche: honesty is the best policy. This, undoubtedly is an over-simplification of a rather complicated relationship between my products, my sponsors, my listeners, and my radio program. I have a genuine affection and respect for all of these, and this big love-fest is what has hung the label of 'saleswoman' on me.*
>
> —Mary Margaret McBride,
> (radio broadcaster and columnist)

During the 1920's Malone was reported to have been worth fourteen million dollars. Her fortune was made with the development of non-damaging hair straightening products, hair growers and conditioners. Under the "Poro" name Malone built a financial empire as well as the Poro College (1917), aimed at educating St. Louis' Black community and training women as agents for Poro products. Later, the college was moved to Chicago. By 1926 the college claimed to have graduated 75,000 agents, serving customers worldwide. The college no longer exists.

> *Rock and roll Hall-of-Famer Chuck Berry graduated from the Chicago-based Poro College in 1952.*

A philanthropist in her later years, Malone made substantial contributions to Howard University and donated monies for the construction of the St. Louis Colored Orphan's Home, now known as the Annie Malone Children and Family Service Center.[6]

It is probably fitting that Sarah Breedlove Walker, 1867-1919, shares with one other the honor of being the first American woman of any race or rank to become a millionaire through her own efforts. That other—Annie Turnbo Malone, Walker's early teacher and boss.

Madame C.J. Walker, as she would eventually become known, worked for nearly two decades as a domestic and laundress before she became an entrepreneur. In the early 1900s she became a commissioned agent for Malone in St. Louis who was selling her own hair products to African Americans.[7]

> *There is little difference in people, but that little difference makes a big difference. That little difference is attitude. The big difference is whether it is positive or negative." ... "You are a product of your environment. So choose the environment that will best develop you toward your objective. Analyze your life in terms of its environment. Are the things around you helping you toward success—or are they holding you back?" ... "We have a problem. 'Congratulations.' But, it's a tough problem. 'Then, double congratulations.'*
> —W. Clement Stone

A very successful sales representative for Malone, Breedlove moved to Denver in 1905 to sell Malone's products. During that year, Sarah Breedlove Walker emerged a changed women, as "Madame C.J. Walker," an independent hairdresser and door-to-door saleswoman for her own very successful formulated cosmetic products and the Walker System—a shampoo, a pomade 'hair-grower,' vigorous brushing, and the application of heated iron combs to the hair.[8]

> *I would like to leave you now with my best three words of advice: Work for yourself... If you're a good salesperson, you can make more money in one month selling a product that you make or market than you can in a year working for an employer... Have a quality product, believe in it thoroughly, and go out and sell it. And don't forget: Make sure it's a great gift.*
> —Ron Popeil

Madame Walker's appeal to African American women was star-like. Author Harold Evans compares Walker's eventual celebrity status to that of current day Oprah Winfrey, "and in doing so, she liberated millions of women."[9]

Madame Walker, moving her headquartered to Indianapolis in 1910, was now heading up a corporation with a quarter of a million dollars annual sales, making the Walker Company one of the largest Black businesses in the country. Walker began marrying philanthropy with business, organizing her 20,000 agents into Walker Clubs. She rewarded those who raised the most money for charity along with those who registered the highest sales.

Walker eventually left Indianapolis in 1916 for New York City and constructed a nearby Hudson Valley estate, "Italianate Villa" at Irvington-on-the Hudson. She died in 1919.

> *We can let circumstances rule us, or we can take charge and rule our lives from within.*
> —Earl Nightingale

Walker's contributions were substantial—exceptional saleswoman, insightful manager, clever marketer, generous philanthropist, and an example to those who would follow as someone from the humblest of beginnings, reaching the very highest pinnacles of success.[10]

In 2006 playwright/director Regina Taylor introduced her play about Sarah Breedlove—*The Dreams of Sarah Breedlove*. Breedlove attributed her transformation—from washerwoman to millionaire business magnate Madam Walker—to a dream in which an African man whispered the secret ingredients of a scalp conditioner and hair growth product. (Thus, the name for the play, "The Dreams of Sarah Breedlove.") [11]

What's in a Name?

Johnny Appleseed, as an early environmentalist, was honored with his own 5-cent U.S. postage stamp in 1966. (Johnny Appleseed Museum)

Could it be? I asked myself why I hadn't noticed this before. There's the ongoing discussion about nature and nurture. Are we who we are because we were born that way? Or has the environment to which we were born molded us into what we are to become? Probably a mixture of both, I had finally concluded.

But, then along came Johnny Appleseed — a peddler like no other; so outstanding in his accomplishments and distinctive in his ways that it's difficult to separate fact from fiction and reality from legend. He has been portrayed and reported on in literally hundreds of different venues—biographies, folklore and popular tradition, poetry and novels, children's fiction, music, film, and several festivals and memorials. Even a Johnny Appleseed Society celebrates his life and contributions both in a museum housed at Urbana University, Urbana, OH, and on the website, *www.urbana.edu/appleseed/museum.htm.*

I wondered about this man, born in 1774 in Leominster, MA, of a father who was a farmer and carpenter who served in the Revolutionary War as one of the original "Minute Men" and later was with Washington's army in New York. Chapman's mother who died when he was only two, was related to the "notorious" Englishman, Count Rumford, politician, scientist, who possessed a vast fortune.

Little is known of "Johnny" before the age of 23. It was then, in 1797, that he began his trek westward from eastern Pennsylvania up the Susquehanna River with apple seeds in tow. As he traveled he stopped to plant his seeds in nurseries that would eventually total more than 30 in the states of Pennsylvania, Ohio, and Indiana. In Ohio and Indiana, the traces of such orchards that were started from John Chapman's stock alone extend over hundreds of square miles."[12] In fact, it is estimated that by 1838 Johnny had planted seeds that had grown into trees bearing fruit over an area of 100,000 square miles. In addition, his eventual land holdings that he owned by deed outright or on long-time lease were nearly 1200 acres.[13]

> *Anyone can count the number of seeds in an apple, but only God can count the number of apples in a seed.*
> —From a "Sayings of Holmes County, OH."
> (Plaque on wall at the Johnny Appleseed Museum, Urbana, OH)

In 1881 David Ayres, whose family had secured trees from Chapman, remembered him as follows: "I was acquainted with Jonathan Chapman, alias Johnny Appleseed, in Richland County, OH, in 1822, when I was yet in my teens. I lost track of him in 1837 or 1838.

"He was a spare, light man of medium height, and would weigh about 125 pounds. He had fine, dark hair, which he allowed to grow down to his shoulders and brushed back of his ears. His beard was grayish and clipped with shears, never close. He was always clad very poorly — old slipshod shoes without stockings, the cast-off clothes of some charitable miser. He would not ask for any, and I suppose he never purchased any. He would eat at the table with any family and liked good victuals, but he would also eat scraps which were designed for the slop barrel. He slept on the floor on an old blanket.

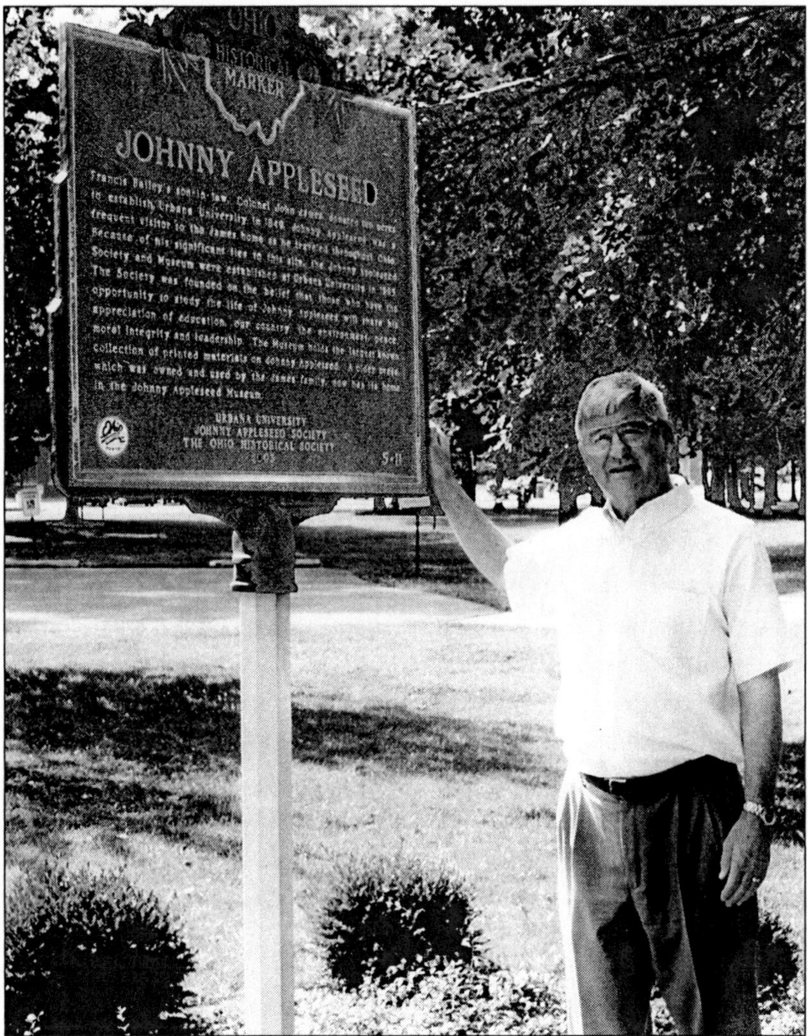

Mr. Joe Besecker, director of The Johnny Appleseed Society, stands next to the marker designating the grounds as an official Johnny Appleseed historical site. The marker reads: "Francis Bailey's son-in-law Colonel John James donated ten acres to establish Urbana University in 1849. Johnny Appleseed was a frequent visitor to the James home as he traveled throughout Ohio. Because of his significant ties to this site, the Johnny Appleseed Society and Museum were established at Urbana University in 1995. The Society was established on the belief that those who have the opportunity to study the life of Johnny Appleseed will share his appreciation of education, our country, the environment, peace, moral integrity and leadership. The Museum holds the largest known collection of printed materials on Johnny Appleseed. A cider press which was owned and used by the James family now has its home in the Johnny Appleseed Museum." (Photo by Ronald Solberg)

His old slipshod shoes were untidy looking and he seemed to care very little about his person. I never heard of his being sick."[14]

Author Edward Hoagland in a December, 1979 *American Heritage* article tells us that at his death in 1845, Johnny was dressed in his coffee sack "as well as waist sections of four pairs of old pants cut off and slit so that they lapped 'like shingles' around his hips, under an antiquated pair of pantaloons."

Johnny Appleseed's curious dress, including the cooking pot hat, has made it into many a modern medium—books, posters, and film. Current historians, though, tend to consider his hat an amusing, if not eccentric, part of Appleseed's "rural legend." On the other hand, early eyewitnesses support the fact that Johnny did indeed wear the metal hat. John Henry Cook who actually accompanied Johnny on many of his travels, described his headgear as "a pyramid of three hats" in which he carried his religious tracts. "The first was only a brim. Next came his cooking pot. Surmounting all was a hat with a crown. The sum total, if extremely odd, it was still rather ingenious. It enabled him to carry not only his kettle but his treasure of sacred literature, sandwiched between the pot and the crown of the uppermost hat. The books were kept dry and his hands were left free to deal with seed bags and tools."[15] (Author's note: Another legendary American, President Abraham Lincoln, used his stove-pipe hat as a depository for legal papers, according to author Andrew Ferguson in his *Land of Lincoln*)

> *Johnny Appleseed's name will never be forgotten ... We shall realize more and more the value of the work he has done. We will keep his memory green and future generations of boys and girls will love him as we, who knew him, have learned to love him.*
>
> —General William Tecumseh Sherman
> (Johnny Appleseed Museum)

Although in demeanor he appeared penniless, he was in no way a pauper. Permitting people along the way to think that he was an innocent bumpkin to whom money meant nothing may have been an intentional "act" on his part, considering that he was occasionally

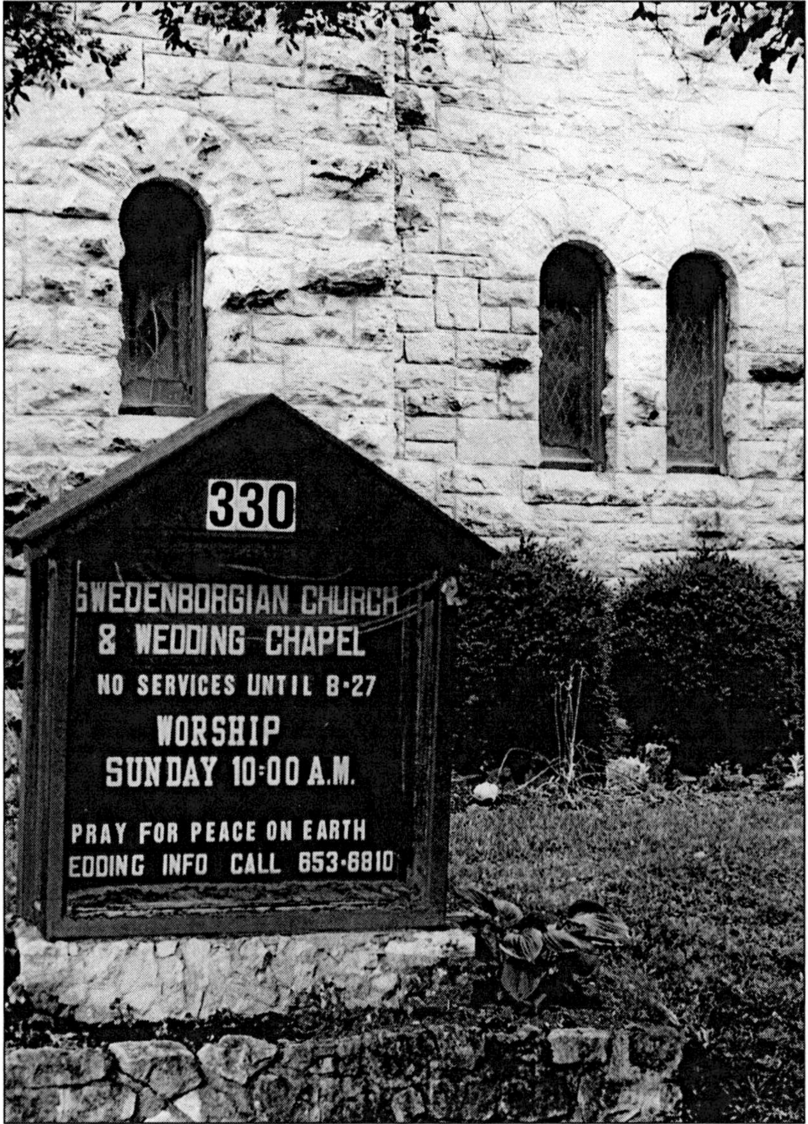

It is no coincidence that this Swedenborgian Church is just around the corner from Urbana University and the Johnny Appleseed Museum as the University was founded in 1850 by Swedenborgians. The land for the University was donated by Swedenborgian Colonel John James and he was probably encouraged to do so by friend Johnny Appleseed. As a Swedenborgian missionary, Johnny was regularly attracted to this area of Ohio. In addition to the museum, the University houses an extensive archival collection of Swedenborgian-related books and other materials. Swedenborgians claim about 50,000 members internationally. (Photo by Ronald Solberg)

carrying large sums with him on "the lonely ways he traveled."[16] He lived simply, had no family and no home. He was the penultimate peddler of apple seeds and seedlings.

One cannot overestimate the value of the product Johnny was selling and distributing to the settlers of frontier America. The need for the apple was urgent. No other fruit could be so easily cultivated and put to so many uses—apple butter, sweet cider, a sweetener (sugar as we now know it was unavailable), and flavoring and preservative. As an important use not to be overlooked, apples were basic for apple brandy and apple jack, the alcoholic drinks of choice for these early Americans. American-raised grapes were unacceptable (and unavailable) to the19th century settlers to be used for making wine. The American grape was the apple. Perhaps, and probably even more important, Ohio required some indication of permanency from those laying claim to land. The planting of appleseeds or peachstones was a common guarantee, warranting the establishment of a legal title.

Johnny's sales technique was unique. He moved his seedling tree business westward with the frontier. "Few other nurserymen could adjust their lives and their business to such a plan. So far as records now make known, no one else ever did."[17]

The stories that have come down to us about Johnny, though possibly fictional, do tell us something about his manner. All his life, bare feet, concern for animals, and ice competed with apples as symbols of his career. One story tells about the time Johnny punished his foot because it had accidentally trampled a worm (or, more realistically, a snake). He would even entertain children he met along the way by pressing needles and hot coals into the horny soles of his feet.[18] An ice story has him hitching a ride on a cake of ice on a fast flowing river. He fell asleep in his canoe that was resting on the ice and, eventually, waking up hours later, found himself nearly 100 miles below his intended destination.[19]

"By occupation,
a gatherer and planter of seeds."
John Chapman's description of himself
(Johnny Appleseed Museum)

It would be a disservice to the man to focus only on his apple business. As it turns out, he was also something of a colporteur, a distributor or peddler of religious tracts. On his frequent visits with settlers, he would give them "some news right fresh from Heaven." Then he would produce a Swedenborgian tract or two for their reading. The Swedenborgians, followers of Emanuel Swedenborg, held that everything on earth corresponds directly to something in the afterlife. "Chapman saw himself as a bumblebee on the frontier, bringer of both seeds and the word of God—of both sweetness, that is, and light."[20]

Philip Roth in his 1997 Pulitzer Prize winning book *American Pastoral* offers a somewhat different (and partially mistaken) appraisal of Johnny Appleseed through one of the novel's characters: "Johnny Appleseed, that's the man for me. Wasn't a Jew, wasn't an Irish Catholic, wasn't a Protestant Christian—nope, Johnny Appleseed was just a happy American. Big. Ruddy. Happy. No brains, probably, but didn't need 'em—a great walker was all Johnny Appleseed needed to be. All physical joy. Had a big stride and a bag of seeds and a huge spontaneous affection for the landscape, and everywhere he went he scattered seeds."[21] So, Johnny's legend continues to grow.

Finally, however, Johnny Appleseed's greatest contribution, according to botanist and author Michael Pollan, may have been the preservation and dissemination of a vast assortment and varieties of the "wild" apple, thus ensuring its continued existence, at least for the time being. Pollan explains that "to domesticate another species is to bring it under culture's roof. But when people rely on too few genes for too long, a plant loses its ability to get along on its own, outdoors. Something like that happened to the potato in Ireland in the 1840s—and it may be happening to the apple right now."[22]

He said he'd bring them apple trees,

Our Lord's gift to the earth,
He said the sun would warm his seeds,
The rain would give them birth.
He said that each good orchard grown
Would bear fruit as God planned,

This apple cider press was owned by John James, the man who contributed the land for the establishment of Urbana University. Johnny Appleseed had planted apple trees nearby for the James family. Over the years the fruit from those trees was pressed for cider. (Johnny Appleseed Museum)

And give the yearning pioneers
A taste of Promised Land.[23]
—Reeve Lindberg
(daughter of Charles and Anne Morrow Lindberg)

Through all of this I had wondered where or how "Johnny Appleseed," the itinerant peddler and salesman of the apple, had learned his art and craft. He did things right for his time. He loved and had an intimate knowledge of his product. He understood the need. He had compassion for his customer. And he certainly had an uncanny sense about the territory. Did he learn all of this, or, was he born to be the wondrous peddler of myth and legend? The answer, I discovered, may be in his name. No, not the moniker "Johnny Appleseed" pinned on him by later generations. Rather, it was his surname, "Chapman."

According to historian Philip Bruce, "The authors of the *Present State of Virginia*, 1697, referred to the general class of merchants in the Colony as being simply country chapmen, but this was true only to the extent that they supplied the wants of a rural and scattered population."[24]

Even more interesting, the name "Chapman" comes from the Old English word, *ceapman*, meaning "trade" + "man." The British used the word "chapman" for itinerant dealer or PEDDLER!

"Johnny Appleseed"
John Chapman
He lived for others.
1774-1845
—Johnny's gravestone near Worth cabin,
Fort Wayne, IN (Johnny Appleseed Museum)

It's Location, Location, Location

Though one couldn't count Ron Popeil in officially as the traditional "traveling salesman," he certainly should be identified as the new breed of salesman that travels the airwaves, visiting his customers where they live, through television.

Ron Popeil has become the model of his type, successfully promoting and selling more than 30 different products, many of which he created himself. The sale of such products as the Veg-O-Matic, Pocket Fisherman, Automatic Pasta Maker, and Ronco Power Scrubber contributed to a telemarketing gross of more than $1 billion over 40 years.[25]

At age 16 Popeil officially began hawking his father Samuel's food-preparation products on Chicago's Maxwell Street, a sort of open-air flea market. Popeil admits that this daily work on the street honed his pitching and selling style that he would eventually use on-the-air.[26]

Soon Popeil supplemented his Maxwell Street activity by making arrangements with Woolworth's flagship store in Chicago to sell his father's food choppers, shoeshine spray, and plastic plant kits just inside the store's door. After a time, he was making $1,000 a week when the average salary was $500 a month.[27] Popeil expanded his business by touring the state fair circuit—Illinois, Wisconsin, Ohio, North Carolina, and Massachusetts—selling products such as the Feather Touch Knife and the Kitchen Magician (a peeler, grater, and serrater all-in-one).[28]

Popeil moved his spiel to television in the late 50's, producing 30-, 60-, 90-, and 120-second commercials to sell the Ronco Spray Gun (garden hose nozzle dispensing soap, wax, weed killer, or insecticide). Heeding the advice of such salesmen as King Camp Gillette, Popeil indicated that the Gun's tablets would run out. "And, I was in the razor blade business, the business of selling tablets."[29]

Popeil continued his on-the-air campaign to sell the Chop-O-Matic, using his unscripted presentation, a successful style that persists to this day. Of all of his father's products sold over television, the Chop-O-Matic was the greatest success.

Because of his success with the television venue, by the early 1960's Popeil was selling his own line of products exclusively over television under the name of Ronco. "Commercials for products like Mr. Microphone, the Inside-the-Shell Egg Scrambler, and the Showtime Rotisserie have become classics of the genre and were major influences in shaping the present-day advertising phenomena known as the infomercial."[30]

Demonstrating important elements of Popeil's "pitch"—Make the product sound indispensable; Repeat important points; Don't be afraid to use superlatives; Don't reveal the price until the end; But wait, there's more (the bonus)—is Popeil's 1963 transcript for the Veg-O-Matic: "This is Veg-O-Matic, the world famous food appliance. Slice a whole potato into uniform slices with one motion. Hamburger lovers, feed whole onions into the Veg-O-Matic and make these tempting thin slices. Simply turn the ring and change from thin to thick slices. Isn't that amazing? Like magic, you can change from slicing to dicing. No one likes dicing onions. The Veg-O-Matic makes mounds of them fast. The only tears you'll shed will be tears of joy. You can make hundreds of French Fries in one minute. Isn't that sensational? Here's your chance to own one for only $9.99. At no extra cost we'll throw in this extra booklet of recipes from world famous chefs."[31]

What will we remember about Ron Popeil? "I think people perceive me as a very successful marketer and inventor of products, but what they really remember is that I was a part of their lives in their bedroom, living room, anywhere they had a TV set. It was my voice, my face, my hands, and it always ended in 'And it's only four easy payments of $39.95' or 'Still just $2.98 and it makes a perfect gift'!"[32]

Worth More Than A Thousand Trees

As is the case with many good traveling salesmen, they understand what the customer wants and needs and then go about creating or modifying the product to meet that need. So it was with Mason Locke "Parson" Weems, (pronounced "wems" as in "gems or "hems"), "the best known and most romantic book peddler of all"[33] who was born in Maryland in 1759.[34]

In 1784 he was ordained a deacon in England by the Bishop of Chester and a week later consecrated a priest by the Archbishop of Canterbury. At that point he returned to Maryland to become Rector of All Hallows Parish, at South River Creek, in his native Anne Arundel County.

Not entirely satisfied with remaining ensconced in a church, the Parson became a kind of evangelist for books, observing that he found

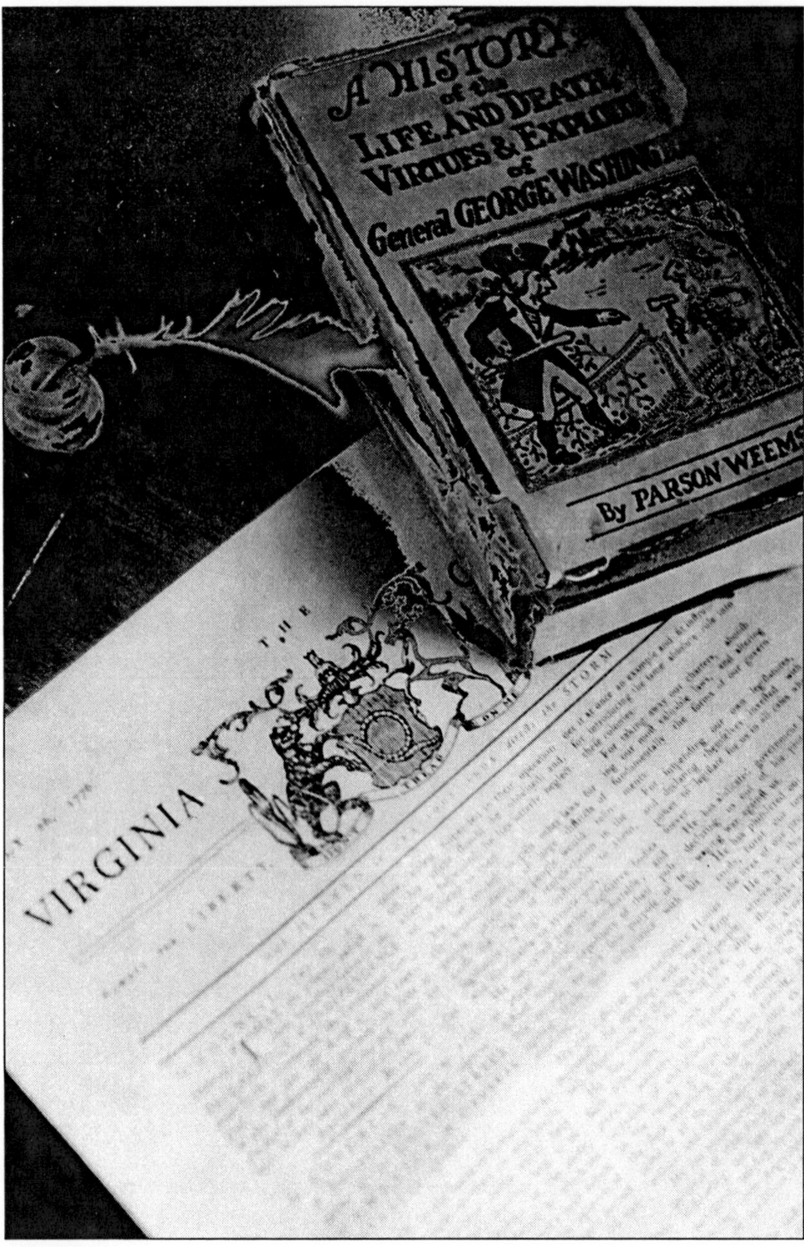

A desktop as it might have looked to Weems in his day: quill pen, copy of the Virginia Gazette (published weekly in Williamsburg, 1736-1780) and Weems' very popular A History of the Life and Death, Virtues & Exploits of General George Washington. *The book cover depicts the enduring, but fictional, "I can't tell a lie" episode. (Weems-Botts Museum, Photo by Ronald Solberg)*

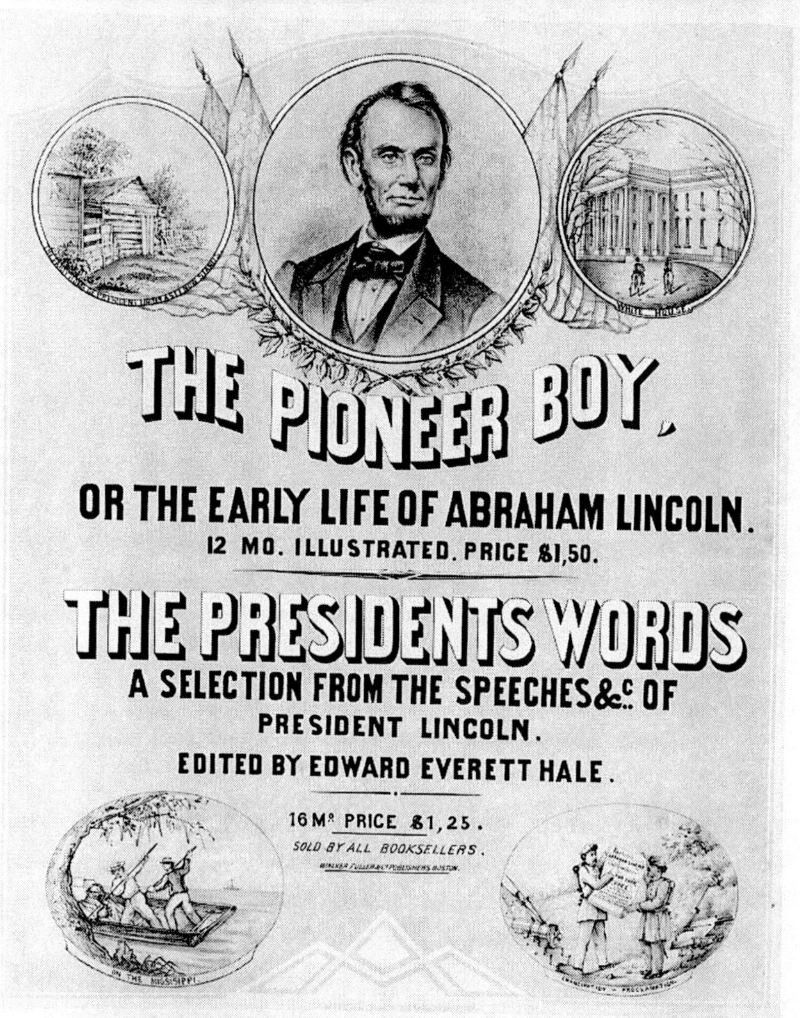

Two subscription publications about Abraham Lincoln, Pioneer Boy *and* The President's Words, *are promoted in this 1865 advertisement. Weems' book about George Washington and, in particular, the cherry tree episode, made a great impression on the President. So much so, that it is likely that the "Honest Abe" moniker was personally cultivated and promoted by Lincoln.*
(Library of Congress)

The Weems-Botts Museum in Dumfries, VA,, the state's oldest chartered town, houses extensive library material and artifacts documenting the lives and accomplishments of the Rev. Mason Locke Weems and attorney Benjamin Botts. Weems used the house as a bookstore while Botts had used the building for his law office. Botts is best remembered as one of the lead lawyers who successfully defended Aaron Burr during his infamous treason and conspiracy trial. (Photo by Ronald Solberg)

people, especially in the backcountry, "unformed, their minds bitter, and their manners savage. Humanity and Patriotism both cry aloud," he said, "for books, books, books." Such would be the Parson's battle cry, the remaining years of his life.

On his local book tours he took with him his fiddle, a device that would continue to serve him well as an attention-getter at various gatherings—fairs, "hoe downs," horse races, and public sales.[35] "What a merry picture he must have made, this white-haired parson who would play for you to dance, would sell you a book, pray with you, or preach you a sermon."[36]

The "Shakespearian" origins of the Weems name

The earliest known individual ancestor of the Weems family was Malcolm Canmore I, King of Scotland, who passed his title on to his son, Malcolm II. When Malcolm II died, the throne of the King of Scotland was available. The main contenders for the throne were

Duncan I and Macbeth, both grandsons of Malcolm I. In 1040 Macbeth killed Duncan in battle and made himself king. Malcolm Canmore, eldest son of Duncan, returned to Scotland leading a small army to kill Macbeth. His cousin, Macduff, was the one who killed Macbeth and restored the throne for the Malcolm line and Malcolm Canmore became King Malcolm III. These are the events that gave rise to Shakespeare's famous (but historically inaccurate) play, "Macbeth," 600 years later.

> *The beginning of the Wemyss name occurred after these events when 11th century Macduff inherited all of the lands in Fife on the Forther, a large Wemyss estate in Scotland, as a reward for killing Macbeth. Many underground caves or wemyss, as they were called, were located on this estate; therefore, Gillemichael Macduff became known as Michael Wemyss—Michael de Wemyss, Earl of Weymss.*
>
> (Author's note: this brief narrative of the Weems' geneology may help to explain why the "Parson" probably pronounced his surname with a "short 'e'" rather than with a "long 'e'.")
>
> The above information obtained from: 1) Bertrand Family Records; 2) *Virginia Genealogies* by Rev. Horace Edwin Hayden; 3) *Americans of Royal Descent* by Chas. H. Browning; 4) *An Encyclopedia of World History* by William L. Langer; 5) *The Columbia Encyclopedia* by Columbia University Press; and 6) *The Encyclopaedia Britannica.* Weems-Botts Museum.

In 1791 The Parson began reprinting and publishing "improving books," and "little paperbacks on the necessity for tolerance, on the dangers of drink, gambling, dueling, and marital infidelity sold widely in many editions, most of them at twenty-five cents each."[37]

Weems found an especially good market for his books in the South where people didn't have access to the bookstores that flourished in the urban centers of Boston, New York, and Philadelphia. It was at this time—in 1794—that Weems partnered up with Mathew Carey, the famous pioneer publisher. Though it was a tempestuous relationship, the two made most of what the other provided—inexpensive published works sold by a determined and persuasive salesman who traveled the Southern hinterlands, "selling books, it is said, as if they were bottles of snake oil."[38]

When suitable books were unavailable from Carey, Weems went ahead and authored his own pamphlets and booklets, many of which were "ripoffs" of other authors. He had almanacs printed off by the hundreds ... and, selling them by many different titles—*The Bachelor's Almanac*, *The Virginia Almanac*, *The Washington* Almanac, and *The Franklin Almanac* were some examples. Though none was more appealing than his 1799 *Lover's Almanac*. Besides containing the usual helpful information, it offered "a very seasonable, savory Dissertation on Love, Courtship and Matrimony—with a most enchanting Flourish on Beauty, admirably calculated to disclose those two most delectable and desirable of all Secrets, how the homely may become handsome, and the handsome, angelic."[39]

In the early years the real staple of Weems' plethora of books was the *Bible*. It pleased Weems no end that he was able to convince the Roman Catholic Carey into printing Protestant Bibles with the promise, "If due attention be paid, you may monopolize the Bible business of America." Weems never really fulfilled that promise, though his Bible sales did contribute to an annual income of $15,000 to $20,000.[40]

Weems eventually discovered that his customers had a real interest in his biographies of notables of the day. Though the Weems-written biographies tended to be more fiction than fact, that seemed to make little difference to the readers. "Quite frankly, he preferred interest to accuracy ... and made no pretense of their being no more than biographical fiction."[41]

He wrote "biographies" of General Francis Marion, Benjamin Franklin, William Penn, and his most popular subject, George Washington.

Weems' book The Life *The Life and Memorable Actions of George Washington* began as a pamphlet, as many of Weems' works did. Because of the growing sales success of the biography, Weems expanded the "little book" into a much longer narrative, "a potpourri, with something for everyone." No wonder it sold, and kept selling. "I could maintain my family handsomely on that single book," said Weems.[42]

Weems' tale of Washington's chopping down of a cherry tree remains an important and enduring addition to America's collective legend about the country's heroes. Supposedly, Weems heard the story from an "amiable 'aged lady, who is a distant cousin' of Washington, 'and when a girl, spent much of her time in the family.'"

Weems has the aged lady saying: "When George was about six year old, he was made the wealthy master of a hatchet! Of which, like most little boys, he was immoderately fond, and was constantly going about chopping every thing that came in his way. One day, in the garden, where he often amused himself hacking his mother's pea-sticks, he unluckily tried the edge of his hatchet on the body of a beautiful young English cherry-tree, which he barked so terribly, that I don't believe the tree ever got the better of it.

"The next morning the old gentleman finding out what had befallen his tree, which, by the by, was a great favourite, came into the house, and with much warmth asked for the mischievous author, declaring at the same time, that he would not have taken five guineas for his tree. Nobody could tell him anything about it.

"Presently George and his hatchet made their appearance. 'George,' said his father, 'do you know who killed that beautiful little cherry-tree yonder in the garden?' This was a tough question; and George staggered under it for a moment; but quickly recovered himself; and looking at his father, with the sweet face of youth brightened with the inexpressible charm of all-conquering truth, he bravely cried out, 'I can't tell a lie, Pa; you know I can't tell a lie. I did cut it with my hatchet.'

'Run to my arms you dearest boy,' cried his father in transports, 'run to my arms; glad am I, George, that you killed my tree; for you have paid me for it a thousand fold. Such an act of heroism in my son, is more worth than a thousand trees, though blossomed with silver, and their fruits of purest gold.'"[43]

Is this "Cherry Tree" tale true? Maybe. Maybe not. Though it is interesting to take note of an anecdote about Weems, himself, as told by his grandson. Not long after Washington's death, Weems' own son cut down a favorite rose bush in his garden in Dumfries, VA. The child confessed to the deed—and was soundly whipped by Weems.[44]

True or not, the cherry-tree tale made a great impression on one of America's most honored presidents—Abraham Lincoln. Weems' *Washington* was among four books that Lincoln maintained in his "fireside library." The other books were *Robinson Crusoe, Pilgrim's Progress* and the *Bible.* [45]

Author Ida Tarbell recounts that by night Lincoln read and worked as long as there was light and he kept a book in the crack of the logs in his loft to have it at hand at the crack of dawn. Once, during a heavy storm, the rain seeped through the logs and damaged a copy of the *Life of Washington*, which he had borrowed from a neighboring farmer. The farmer demanded that Lincoln pay for the book, valued at 75 cents, by pulling fodder for three days in his fields at the rate of 25 cents a day. But Lincoln did the job in two days, as he later explained to a friend: "You see I am tall and long-armed, and I went to work in earnest. At the end of the two days there was not a corn blade left on a stalk in the field. I wanted to pay full damage for all the wetting the book got, and I made a clean sweep."[46]

Weems historian William Flory indicates that, thereafter, Lincoln kept the book close at hand and read it over and over again until he knew it almost by heart. "We may recall that Lincoln once said that the greatest asset he had throughout his life was that he was known among people as 'Honest Abe.' Land, a Lincoln biographer, says, 'Nor is it unlikely that this admirable trait of truthfulness was inspired, at least in part, by the example of George Washington, and the story of his little hatchet and the cherry tree'."[47]

Although Weems' tale about George Washington is probably the best known, Weems' biography of General Francis Marion may have had the greater long-term effect. Illinois historian Charles Chapin reports that the Revolutionary War heroes and comrades Jasper and Newton, mentioned only briefly in five pages of the Marion biography, became the names of many communities and counties, fanning out from the point of origin in South Carolina/Georgia, (Weems' book-selling territory). In many instances, says Chapin, a community named Jasper or Newton resides within a corresponding county named Jasper or Newton. Chapin has identified 17 counties and 31 cities with the name of Marion; 8 counties and 12 cities, named Jasper; 6 counties and 14 cities, Newton. "Not all may be attributed to the book," according to Chapin. "Newton County, AR, is asserted to be named for an Arkansas State Senator named Thomas Willoughby Newton. Remarkably, Jasper is its county seat! Newton County, MO, is supposedly named for Sir Isaac. Coincidentally, it is bordered on the south by Jasper County! The admiration the early settlers had for these Revolutionary soldiers was truly remarkable—and we have Parson Mason Locke Weems to thank for that."[48]

Flory credits Weems for inventing the term "best seller" in the book trade as well as creating in concept, at least, the "blurb"—the brief commendatory publicity notice now found on book jackets. Flory also suggests that "Weems may have popularized the term 'puffery,' the exaggerated product claims that we see in the advertisements today and which consumer groups deplore."[49] The English dramatist Richard Sheridan introduced the word, "puffery," in his 1779 play *The Critic,* featuring "the bogus, verbose critic and author Mr. Puff."[50]

Furthermore, it is likely that Weems pioneered the use of endorsements by prominent personalities. He also pinpointed the economic principle of price-cutting and its effect on sales and profit. In the end, Flory claims that Weems developed a total marketing system which, with little modification, is used today in the book publishing trade. "By the use of energy, imagination and a determination to succeed, Weems evolved in his lifetime a philosophy and practice of marketing which are strikingly similar to the philosophy and practice taught today in virtually all schools of business and to which most progressive businesses, at least, give lip service ... It represents an alternative to the older concept that the function of marketing is to sell whatever products the company chooses to make."[51]

For thirty years, Parson Weems traveled the South, "providing gypsy-like with horse and wagon, traveled his long route year after year, sleeping in wayside inn, farmhouse, or forest, fiddling, writing, selling books, living in the open, and learning some new road lore, field lore, or wisdom of the road with each new day that passed." While on business in Beaufort, SC, in 1825, he died in an inn, "far from his wife and home."[52] (*For a narrative depicting the life of a colporteur like that of Weems, see Chapter 7.*)

CHAPTER 4

Salesmen and Humor

"Hey Hiram, which way to Pittstown?"

American traveling salesman humor is a genre unto itself, in that it is both utilitarian and entertaining, filling literally dozens of turn-of-the-century pamphlets and books.

The jokes and the news he carried were a way for the salesman to ingratiate himself to the customer. One merchant at the time wrote, "I like his breezy ways, his unaffected and easy style of approach, the bits of news he brings me of trade changes and conditions, and the ... insincere deferences (which never deceived, nor is it intended they should) that he seeks opportunity to ladle out. He is a newspaper-market report, funny column, society and police news, and all the rest of it, with editorials upon every page. He is a blessed nuisance; a pervading, invading, awakening influence with a mixed tendency to good and evil.[1] "Salesmanship by the numbers" supports the merchant's characterization.

The jokes, originally perpetuated more by the salesmen than by those who might be characterizing them and their ways, are quite enlightening as to how to these men (and women) of the road and their working conditions were seen by people of the times. One historian has asserted that the "life of a drummer is more graphically described in the jokes about it than in any of the many autobiographies of traveling salesmen written during this era."[2]

Because so much of our salesman humor is of an oral tradition and its origins cannot be associated with particular authors, we are unable to cite original sources for all pieces. In fact, some of the humor, such as "Think twice about what you wish for," was shared with me by friends and associates who knew that I was collecting salesman humor. Furthermore, citing original sources became somewhat more complicated as we discovered that the same jokes with some alterations regularly appeared in several different sources.

One source does appear frequently—the early 1900's humor magazine *Capt. Billy's Whiz Bang*. Numerous jokes we reprint here appeared singularly in this "little publication," (many of which are in this author's personal collection). We understand that 20th century American comedians were about collecting Capt. Billy's magazines, mining them for "original" material. One story goes that "back issues have long since been exhausted as the publisher recently had to inform a prominent radio comedian who had lost his file of old *Whiz Bangs* in a fire, and thus his supply of gags. The comedian had offered $1,000 for a file of back issues."[3]

As the jokes presented here indicate, much of the humor chronicles the "city-slicker" salesman encounters with the country "hick." Sometimes the commercial traveler may best the farmer, but more often than not the farmer raps the salesman with a zinger or two as in "Just lucky" and "Which side of the fence are you on?" On the other hand, "He might at that" implies that in some instances they come out about even.

Although another common theme is the farmer's daughter, a more modern rendering of the story puts a real twist on it in "The tables are turned" as it's about a saleswoman and a farmer's two sons. The "men" still have romantic intentions toward the "woman" in this piece of humor—but with unanticipated consequences. Though you won't find some of the more bawdy stories here, "telling jokes, particularly dirty jokes, brought salesman face to face with customers and established a masculine context for laughing about titillating material—and ultimately selling goods."[4]

The early salesman, probably more than any other business person of the day, used the business card as an important sales tool. In addition to communicating the salesman's business and products, it was frequently used to characterize, through words and/or graphics, the salesman in a humorous and self-deprecating manner. The business card is central to the telling in "Come to think of it ..."

The salesman's on-and-off-again relationship to the home office is a common theme of many jokes and stories. "Birds of a feather" and "Send any pocket change, as well" suggest that all was not always copasetic between the salesman and his bosses. Someone, probably a salesman, is downright disdainful of his sales manager in "Must be an Irish Sitter."

In several of the one-liners, the manager indicates an equal degree of contempt for his sales team: "We just got a painting of our sales department. It's a still life" and "Do you ever get the feeling that your sales staff couldn't sell pickles in a maternity ward?" and "I'd like to say that our sales department has had the best year in its history. Wow, would I like to say that!"

"Seedy" hotels and "slow" trains are also common themes in our jokes. "Just checking" suggests that the salesman was competing for the hospitality of the hotels with other "guests," while "Faster than a speeding slug" tells us a cow won the race with the train.

Train and hotel service was a little uneven, as well. Less than attentive porters inhabit "Still thinking about that poor fellow in Detroit" and "A remarkable coincidence." We also find that it was not unusual for the salesman of the day to have to share a bed with another in "He got the point."

As it was with his sales manager, the salesman's relations with his spouse were sometimes rocky. Since he might be away from the wife for several days at a time, some traveling salesmen resorted to severe tactics to reconcile matters at the homestead with "The ultimate sales tool: the baseball bat."

Apparently it was not uncommon for the wandering salesman to develop "wandering eyes," according to "Watch whom you call 'honey,' honey" and "The Drummer."

The jokes frequently introduce us to creative sales techniques. In "First rule: Always let the business go to the dogs" a young entrepreneur hones his sales skills on the first day, making a very "big" sale. In another, "The power of 'the word'," a salesman turns a shortcoming into a strength. And "How about stockings, dodo?" testifies to the fact that a salesman may all too easily overlook a ready market for his products.

Many stories represent the traveling salesman's morals as being questionable, at best. In "The Devil you say?" and "What's your line?" our salesman finds himself in Hell, but for reasons unclear. On the other hand, "Ask me about good little girls" tells us where "bad little girls go. " (Hint: Hell, it isn't).

Frequently, local merchants disliked the salesman because he was competing with them for their business. "And probably 'on the lamb' as well" is an example of one merchant's hatred for his itinerant competitor. One way that local merchants "leveled the playing field" was to get local city and county officials to impose licensing requirements on the salesman. "You salesman, me sheriff" tells us about a sheriff who confronts a potential offender for selling without a license.

FARMERS AND RURAL AMERICA

Just lucky

"Hey, Hiram, which way to Pittstown?"

"How'd you know my name was Hiram?"

"Just guessed it."

"Then guess the way to Pittstown."[5]

Which side of the fence are you on?

"Not much difference between you and a fool is there?"

"No," said the farmer. "Just this fence."

Another pig tale

It was in the hills of Kentucky that a traveling saleswoman came upon a farmer holding a pig in his arms so that the creature could eat the apples right off the tree.

"Won't it take a long time to fatten your hog that way?" asked the lady traveler.

"I suppose so," replied the farmer. "But what's time to a durned old hog?"

Then there's Donner and Blitzen

A Vermont farmer, who was plowing a field with his one mare, kept on calling, "Giddap Babe, Giddap Lady, Giddap Sweetheart, Giddap Queenie."

"But," said the passing traveling salesman, "why has that mare got all those names?"

"Sh!" said the farmer. "Her name's Bess. But when I put blinders on her and yell those other names, she thinks she's got all those other horses helping her."

Catalog farmer

The catalog farmer sat on a fence,
Waiting for his corn to grow to ninety cents;
But his corn went down to thirty cents
And he slipped on the railing and fell off the fence.
There he lay in the dismal sun
This poor deluded son of a gun.
The grasshoppers ate all his clover grass
The bumble bees sucked all his honey,
The hornets made a nest in the eaves of his house
And Sears-Roebuck got all his money.
(*Capt. Billy's Whiz Bang,* January, 1925)

He might at that

A salesman was driving through a rural area when his car ran out of gas. He went to a nearby farmhouse for help but the farmer insisted he had no gas, adding that the nearest gas station was twelve miles on up the road. "Well," said the salesman, "could you lend me a horse and wagon so I can get the gas?"

"Don't have one," said the farmer, eyeing the salesman suspiciously.

"Do you have any kind of transportation?" asked the salesman. "Even a donkey will do."

"Nope," said the farmer," don't even have a donkey."

Just then a donkey lit out a mighty bray from the confines of the farmer's barn. "What do you mean by saying you don't have donkey?" declared the salesman. I just heard one braying.

"Look here, young feller," retorted the farmer. "Are you going take the word of an ass in preference to mine?"

Those add-on's will get you every time

The implement salesman stopped by the farm to close the deal on a tractor in which the old farmer had earlier expressed an interest. After telling the salesman which tractor he wanted, they sat down to do the paperwork. The salesman handed the farmer the bill, and the farmer declared, "This isn't the price I was given!" The salesman went on to tell the farmer how he was getting extras such as power steering, power brakes, an enclosed cab with air conditioning and stereo radio/CD player, special tires, etc. and that was what took the price up. The farmer, needing the tractor badly, paid the price.

A few months later the salesman called up the farmer and said, "My son is in 4-H and he needs a cow for a project. Do you have any for sale?"

The farmer replied, "Yes, I have a few cows I would sell for $500 apiece. Come and look at them and take your pick." The salesman said he and his son would be right out. After spending a few hours in the field checking out all the farmer's cows, the two decided on one and the salesman proceeded to write out a check for $500.

The farmer said, "Now wait a minute, that's not the final price of the cow. You're getting extras with it and you have to pay for that too."

"What extras? asked the salesman. The farmer gave the salesman the following list:

Basic Cow: $500. Two-tone exterior, $45; Extra stomach, $75; Product storing equipment, $60; Straw compartment, $120; 4 spigots @ $10 each, $40; Leather upholstery, $125; Dual horns, $45; Automatic fly swatter, $38; and Fertilizer attachment, $185.

Look who's talking

A traveling salesman was driving down a country road when his car sputtered to a stop near a field filled with cows. The salesman, getting out to see what was the matter noticed one of the cows looking at him. "I believe it's your radiator," said the cow.

The salesman nearly jumped right out of his city slicker britches. He ran to the nearest farmhouse and knocked on the door. "Sir, a cow just gave me advice about my car!" he shouted, waving his arms frantically back toward the field.

The farmer nonchalantly leaned beyond the doorframe to glance down the field. "Was it the cow with two big black spots on it?" the farmer asked slowly.

"Yes, yes! That's the one!" the excited salesman replied.

"Oh, well, that's Ethel," the farmer said, turning back to salesman. "Don't pay no attention to her. She don't know a thing about cars."

Never kick a feller when he's down

The salesman's car was mired in a muddy country road. While he was walking along looking for a service station, the salesman noticed a hat in the mud. He gave it a kick.

"Cut that out, mister," gurgled the voice of a farmer beneath the hat.

"I'll be darned," said the salesman. "Is the mud as deep as all that?"

"Don't be crazy, mister," said the voice. "I'm standin' on my mule."

It's about where you place your values

"What you really need is this fine bicycle."

"I got only enough money to buy a cow."

"But think how funny you'll look riding to town on a cow."

"Not half as funny as I'll look trying to milk that bicycle."

What would "The Colonel" say about this?

One day, a traveling salesman was driving down a back country road at about thirty miles an hour when he noticed that there was a three-legged chicken running along beside his car. He stepped on the gas, but at fifty miles per hour, the chicken was still keeping up. After about a mile of running, the chicken ran up a farm lane and into a barn behind an old farmhouse. The salesman had some time to kill, so he turned around and drove up the farm lane. He knocked at the door, and, when the farmer answered he told him what he had just seen.

The farmer said that he knew about the chicken. "As a matter of fact," the farmer said, "my son is a geneticist and he developed this breed of chicken because the three of us each like a drumstick when we have to kill only one chicken."

The salesman said, "That's the most fantastic story I've ever heard. How do they taste?"

The farmer said, "I don't know. We can't catch 'em."

Come to think of it, I could use a broom

The vacuum cleaner salesman was driving down the dusty road towards the farmhouse. It was Kansas in 1930. The Great Depression had struck but no one knew how hard it would become or how long it would last, except the farmers. They knew, they always knew.

Farmer Smith was sitting on his porch watching the car approach. He didn't get a lot of visitors and not many that drove1928 Ford Model A's. Must be a salesman. He never bought from them but he always listened to them. He thought that if they were making the effort he should hear out their spiel.

The salesman introduced himself and presented the farmer with a very nicely engraved card showing the salesman to be an accredited representative of Acey-Duecey Vacuum Cleaners. He told the farmer of all the advantages to having a cleaner, easier way to clean his carpeting.

"That's nice, son, real nice. Thing of it is, I don't have any carpeting." The salesman presented the farmer with a very nicely engraved card showing the salesman to be an accredited representative of the Persian Carpet Company. He told the farmer of all the advantages to having carpeting, from the extra insulation on cold winter nights to the envy of his neighbors. When he was done the farmer said,

"Well, that's just fine, son. You did a real nice job there. Thing of it is, I don't have a floor down you can carpet over. I have packed dirt floors. That sort of makes carpeting useless to me."

"Well, Mr. Smith," the salesman said as he gave the farmer another very nicely engraved card showing him to be an accredited representative of Fine Quality Flooring. "I can have a floor down in two days. Then the carpeting down in another one."

"Well, son, you certainly are an industrious man. You came here well prepared, I'll give you that," the farmer said.

"Why, thank you, sir! I try to be of service to my customers. I don't just pawn off some vacuum cleaner and hit the road never to be heard from again. If you ever have any problem, I will take care of it. You can count on that. Yes, sir, just plug this baby in and it'll clean just like magic."

"Plug it in? What's that mean?" the farmer asked.

"Plug the vacuum cleaner into a wall socket and turn her on."

"Well, son, that's real nice, real nice. Thing of it is, I don't have any electricity here," the farmer told him.

The salesman pulled out another very nicely engraved card showing him to be an accredited representative of Kansas Power and Light.

"Well, son, you really are a busy, industrious man."

"Thank you again, sir. I can have that power line here inside a week."

"Well, son, that's nice, real nice. Is this some sort of advertising to get my neighbors to do it? I sure don't have that kind of money, that's for sure," the farmer said.

The salesman pulled out yet another very nicely engraved card indicating that he was an accredited representative of Central Capital Finance. "Sir, I can get this whole thing done for $3000. We can set up very small monthly payments for you."

"Yes? That's nice, real nice, son. Now, if this depression gets to be real bad and I can't make those payments, what happens then?"

"Mr. Smith, we'd have no choice but to, umm, get a court order to sell your farm to cover the $3000. We wouldn't be happy about it but we'd really have no choice. I'm sorry," the salesman told Farmer Smith.

"Oh, don't be sorry. Of course you'd have to do that. The thing of it is, I know things are going to get a lot worse before they get any better. I know I won't be able to make your payments and you'll have to get some lawyer to get a court order and some auctioneer to sell the place, They both want a cut of the money. You'd be very lucky to get your $3000 back."

"Sir, if the worse happens, we'd just have to settle for what we could get," the salesman said.

"The thing of it is, you could just give me the $3000 and not have to put down a floor, then carpet it, then run a line from two miles down and give me a vacuum cleaner. You wouldn't get the $3000 back, but you'd lose less this way. Sounds like a good deal to me. What do you say? We got a deal?" asked the farmer.

Let's keep it clean

"I'm a sanitary engineer," said the bathtub drummer to the farmer. "What are you doing to protect your family from the flu epidemic raging the country?"

"I bought a sanitary cup and we all drink from it."

This ain't no pig in a poke joke

A traveling salesman came to a farm house with a three-legged pig in the barnyard. The salesman said to the farmer, "That pig is amazing!"

To which the farmer replied, "Son you don't know the half of it. That pig saved our lives. One night our house was blazing. The pig woke us up and pulled the baby from its burning crib to safety. We wouldn't be here without that pig!"

The salesman said, "Wow, what an amazing pig!"

The farmer said, "That's nothing! We were having some money trouble, and we were going to lose the farm. This pig went out back of the farm, rooted around and struck oil. We never have had to work another day in our lives."

The salesman said, "That's just incredible."

The farmer said, "There's more! That pig can do math. He tutored my daughter, and now she's getting straight A's!"

The salesman said, "I can't believe it. What a pig! But tell me why does he only have three legs?"

The farmer looked at the traveling salesman and said, "Man, you don't eat a pig like that all at once!"

This well-dressed rooster has his hands full

A traveling salesman was passing through the countryside and stopped at a farm, asking for some cool water. The old farmer's wife invited him to sit in the shade of the porch with her and she would get him some cold lemonade. They sat and talking for awhile when suddenly a hen went running by with a rooster wearing a pair of coveralls chasing her.

The salesman asked, "What in the devil was that?"

The old farmer's wife told him, "Well you see, some years ago we had a tornado come through here and hit the hen house. It killed all our chickens except for that rooster, but it plucked every feather off of him. I felt kind of sorry for him, seeing how as he did survive a tornado, so I knitted him a pair of coveralls."

The salesman said, "Well that is just about the funniest thing I have ever seen."

To which the farmer's wife replied, "You think that's funny, you ought to see that rooster hold a hen down with one leg while trying to get those coveralls off with the other!"

Say, mister, got a match?

Some of these corn-fed damsels around the farm are sure coy. Not long ago one of them was hiking along a cross road, when she caught up with a peddler who was carrying a large iron kettle on his back; in one hand he held the legs of a live chicken, in the other a cane, and he was leading a goat. They sauntered along together until they came to a lonely clump of woods, when the simple maid drew back.

"I'm afraid to go on," she said. "You might overpower me and kiss me."

"How can I possibly do that?" the peddler retorted. "I have this iron kettle, a live chicken, a goat, and a cane. I might as well be tied hand and foot."

"Well," responded the coy young thing, "if you stick your cane in the ground and tie your goat to it and turn the kettle upside down and put the chicken under it, then you might wickedly kiss me in spite of my resistance." (*Capt. Billy's Whiz Bang,* June, 1924)

Liar, liar, pant's on fire

A traveling salesman stopped alongside a field on a country road to rest a few minutes. The man had just closed his eyes when a horse came to the fence and began to boast about his past. "Yes, sir, I'm a fine horse. I've run in 25 races and won over $5 million. I keep my trophies in the barn."

The salesman computed the value of having a talking horse, found the horse's owner and offered a handsome sum for the animal. "Aw, you don't want that horse," said the farmer.

"Yes, I do," said the salesman, "and I'll give you $100,000 for the horse.

Recognizing a good deal the farmer said without hesitation, "He's yours."

While he wrote out his check, the salesman asked, 'By the way, why wouldn't I want your horse?"

"Because," said the farmer, "he's a liar. He hasn't won a race in his life."

It's better than watching grass grow

A commercial traveler having missed the bus found himself with two hours to spend in Brushville. He approached an ancient porter.

Traveling Man: "Got a picture show here?"

Porter: "No."

Traveling Man: "A pool room, or library?"

Porter: "No."

Traveling Man: "Well, how on earth do you amuse yourselves?"

Porter: "We go down to the grocery store in the evenings. They have a new bacon slicer."

Think twice about what you wish for

After a morning of walking from house-to-house to sell his brushes a traveling salesman stopped by the rural community's only restaurant for lunch. He entered the eatery accompanied by an ostrich. As they sat at the counter, the salesman looked over the menu and told the waitress he wanted a hamburger, fries, and a cola.

The ostrich hesitated briefly, then said, "I think I'll order the same." When the two completed their meals, the waitress handed the salesman the tab for $10.56. Immediately the salesman reached into his pocket, pulling out the exact amount owed, handing it to the waitress. At that point, the salesman and ostrich left the restaurant.

The next day, the salesman and ostrich visited the same restaurant for lunch. The salesman ordered his hamburger, fries, and cola, just as he had the previous day. The ostrich repeated the same order. Again, the waitress handed the salesman a tab for $10.56. The salesman reached into his pocket and took out the precise amount owed.

The next day, the salesman and ostrich stopped at the same restaurant for lunch. However, on this day, the salesman decided to order a hot beef sandwich with mashed potatoes and gravy along with a cup of coffee. After some thought, the ostrich ordered the same hot beef sandwich meal. This time the waitress presented the salesman with a tab of $15.40. The salesman reached into his pocket, pulling out the $15.40.

Staring at the salesman, the waitress couldn't stand it any longer. She said, "How do you do it? Pulling out the exact amount owed every time. And then, what's with this ostrich who is sitting with you?"

The salesman replied that this all came about on one of his sales trips. While walking down a secluded path in a community park, he saw something shiny behind a bush. He stopped and retrieved an ancient-looking lamp. As he rubbed the dust off of it, a genie, who had been imprisoned in the lamp for centuries, emerged. Happy at finally being free of the lamp, the genie granted the salesman two wishes.

After some thought, the salesman said, "As my first wish, I want to be able to reach into my pocket and pull out the exact amount of money required for any and all purchases."

"Granted," said the genie. "And, now for your second wish."

The salesman thought some and said. "I would like to be accompanied everywhere I go by a chick who agrees with everything I say."

Just a shot in the dark

The traveling man riding over the Montana prairies inquired of a native, "Does Walter Malter live near here?"

"No," was the reply.

"Well, do you happen to know where I can find him?"

"No," said the other.

The traveling man was puzzled. "Dear me," he said, "I must have lost my way. Perhaps you can tell where Mr. William Bluff, familiarly known as 'Grizzly Bill,' hangs out?"

"I can. Right here. I am Grizzly Bill."

"But," expostulated the tenderfoot traveler, "they told me that Malter lived within gunshot of you."

"Well," said the other, "he did."

(*Capt. Billy's Whiz Bang,* May, 1920)

His name fits him to a "T"

One fine day an insurance agent stopped by a particular farm house to introduce a farmer and his wife to his new line of financial products. As he walked up to the farm house, our salesman noticed that there were literally dozens of golf balls strewn about the front lawn. The salesman began to walk up the steps to the front door when an aged farmer happened around the corner of the house.

"Howdy, stranger," said the farmer.

"And a good day to you," replied the agent. After introducing himself, the salesman made mention of the plethora of golf balls laying about. "Someone here looks to have a golfing interest," he said.

"You betcha," said the farmer, pointing off to a nearby barn and pen. "That's good Ole Beef, down yonder, practicing his drives."

"Ole Beef?" asked the salesman.

"Yes, that cow of ours has a real mean chip shot, too."

"That's amazing," exclaimed the salesman. "A cow that swings a club and plays golf? But tell me, is "Beef" his name."

"Actually," said the farmer, "that's a kind of nickname fer him. "His whole name is Bee ..." At that moment the farmer abruptly halted in mid-sentence as he sighted a hard hit ball flying through the air toward the two men.

He finished with a shout, " ... Fore!"

FARMERS' DAUGHTERS (AND SONS)

Baby, it's cold outside

A young salesman wandered into a lonely farmhouse to ask for shelter for the night and was informed the old couple that if he wanted a bed he would have to sleep with the baby. Anticipating wet sheets and similar inconveniences, he begged them for permission to spend the night in the hayloft. The next morning, bright and early, he was just opening his eyes when the barn door opened and a beautiful young woman showed herself. He had never in his life had seen anything so lovely. "Who are you?" he asked her.

"I'm the baby," she replied. "Who are you?"

"Oh, I," he stammered. "I'm the jackass who spent the night in the barn." (*William Faro, 1933*)

Some kind of hospitality!

A traveling salesmen was driving through upstate New York when it began to pour. Soon, the visibility became so bad that he couldn't see five feet in front of him. As he was driving, he spotted a farmhouse and pulled into the driveway. He jumped out of the car, raced to the house, and knocked on the door.

In a few moments, the farmer appeared at the window, spotted the salesman, and quickly opened the door. "Come on in, young feller," he said. "It's kinda wet out there." When the salesman was inside, the farmer told him to set by the fire and warm himself. Then he got the salesman a towel and made him a cup of hot tea. After he was warm and dry, the salesman went to the window and looked out. It was still pouring.

Turning to the farmer, he said, "It's awful outside. It would be treacherous to drive. Do you think you could put me up for the night?"

"I guess so," said the farmer, "but there's one thing I gotta tell you first."

"What is it?' asked the salesman.

"I ain't got a daughter."

"What!" screamed the salesman, as he picked up his hat and coat and raced to the door. "Of all the nerve ... to think that I would stay with a farmer who didn't have a daughter. How far is the next farmhouse?"

We got education here, ya hear?

Another salesman stopped at a farmhouse and asked the farmer, "Do you have a daughter?"

"Yup, and a real pretty one, too."

"Good," said the salesman. "I'll stay here for the night."

The next morning the salesman got up, packed his bag, and started to leave. As he was walking to his car, he spotted the farmer. "You old liar, you," he yelled. "I thought you said you had a daughter."

"I do, said the farmer."

"Don't lie to me," hollered the salesman, getting madder by the moment. "I was here all night, and I didn't see her once. Did you hear of a traveling salesman who stayed in a farmhouse for a whole night without seeing the farmer's daughter?"

"There's a simple explanation," said the farmer.

"What is it?"

"My daughter is away at college."

What kind of insurance is that?

An insurance salesman was getting nowhere in his efforts to sell a policy to a farmer. "Look at it this way sir." he said finally. "How would your wife carry on if you should die?"

"Well ... " drawled the weather-beaten man, "I don't reckon that'd be any concern of mine—long as she behaves herself while I'm alive."

This is all about eggs. No yoke.

A traveling salesman was passing through an old farming town when he decided he needed to get some sleep. He stopped by an old farmer's house to see if he could get a room for the night. The farmer agreed to let the stranger stay at his house, but warned him to stay away from his young daughter. The salesman agreed.

To make sure the salesman kept his word, the farmer discreetly placed three fresh eggs above his daughter's door. If the eggs fell and broke, then the farmer would know of the salesman's hanky-panky with his young innocent daughter.

Temptation got the best of the salesman and he snuck into the young girl's room. And of course, broke all the eggs. He and the young girl spent the rest of the night gluing the eggshells back together and placing them back on the top of the door.

The farmer got up the next morning and checked his daughter's room. All three eggs appeared to be in place. He felt good about his daughter and the salesman and decided to fix them breakfast with the eggs he had used. He cracked the first one. Nothing inside. Same the second and third eggs. Nothing inside.

The farmer thought to himself, "I'm no dummy! Nobody can fool me!" And stormed out the door in sheer anger. He stood on his porch and hollered, "Okay, I want to know the truth … Which one of you roosters is wearing a condom!?"

I ain't got no time for you

There was an old farmer who lived beside a little branch-line railroad in South Jersey, and every so often he'd get on the train and go over to Trenton and buy himself a crock of applejack. He'd buy it right at the distillery door, the old Bossert and Stockton Apple Brandy Distillery, and save himself a penny or two.

One morning he went to Trenton and bought his crock and that afternoon he got on the train for the trip home. Just as the train pulled out, he took his watch from his vest pocket, a fine gold watch in a fancy hunting case, and he looked at it, and then he snapped it shut and put it back in his pocket.

And there was a drummer sitting across the aisle. This drummer learned over and said, "Friend, what time is it?"

The farmer took a look at him and said, "Won't tell you."

The drummer thought he was hard of hearing and spoke louder. "Friend," he shouted out, "what time is it?"

"Won't tell you," said the farmer.

The drummer thought a moment and then he said, "Friend, all I asked was the time of day. It don't cost anything to tell the time of day."

"Won't tell you," said the farmer.

"Well, look here, for the Lord's sake," said the drummer, "why won't you tell me the time of day?"

"If I was to tell you the time of day," the farmer said, "we'd get into a conversation, and I got a crock of spirits down on the floor between my feet, and in a minute I'm going to take a drink … and if we were having a conversation I'd ask you to take a drink with me, and you would, and presently I'd take another … and I'd ask you to do the same, and you would, and we'd get to drinking, … and by and by the train'd pull up to the stop where I get off … and I'd ask you why don't you get off and spend the afternoon with me, and you would … and we'd walk up to my house and sit on the front porch and drink and sing … and along about dark my old lady would come out and ask you to take supper with us, and you would … and after supper I'd ask if you'd care to drink some more, and you would … and it'd get to be real late and I'd ask you to spend the night in the spare room, and you would … and along about two o'clock in the morning I'd get up to go to the pump, and I'd pass my daughter's room, and there you'd be, in there with my daughter … and I'd have to turn the bureau upside down and get out my pistol … and my old lady would have to get dressed and hitch up the horse and go down the road and get the preacher … and I don't want no goldurn son-in-law who don't own a watch." (*Benjamin A. Botkin, 1957*)

The tables are turned

Here's one that repeated scrubbings with soap made printable. It concerns a traveling saleswoman and the two farmer's sons. It seems this pert young miss was traveling for a medical supply house. Her car broke down one night on the road and she was forced to seek shelter in a farmhouse. After dinner the farmer went out to the barn to take care of some chores, and the traveling saleswoman and the two sons found themselves alone in the house.

Passion began to rise in the bosoms of the two stalwart young men. So, after a certain amount of amorous byplay the older son finally said, "Gee, golly, lady, you're pretty. I'd sure like to kiss you."

"Me too, gurgled his brother.

"I wouldn't object," said the lady, always willing to please. "But I do have one request."

"What's that, lady?" they chorused.

"As you know, I travel for a medical supply house and we believe that kissing is dangerous. Too many germs are passed that way. If you want to kiss me, you'll have to wear these gauze masks to prevent my catching some disease."

"That's OK with us, lady," said the boys, their ardor rising by the minute. The young stalwarts donned the masks and each got their antiseptic kisses. The next morning the saleswoman left.

About two months later, the boys were working in the north pasture. The older turned to the younger, "You know," he said. I don't care if that traveling lady gets a disease."

"Me neither," responded his brother.

"Then, let's take off these goldurn masks," said the older boy.

Say, what?

The girl who used to trust the traveling men now has a daughter that even the traveling men don't trust. (*Capt. Billy's Whiz Bang,* May, 1920)

Wrong time, wrong place

A traveling salesman's car broke down in front of a farm and he sought shelter at the farmhouse.

"Sure, we can put you up for the night," said the farmer, "but you will have to share a bed with my son."

"Excuse me," said the salesman, "but I think I'm in the wrong joke."

GRIPS, TRUNKS AND VALISES

A case of mistaken identity

If the trunk manufacturers do not quit making so many thousands of valises exactly alike, somebody is going to get into some awful trouble about it sometime, and some trunk maker will be sued for damages enough to build a court house.

The other day an omnibus full of passengers drove uptown from the Union Depot. Side by side sat a commercial traveler named William MacCaby, and Mrs. Winnie C. Dumbleton, the eminent lady temperance lecturer. When the omnibus reached the Barrett House, the commercial traveler seized his valise and started out. The lady made a grab after him and he halted.

"I beg your pardon," she said, "but you have my valise."

"You are certainly mistaken, madam," the traveler said, courteously, but firmly, "this is mine."

"No, sir," the lady replied, firmly, "it is mine. I would know it among a thousand. You must not take it."

But the traveler persisted and the lady insisted, and they came very near to blows. Presently one of the passengers pointed to a twin valise in the omnibus and asked:

"Whose is that?"

"It isn't mine," said the traveler; "it is just like it, but this is mine."

"And it isn't mine," said the lady. "He has mine, and I'll have it or I'll have the law on him. It's a pity if a lady can't travel alone in this country without being robbed of her property in broad daylight."

Finally the traveler said he would open the valise to prove his claim. The lady objected at first, saying she did not want her valise opened in the presence of a crowd of strangers. But as there was no other way of settling the dispute, she at length consented. The traveler sprung the lock, opened the valise, and the curious crowd bent forward to see.

On the very top of everything lay a big flat flask, half-full of whiskey, a deck of cards, and one or two things that nobody knows the name of.

The traveler was first to recover his self-possession and speech.

"Madame," he said, "you are right; the valise is yours. I owe you a thousand apolo-"

But the lady had fainted and the traveler relocked his valise with a quiet smile.

Early in the afternoon a sign painter downtown received a note in a feminine hand, asking him to come to the Barrett House to mark a red leather valise in black letters a foot-and-half high. (*Burlington Hawkeye.*)

According to Hoyle

The traveling salesman arrived at a small rural hotel. He placed his sample case in the lobby and prepared to leave for dinner. "Better mark that valise," advised the room clerk.

"Suppose I put my card on it? queried the salesman.

"That ought to do the trick," responded the clerk. The salesman hunted in vain for one of his business cards but couldn't find one. In the absence of a better solution, he a took a pack of playing cards from his pocket, withdrew a card and marked his sample case that way.

About an hour later he returned to find his bag missing. "Say, you there," he shouted to the clerk. "What happened to my sample case? I had it marked."

"That's just it, mister," replied the clerk. "You marked the valise with a jack of diamonds. A guy came along with a king and took it."

Why don't you call in the militia!?

"Will you be kind enough to take the gripsack off that seat?" said a countryman who got on a train at Luling, Texas.

"No sir, I don't propose to do anything of the sort," replied the drummer, who was sitting on the other side of the seat.

"Do you say that you are going to let that gripsack stay right there?"

"Yes sir, I do."

"In case you don't remove that gripsack, I shall be under the painful necessity of calling the conductor."

"You can call in the conductor, the engineer and the brakeman, if you want to. Perhaps had better stop at the next station and send a special message to old Jay Gould himself about it."

"The conductor will put you off the train."

"I don't care if he does. I am not going to take that gripsack from that place where it is."

The indignant passenger went through the train and soon returned with the conductor.

"So you refuse to remove that gripsack, do you?" asked the conductor.

"I do."

"Why do you persist in refusing to remove that gripsack?"

"Because it's not mine."

"Why didn't you say so at once?"

"Because nobody asked me." *(Texas Siftings)*

The gripe: Get a grip on your grip

By George W. Peck

There was one of those old-fashioned mistakes occurred on the train from Monroe to Janesville a week or so ago. A traveling man and a girl who was going to Milton College sat in adjoining seats. Their satchels were exactly alike and the traveling man took the wrong satchel and got off at Janesville and the girl went on to Milton.

The drummer went down to Vankirk's Grocery store and asked Van how his liver was getting along, while he picked off a piece of codfish and ate it. Then he smelled of his hands and said "Whew!"

Van said his liver was "not very torpid, thank you; how are you fixed for tea."

The drummer said he wished he had as many dollars as he was fixed for tea and began to open his sample case. Van cut off a piece of cheese and was eating it while he walked along toward the drummer.

When the case was opened, the drummer fell over against a barrel of brooms, and, grasping a keg of maple syrup for support, turned pale, and said he'd be dashed. Van looked in the sample case, and said, "Fixed for tea! I should think you was, but it wasn't the kind of tea I want." There was a long female night-shirt, clapboarded up in front with trimming and starch, and buttoned from Genesis to Revelations. Van took a butter tryer and lifted it out, and there was more than a peck measure full of stuff that never belonged in no grocery. Van said: "If you are traveling for a millinery house, I will send a boy to direct you to a millinery store."

The drummer wiped the perspiration from his face with a coffee sack and told Van he would give him a million dollars if he never would let the house in Milwaukee know about it and he chucked the things back in.

"What's this?" said Van, as he held up a pair of giddy-looking affairs that no drummer ever wore on his own person.

"Don't ask me," says the drummer, 'I am not a married man." He took the satchel and went to Milton on the next train.

The girl had opened the satchel, which fell to her in the division, to show her roommate how to make a stitch in crochet, and when the brown sugar, coffee, tea, rice, bottles of syrup, macaroni and a pack of cards came in sight, she fairly squealed.

Along after dinner, the drummer called and asked for an exchange, and they exchanged, and it was hard to tell which blushed the most. (*The Complete Traveling Salesman's Joke Book,* Bill Brower, 1952)

HEAVEN, HELL, AND THE CLERGY

The devil, you say?
Those Chicagoans gotta be real wet behind the ears

Some salesmen were chewing the rag recently in the lobby of the Astor, and the Chicago salesman was being particularly arrogant when a bystander interrupted with the following.

"A Chicago salesman sold his last bill of goods, died, and went straight to Hell. There the devil immediately took him in hand began to show him about. Here were the pits of molten lead for the New York drummers, the sulphur caves made especially for the torture of St. Louis drummers, and the lake of fire for drummers from Cleveland. Then he was shown into a very hot room where a lot of people were suspended by their necks from the ceiling.

"'This,' said the Devil, 'is the drying room.'

"'The drying room?'

"'Yes, these are your Chicago drummers. They're so green we've got to hang 'em up to dry before we try to burn 'em.'" (*Reveries of a Drummer,* Wm. Walter Shaw, 1926)

What's your line?

But at the gate I met my fate,
For I found the blamed thing locked,
I waited around and I pawed the ground
While I knocked, and knocked, and knocked.
At last it turned and I discerned
Old Peter inside the gate,
As he grinned at me, says he, "Let's see
Just what your papers state."
He looked them o'er and he grinned some more,
And the chills went down my spine;
"Oh, you're one, then, of those drummer men;
Tell me, what is your line?"
My legs grew weak, I could scarcely speak,
As I answered, "Coal," and I know
That he shook with glee as he beckoned to me,
And motioned me down below. (Wm. Walter Shaw)

Not my job

An elderly woman was taking her first airplane ride. She wasn't too enthused about it. Fortunately, though, she was seated next to a clergyman. She thought that would help, but it didn't. After they were up for awhile, the plane hit some pretty traumatic turbulence. They bounced around and she got whiter and whiter. Finally, in anger she turned to the clergyman and said, "You're a religious person. Can't you do something about this?"

He said, "I'm sorry, Madam. I'm in sales, not management."

Ask me about good little girls

Parson: "Do you know where bad little girls go?"

Nellie: "Of course I do!"

Parson: "Where do they go?"

Nellie: "They go down to the railroad station to see the traveling salesmen come in."

He should have approached his wife with hat in hand

Four or five jolly drummers gathered in the smoking compartment of a Pullman car, and soon their conversation drifted to the great problem of the day—women. In the compartment also was a frock-coated pastor of serious mien.

The salesmen winked at each other as the minister entered, and then, as if to have some harmless pleasure, one after another started telling of the wonderful virtues of the knights of the grip.

"I am often away from home for four weeks at a time, one salesman commenced, "and I never even look at another woman."

"And I am so bound up in the charms of my wife that I'm ashamed to tip the check girls," declared the next one.

"Why, my wife is so good to me that I won't allow a woman to wait on me in a restaurant," said another.

Their conversation sounded too much like unadulterated bunk for the good minister to swallow, and he joined the party by offering a silk hat to any salesman present who could truthfully say he had always been faithful to his wife. The pastor won his point and the conversation soon drifted to other subjects.

The next day one of the salesmen arrived home and soon told his wife of the jolly party in the Pullman smoker.

"But, John," she said, "why didn't you take him up?" John's active salesman brain worked quickly.

"Why, Mabel, you know I look like hell in a silk hat." (*Capt. Billy's Whiz Bang,* October, 1921)

Now, that is a matter of principle

Salesman: "Listen, girlie, how come you're so wild?"

Little Nell: "Say, mister, I'm tough. I went to an immoral school."

Salesman: "Whaddaya mean, immoral?"

Nell: "We didn't have any principal."

(*Capt. Billy's Whiz Bang, Winter Annual,* September, 1929)

And what are your relations with the home office?

Bishop Watterson of Nebraska was once mistaken for a traveling salesman by a commercial traveler who met him in a railway train. "Do you ever represent a big house?" asked the traveler of the bishop.

"Biggest on earth, " replied the bishop.

"What's the name of the firm?"

"Lord and Church."

"Hum! 'Lord and Church.' Never heard of it. Got branch houses anywhere?"

"Branch houses all over the world."

"That's queer. Never heard of 'em. Is it boots and shoes?"

"No."

"Oh, dry goods, I suppose."

"Yes, they call my sermons that sometimes." (*Christian Endeavor World*)

HOTELS AND RESTAURANTS

What about the pillows?

A drummer went to the front desk to leave a wake-up call. "Never mind," said the clerk. "We get everybody up at six, so we can use the sheets for tablecloths."

A Yankee trick

An eastern pedlar lately desired accommodation for the night at a tavern in the south part of Virginia; but from the prejudice frequently existing against this class, our host for a long time refused. At last, he consented, on condition that the pedlar should play him a Yankee trick before he left him. The offer was accepted.

On rising in the morning, Jonathan carefully secured the coverlet of the bed, which, among other articles he pressed the landlady to purchase. The low price of the coverlet operated at once upon the latter, who insisted that her husband should buy it, adding, that it would match hers exactly.

Jonathan took his money, mounted his cart, and had got fairly under way, when our host called to him that he had forgotten the Yankee trick he was to play him.

"O never mind," says Jonathan, "you will find it out soon enough." (*The Galaxy of Wit or Laughing Philosopher*, 1830)

Say, is this "Let's Make a Deal?"

The very young (and inexperienced) traveling man checked into a hotel for the first time in his life and goes up to his room. Soon he called the desk and said, "You've given me a room with no exit. How do I leave?"

The desk clerk responded, "Sir, that's absurd. Have you looked for the door?"

The traveling man said, "Well, there's one door that leads to the bathroom. There's a second door that goes into the closet. And there's a door I haven't tried, but it has a 'Do Not Disturb' sign on it." *(A Prairie Home Companion Pretty Good Joke Book,* 2005*)*

But I do read tea leaves

The traveling man who was eating his dinner in Charley's Fly Trap started such an uproar that Dolly, the blond waitress, sauntered over to see what was the matter.

"Look!" he growled, "I come in here expecting wholesome food and what do I find? A fly in the bottom of my cup! What does it mean?"

"Don't ask me, big boy," Dolly shot back as she flipped away, "I'm a waitress, not a fortune teller. " (*Calgary Eye Opener)*

Just how nervous was he?

As the drummer was checking in late at night the night clerk warned him that the man in the room below was extremely nervous. The drummer retired to his room and began to undress for bed. He dropped one shoe loudly to the floor, then remembering the nervous man downstairs, put the other shoe down quietly. Just he was falling asleep, there was a hammering at the door. It was his nervous neighbor. "When in tarnation are you going to drop that other shoe?"

Man, did they get sucked in

A hotel maid was talking to her supervisor. She said, "Excuse me, M'am, but there are a half a dozen vacuum cleaner salesmen downstairs. They say they have appointments to give demonstrations."

The supervisor said, "That's right. Put them all in separate rooms and tell them to get busy."

He got the point

There was a convention in town and the salesman managed to get only half a bed at the town's leading hotel. He was determined to get the best half of the bed and, with this end in mind, fastened a pair of spurs to his heels before turning in. The other occupant of the bed stood it as long as he could. Finally, he spoke up. "Say, mister," he wailed, "if you were any kind of a gentleman at all, you'd cut your toenails."

Origin of species

Salesman: What on earth do you put in your mattresses?"

Hotelkeeper: "The very finest straw, sir."

Salesman: "Now I know where the straw that broke the camel's back came from."

In this corner

The traveling saleswoman was unhappy. "There are two mice fighting in my room," she complained to the clerk.

"What room are you in?" inquired the clerk.

"506," said the lady drummer.

"Oh, madam," declared the clerk, "that's a two-dollar room."

"What difference does that make?" responded the lady.

"Madam," said the clerk, "what do you want for two dollars—the Tunney-Dempsey fight?" (Brower, 1952)

Just checking

The salesman was writing his name in the register of a Leavenworth hotel when a bed-bug approached and waltzed blissfully across the page. The salesman paused in wonderment and then remarked: "I've been bled by St. Joe fleas. I've been bitten by Kansas City spiders. But this is the first time I was ever in a place where the bed-bugs looked over the register to find out where my room was."

A La Mode Muskegon.

Waitress: "Wevhamneggsanbeefanlamanporkantatersanteaan coffeeanbiskitswotlyerhave?"

Drummer: "Yes."

Waitress: "Wellwotlyerave?"

Drummer: Gimmesomehamneggsanbeefulambnporkan tatersanteancoffanbiskits."

Waitress informs proprietor that drummer insulted her. *(O'er Rail and Cross-Ties with Grip Sack,* George L. Marshall, 1891)

THE HOME OFFICE

Birds of a feather

A salesman wired his firm: "Saw Marshall Field today. No orders but a feather in my cap." Later he wired: "Saw Rothman today, no orders, but a feather in my cap." And so it went as the salesman traveled across the country.

When he reached the last stop in California, he received a wire from his sales manager: "Remove feathers from cap. Make wings. Fly home. Firm bankrupt, cannot send carfare."

Yea, stick it to 'em

The boss and his sales manager looked gloomily at the sales chart on the wall. In one corner was a graph showing the company's descending profits. The rest of the chart contained a map of the territory with pins stuck in it, showing the location of each salesman.

"Frankly," the sales manager sighed. "The only hope is to take the pins out of the map and stick them in the salesmen."

I miss that radio most of all

"I can't get back to the office this afternoon," reported the salesman to his sales manager on the phone. "A bunch of thieves stripped my car while I was at lunch. They've stolen the steering wheel, the brake pedal, the accelerator and the entire dashboard."

The sales manager expressed his regrets, suggested a call to the police, and said he'd see the salesman in the morning. A few minutes later the phone rang again.

"I'll be in after all," said the salesman with a slight hiccup. "I got in the back seat by mistake." *(Executive's Treasury of Humor for Every Occasion,* William R. Gerler, 1965)

Ask me no questions and I'll tell you no lies

A sales manager complained to one of his salesmen, "Why is it that your traveling expenses always run above that of every other man on our force?"

The salesman wired back, "I'll bite, why is it?" *(Capt. Billy's Whiz Bang,* October, 1921)

This lady knows her 'punchuation'

Mr. Ego, the hot-shot salesman, was dictating his sales report to a public stenographer. After addressing it to his boss, and detailing his successes, he went on with: "I feel you should know, sir, that in order to obtain the above mentioned contract, I found it necessary to employ every ounce of my personal charm and magnetism, my diplomacy was the most deft, and flawless tact was imperative. With these fine efforts, I am pleased to inform you, I was able to crown my approach with success."

The steno smiled wryly and asked, "'Crowtation' marks on that last paragraph?"

Out of sight, out of mind

Wife: "What's all the excitement about—why are you throwing things out of drawers? What have you lost?"

Salesman Husband: "I got an order today, and I've mislaid the address of my firm."

And "RML" is shorthand for "read my lips"

The production manager was looking over the specifications for some new equipment that had been ordered by one of his firm's largest customers. Attached to the papers was a coded note saying, "MILTDD-41" and signed by the salesman on the account.

These specifications were not familiar to the production man and he spent several fruitless hours searching various technical journals. Finally he gave up and called the salesman. "Hey, Joe," he asked, "what kind of specs are 'MILTDD-41'?"

"The customer wanted me to be sure to put those on," answered the salesman. "They mean, 'Make it like the damned drawings for once.'"

A good old sawbuck will do just fine

As a newly engaged commercial traveler was about to start out on a commercial trip from his place in Chicago the other day, he suddenly turned to the employer, a brave old merchant, and enquired, "I say, boss, what shall I do when I get out of soap?"

"Soap?" said the old man," why save your samples and you won't get out."

"But I mean what shall I do when I get out of greases," continued the young man.

"Grease? Grease?" pondered the old man, "why you don't need any grease—you are not working for a lubricating estab—"

"Oh, but you don't understand me," chimed in the youthful employee, rather embarrassed. "I mean what shall I do if I run out of spondulix—stamps—wealth."

"Spondulix? Stamps? Wealth?" echoed the mystified merchant, looking at the young fellow over his glasses, to see if he had gone crazy.

"Yes, currency—greenbacks," exclaimed the drummer, "cash, money, you know!"

A light seemed to dawn on the old gentleman's mind at the moment, for gazing upon the creature before him with a look of contempt and pity, broke forth: "Young man, what are you giving us? I rather guess you needn't go out, for I don't believe your class of customer could get along very well with you—they all speak English. Pull down your vest, step up to the cashier's desk and get your sugar.

Now cheese it, cully, you're bounced." And that is the way the high-toned kid got bounced—all through the pernicious habit of slinging slang. (*Cincinnati Enquirer*)

The cost of doing non-business

Head of the Firm: "Mr. Perambulator, what is the meaning of this item, 'funeral expenses $24,' in your expense account?"

Traveling Man: "That was the cost of burying my sorrows when I learned that Thin, Skin & Co. had, a day before, given a heavy order to one of our competitors." *(Jeweler's Weekly)*

And send any pocket change, as well

A salesman dies on the road. The hotel manager wires his company, "What shall I do?"

The company wires back, "Search the body for orders and send the samples home by freight."

In fact, I think I'll fire the whole bunch of you

A certain employer called his forty traveling salesmen together recently and made the following speech:.

"Gentlemen, I have been making some interesting calculations, which are just as important to you as to me ... They explain, in fact, why I cannot raise your salaries and why I cannot afford a Rolls Royce this year ... I find that the actual number of days you worked last year was 265 ... You average 100 days off for Sundays, holidays and illness ... Allowing 8 hours a day, this means 2,120 hours ... But this is not your actual selling time. I find that you have averaged 6 calls a day—32 calls a week ... These calls average 15 minute each ... But only half of the calls result in real interviews ... So that leaves only 16 interviews a week ... Only half of these interviews result in sales ... That means that your actual selling time last year was 8 times 15 minutes or, TWO HOURS A WEEK ... You are costing me, in salaries alone, about $50 per hour apiece, for actual selling time ... This seems incredible. But I cannot find any error in these figures. Can any one of you show me where I am wrong?"

The salesmen were silent. There was nothing to be said. (Herbert Casson, 1927)

Salesmanship by the numbers

A certain salesman, who shall remain nameless, gave the following itemized account of his spring operations to the home office: "Miles, 3,964; trunks, 4; shown goods, 116; sold, 98; been asked the news, 5,061; told, 2,210; lied about it, 2,160; didn't know, 691; been asked to drink, 1,861; changed politics, 46; daily expenses allowed by house, $10; actual average, $7; profit, $3; cash on hand, $2.60; been to church, 1."

Economy drive

Two salesmen were bragging about the size of their respective firms. One of them boasted that his company spent $5000 a year just for ink to use for their correspondence. "That's nothing," retorted his competitor. "We save that amount each year by eliminating the dotting of the i's and the crossing of the t's."

Must be an Irish Sitter

The sportsman went to a hunting lodge and bagged a record number of birds with the help of a dog named *Salesman*. The following year the man wrote the lodge again for reservations, requesting the same dog, *Salesman*. As soon as he arrived at the lodge he asked the handler if *Salesman* was ready to hunt.

"The hound ain't no durn good now," said the handler.

"What happened," cried the man. "Was he injured?"

"Nope! Some fool came down here and called him *Sales Manager* all week. Now all he does is sit on his tail and bark."

Ha! Take that in the kisser!

Four people were riding in a train coach. A woman and her beautiful nineteen-year-old daughter were on one side and facing them were a sales manager and his young trainee. The train enters a tunnel and the cabin becomes dark. A kiss is heard, followed by a slap.

The mother thinks, "That young man stole a kiss from my daughter, and she rightfully slapped him."

The daughter thinks, "That young man tried to kiss me and kissed my mother by mistake and she slapped him."

The sales manager thinks, "That young man stole a kiss and I got slapped by mistake."

The sales trainee thinks, "I'm pretty smart. I kiss the back of my hand and get to hit the manager." *(A Prairie Home Companion Pretty Good Joke Book*, 2005)

On second thought, make two

The secretary was leaving the office when she saw the sales manager standing by a shredder with a piece of paper in his hand.

"Listen," said the manager, "this is a very important document. Can you make this thing work?"

The secretary turned the machine on, inserted the paper, and pressed the start button. "Great," said the manager as the paper disappeared inside the machine. "I just need one copy."

LAW, ORDER, WAGERS, AND PRAYERS

What they don't know won't hurt them

The salesman wanted to be excused from jury duty. "You're not trying to tell me," the judge asserted, "that your firm can't do without you?"

"Oh, no, your honor," replied the salesman. "I know they can, but I don't want them to find it out."

Why didn't you say so in the first place?

The weary door-to-door salesman was stopped late one afternoon by a police officer who demanded to see his solicitor's license. "I don't have anything like that," replied the salesman.

"Don't you know you can't sell anything without a license?" the officer asked.

"Thank you for telling me," said the salesman. "I knew I wasn't selling anything but I couldn't figure out why."

And don't forget to lower the toilet seat when you're finished

The salesman was somewhat startled when he arrived at a rough mining town and noticed the rules posted in the local hotel. They ran as follows: "Lodgers inside will rise at 5 a.m.; in the bars at 6 a.m.; each man sweeps his own bed; no quartz taken at the bar; no fighting allowed at the table. Anyone violating the above rules will be shot."

How about, "May I have your attention, please?"

The traveling salesmen had their own lodge. At one meeting, a new man was called upon to act as chairman. Ignorant of the lodge rules, the chairman rapped heavily with his gavel, shouting, "Order, order!" Instantly, three hundred salesmen leaped to their feet, pencils and notebooks ready, and the poor chairman was trampled in the rush.

Older than dirt

Three traveling salesmen were having dinner together in Chicago. They decided the one with the oldest name be exempt from paying the check. "My name is Richard Eve," said the first salesman. "Surely, that's the oldest name."

"Not at all," said the second salesman. "My name is Adam Law. That must be the oldest name."

The third salesman said nothing. He merely took from his pocket a business card that read, "Mr. B. Ginning."

You salesman, me sheriff

A certain sheriff in a certain mid-western county has a reputation of being out to get all traveling salesmen and peddlers for selling without a license. However, the story is told of one salesman named Johnson, who managed to outsmart the peace officer.

Johnson was selling brushes when he was accosted by the sheriff. The sheriff asked him if he had anything to sell. Johnson promptly began his sales talk. At last, the sheriff bought a brush for a dollar, figuring he could arrest the salesman for selling without a license. The sheriff demanded the man's license that Johnson promptly produced.

The sheriff was a bit nonplussed. "I'll have to confess, he said, "that I only bought the brush to trap you and I don't really want it."

"Alright," said the salesman. "No hard feelings. I'll buy it back from you." So the salesman paid the sheriff a dollar and the salesman had him arrested for peddling without a license.

A drummer's prayer

Oh Lord, look with a forgiving eye, we beseech thee, on the buyers who lie to us about the low prices our competitors give them; Lord, soften the hearts of the buyers who as soon as they see a drummer, get as busy as a hen with one chicken and keep us standing around until our feet warp and then buy as much as two dollars and sixty-five cents worth and want that billed out the first of next month.

Good Lord, curb our tendency to flirt with the married women; the single ones don't count, and they expect it.

Teach us not to complain at the roller towels that the multitude has used before we get there.

Lord, give us digestions like alligators, that we may well digest the loin steaks cut from the neck where the yoke worked. Teach us to be thankful for the slum-water served us and called coffee.

Toughen our hides, that we may sleep soundly in hotel beds already inhabited.

Cause us to look with charitable eye on our competitors, who are a sorry lot anyway.

Lord, soften the heart of our employers, that they may render us what little commission is due us in full.

Oh Lord, teach our wives patience, so they won't expect our wages until we get them.

We beseech thee, Oh Lord, to overlook our absentmindedness when we get away from home and forget about being married.

And in conclusion, when we have our last trip, please don't send us below. We have had our part of that place on earth. Amen. *(Capt. Billy's Whiz Bang,* October, 1921)

SALES TECHNIQUES AND TRAINING

Now, watch as I put it back together

A salesman was demonstrating unbreakable combs in a department store. He was impressing the people who stopped to look by putting the unbreakable comb through all sorts of torture and stress. Finally, to impress even the most skeptical, he bent the comb completely in half … and it snapped with a loud crack. He quickly and calmly held both halves up for the onlookers to see and said, "And this, ladies and gentlemen, is what an unbreakable comb looks like on the inside.'"

The perfect news story

Reporter to City Editor: "Here's the perfect news story."

City Editor: "Man bites dog?"

Reporter: "No, this is even better … 'The bull threw the salesman.'"

Wholesale and Retail

In little trades more clients and lying
Are used in selling, than in buying;
But in the great, more unjust dealing
Is used in buying, than in selling. *(The Galaxy of Wit or Laughing Philosopher*, 1830)

He nearly missed the boat

The cub Florida real estate salesman asked his boss if he could refund the money to an irate customer who discovered the land he had bought was under water. "What kind of salesman are you?" demanded the boss. "Go out there and sell him a motor boat."

And the way I figure, it all adds up

Two grads met at the 20th reunion. One had been on top of the class, the other, now a salesman had a tough time getting his diploma, having had particular trouble with math. The latter seemed to have prospered.

"Joe," said the top man, "you seem to have done exceptionally well. How did you do it?"

"Well," said Joe, "after graduation I realized I was pretty dumb, and I had better get into some line where I didn't need to be smart like you and some of the others. So I found a product I could make for one dollar and sell to the public for five dollars and believe me that steady four percent really mounts up over the years."

The Rival Drummers

It was two rival drummers
The merits that did blow
Of safes were in St. Louis made
And safes from Chicago.
They chanced upon a merchant
Who fain a safe would buy,
And in the praise of their houses' wares
The drummers twain did vie,
Each striving to see which could construct
The most colossal lie.
Out spake the St. Louis drummer
"Once a man a cat did take,
And locked the animal in a safe
Of our superior make.
"They made a bonfire round the safe
With tar and kerosene,
And for four-and-twenty hours it blazed
With raging heat, I ween.
"The fire went out, the safe was cooled,
And I will forfeit five
Hundred good dollars if that cat
Did not come out alive."
Then mild upspake and answered him
The Chicago safe-agent:
"With our safe one day we did essay
The same experiment.
"We placed the safe selected on
Of coals a fiery bed,
And pitch-pine we heaped in cool oil steeped
Till the iron glowed bright red;
And in forty-eight hours we ope'd the safe,

And, alas! The cat was dead!"
"Was dead? Aha!" his rival cried,
With a triumphant breath;
But the Chicago man replied:
"Yes; the cat was frozen to death!"
No word that St. Louis drummer spoke,
But silent stood and wan,
While the Kansas merchant an order gave
To the Chicago man (*Fisher's Comic Almanac*, 1885)

Der Drummer

Who puts oup at der pest hotel,
Und dakes his oysters on der schell,
Und mit der frauleins cuts a schwell?
Der drummer.
Who vash it gomes indo mine schtore,
Drowns down his puncles on der vloor,
Und nefer schtops to shut der door?
Der drummer.
Who dakes me py her der handt und say:
"Hans Pfeiffer, how you vas to-day?"
Und goes for peesness rightdt avay?
Der drummer.
Who shpreads his zamples in a trice,
Und dells me "look, and see how nice?"
Und says I gets "der bottom price?"
Der drummer.
Who says der tings vas eggstra vine—
"Vrom Sharmany, ubon der Rhine"
Und sheat me den times oudt of nine?
Der drummer.
Who dells how sheap der goots vas bought,
Mooch less as vot I gould imbort,
But lets dem go, as he vas "short?"
Der drummer.
Who varrants all der goots to suit

Der gustomers unbon his route,
And ven dey gomes dey vas no goot?
Der drummer.
Who gomes around ven I been oudt,
Drinks oup mine bier, und easts mine kraut,
Und kiss Katrina in der mout?
Der drummer
Who, ven he gomes again dis vay,
Vill hear vot Pfeiffer has to say,
Und mit a plack eye goes avay?
Der drummer

Go on, give her the business

The sales manager was urging his men to go after increased volume from their accounts.

"Once upon a time," he said, "a Sultan had twenty beautiful wives. He would sit on his throne and when he had picked out a wife he wanted, he'd send a 10-year-old boy, called a 'runner,' after her. Now, as time went on, the Sultan lived to be 121 years old, while the 'runner' died at 40. Gentlemen, business never hurt anyone—it's the running after it that wears men out!"

It's all about those samples

Receptionist: "There's a lady salesman waiting to see you, sir."

Boss: "Show him in by all means—and tell him to bring some of his samples with him."

A word to the wise

Advice to salesmen: Soft soap in some form pleases all, and, generally speaking, the more lye you put into it the better. (Brower, 1952)

Her testy testimonial

A life insurance salesman asked a Brainerd widow for a testimony. Here's how she obliged him: "On August 9th my husband took out a policy. In less than a month he was drowned. I consider insurance a good investment." (*Capt. Billy's Whiz Bang,* May, 1920)

First rule: Always let the business go to the dogs

A young boy walked into a bank to open an account with $250. The bank's vice president gave him a warming smile and asked him how he had accumulated so much money. "Selling magazine subscriptions," said the lad.

"You've done well. Sold them to lots of people, obviously."

"Nope," answered the little boy proudly. "I sold them all to one family … their dog bit me."

She's a better man than I am

"There is a new racket on the road," said a commercial traveler. "It's a female drummer. I met her the other day, and she is a dandy. Of course she travels for a Chicago house and she sells goods like a January thaw. She has been out so long now that she is as independent as a hog on ice.

"She sits in an ordinary railway car and charges up sleeping berths in her expenses, just like the rest of us. She walks to the hotels from the stations and charges up the hack fares, just as we do. She beats the landlord down to $1.50 a day, and charges the house $2.50 in the regular old style.

"She can take care of herself every day in the week and she knows how to order up a bottle of wine and work it on the expense account, too. Why, when I saw her last she was a new silk dress ahead of the law firm, and by New Year's proposed to have a sealskin sacque out of her expenses.

"And that isn't all. She has half of the hotel clerks in the Northwest mashed on her; and the way the little rascal knocks 'em down on her bill is a caution. She has a regular trick of staying over Sunday where one of her admirers runs the house, and she walks off Monday morning, forgetting to pay the bill.

"What does she sell? That's the funniest thing about it. You would think she would handle jewelry or millinery, or dry-goods, wouldn't you? But she doesn't. She sells gents' furnishing goods; and the sly young men who usually keep that kind of stores buy of her as if they hadn't seen a commercial traveler for six months.

"And she is a dandy poker player, too. She handles the cards awkwardly and acts as if she didn't know a full hand from two pairs, and raises $2 on deuces and nearly cries when t'other fellow shows up three of a kind, and then gets excited in a big jack pot, and raises the opener, and bets the limit, and raises back and scares t'other fellow out, and slides into the deck a little pair of sixes or sevens or a bobtail as innocently as you please. Bluff? Why, she has a bluff on her like the Wisconsin River.

"She's a daisy; and I tell you it's mighty lucky for the boys that there ain't any more like her on the road." (*Chicago Herald)*

When less is more

For more than six months a salesman had been calling on the buyer for a certain firm, but the buyer never bought anything. After each interview the salesman would say, "Thank you very much. I wish I had fifty customers like you."

Mystified, the buyer finally said, "Look here, I don't mind your coming in here every week or two and showing your samples. I buy nothing, but you always say the same the thing—'Thank you very much. I wish I had fifty customers like you.' Why do you make this statement?"

"Well," replied the salesman, smiling, "right now I have about two hundred customers like you. I really do wish that I had only fifty."

Better prospects in a cemetery

A printer recently walked into a certain business house on his rounds to learn who would desire anything in the way of advertisements and noticed that a drummer stood by the counter with his sample valise ready to open.

"Anything you want to say in the paper this week?" queried the printer of the man behind the counter.

"No," said the business man. "I don't believe in advertising; I wouldn't give a cent for all the advertising."

The drummer waited until the printer was half way to the door, and then slowly taking up his valise, remarked, "Well, that let's me out. I do not care to sell on time to any man, who in this age, does not believe in advertising. I prefer to deal with live men. When I want to strike up a trade with a dead man, I will go to the graveyard and swap tombstones. Good-day sir. (*Schenectady Star*)

More than empty space between his ears

A witty knave bargained with a seller of lace in London for as much as would reach from one of his ears to the other. When they had agreed, it appeared that one of his ears was nailed at the pillory in Bristol. (George G. Evans, 1859)

This cat's saucer has more than nine lives

In front of an East Side delicatessen, a well-known art connoisseur noticed a mangy little kitten, lapping up milk from a saucer. The saucer, he realized with a start, was a rare and precious piece of pottery. He sauntered into the store and offered two dollars for the cat.

"It's not for sale," said the proprietor.

"Look," said the collector, "that cat is dirty and undesirable, but I'm eccentric. I like cats that way. I'll raise my offer to five dollars."

"It's a deal," said the proprietor, and pocketed the five-spot.

"For that sum I'm sure you won't mind throwing in the saucer," said the connoisseur. "The kitten seems to happy drinking from it."

"Nothing doing," said the proprietor firmly. "That's my lucky saucer. From that saucer, so far this week, I've sold thirty-four cats."

If it's a bear, it's goin' down

A supersalesman was hunting one Sunday morning out in the woods and went down to a nearby spring with his gun and a water pail to get water with which to make his coffee. Upon straightening up from the spring he found himself face to face with a very vicious looking bear. Dropping the pail but still hanging on to his rifle, he cleared a nearby fence in one bound to find himself confronted by an enraged bull. Being a supersalesman, however, he turned and fired his lone cartridge through the fence, killing the bear. He knew that he could shoot the bull any time.

Speak softly and carry a big wand

An attractive young woman had an amazing record in the house-to-house sale of vacuum cleaners. Questioned as to her success, she confessed to an effective stratagem: "I always make it a point to address my sales talk to the husband—in tones so low that the wife won't want to miss a single word."

Peddling eloquence

"Gentlemen, these razors were made in a cave, by the light of a diamond, in Andalusia, in Spain. They can cut as quick as thought, and are as bright as the morning star. Lay them under your pillow at night, and you will be clean shaved in the morning." *(William E. Burton, 1859)*

We're so poor we can't even afford bankruptcy

Trying to sell a housewife a home freezer, a salesman pointed out, "You can save enough on your food bills to pay for the freezer."

"Yes, I know," the woman replied, "but you see we're paying for our washing machine on the laundry bills we save, and we're paying for the house on the rent we save. We just can't afford to save any more right now."

Would you bring the ketchup, too?

A salesman, Mr. Fillmore, was selling vacuum cleaners in an early 20th century rural area. He was allowed to enter a farmhouse and show off his machine to Mrs. Gander. As he was extolling its virtues he reached into a bag and pulled out a handful of horse manure, which he scattered all over the carpet. Then he said to the missus, "If this machine doesn't sweep up all this manure and have your carpet clean as a whistle, I'll eat it."

At that, Mrs. Gander got up and headed for the kitchen.

"Where are you going?" asked the salesman.

"I'm going to get the salt and pepper. Our house isn't wired for electricity."

How about stockings, dodo?

An American and a British shoe salesman traveled to certain distant islands, each representing different shoe companies. After landing, they looked around, and what struck them first was that all the natives were barefoot. The Britisher cabled his head office: "Nobody here wearing shoes. Coming home by next ship." The American salesman cabled his chief: "Nobody here wearing shoes. Send one million on consignment. Market wide open."

The power of "the word"

A man with a severe stuttering problem applied for a job as a Bible salesman. The sales manager was somewhat hesitant about hiring him, but decided to let the man try out his hand selling the holy scripture. After a week out in the territory, the sales manager called the man in to get a report on his progress.

"And, how are sales?" asked the manager.

"G-g-g-going v-v-v-e-e-ry w-w-w-w-ell," replied the salesman, indicating that he had sold more than 100 Bibles.

"That's great," said the manager, obviously surprised at the novice salesman's early success.

"And how did you make those sales?" asked the manager.

The salesman replied, "I j-j-just t-t-told m-m-my c-c-customers t-t-t-that if t-t-they d-d-didn't b-b-buy the B-b-bible, I w-w-would j-j-just h-h-have to r-r-read it t-t-to t-t-them."

And all the rotten apples are in the back row

The colonel reviewing the troops on parade looked long and hard, frowned, and then barked at the captain: "What's the idea of parading all the big men in front of the smaller men?"

"Sorry, sir," explained the captain, "but it seems the sergeant ran a fruit stand before he enlisted."

She'll need a wide-angle lens for this big shot

The receptionist was pretty, and the visiting salesman lost no time in trying to impress her with his many charms. He bragged on and on about his exploits in selling, his former life as football hero, his success with the fair sex, and everything else he could think of.

The young lady tried to get on with her work, but that didn't dissuade the story-teller. Finally, she looked up innocently and asked, "Tell me, have you ever had a group photograph taken of yourself?"

And probably "on the lamb,"as well

The merchant was bitter. "Salesmen," he said, "are not very much like the month of March."

"How's that?" asked a friend.

"March comes in like a lion and goes out like a lamb. Salesmen come in a-lyin' and go out a-lyin."

Doing the right thing

Even more than the average citizen, comedian W.C. Fields was easily annoyed by a persistent salesman. One insurance salesman, in particular, refused to be shaken, even following Fields into the barbershop. The salesman just kept babbling through his various pitches, hoping eventually to wear down Fields' resistance.

Finally, Fields had had enough. "How many times do I have to say no to you?" he bellowed, spraying shaving cream all over the floor. "Just to get rid of you, I'll call my lawyer this very moment."

Still not satisfied, the salesman asked, "And will you do the right thing if he likes my offer?"

"I certainly will!" Fields shouted. "I'll get a new lawyer."

The Drummers

by Florence Josephine Boyce

I kind o' like to see 'em come,
They look so might smilin,'
They sort of 'liven up the town,
And keep the pot a-bilin';
The landlord hurries in and out,
An' has a brisker walk,
And all the loafers stand about,
An' grin to hear 'em talk.
They ask the merchant o' his health
An' if the trade is pleasin'
An' take an' shake his hand as if

They'd never leave off squeezin';
And then with grip a standin' nigh,
A-tradin' and a-lyin,'
The merchant vows the goods are high,
But still he can't help buyin,'
An' if there's any news a-shore,
They're sure to bring it to you;
I allus like to see 'em come,
It sets us all a-smilin,'
Because they 'liven up the town,
An' keep the pot a-bilin.' (Bill Brower, 1952)

Multiple choice

"Are you a salesman, bill collector, or friend of the boss?" asked the receptionist.

"All three," said the salesman.

"Well, then, he's at a conference, out of town, and step into the office and see him."

Sincerely, yours

The sales manager was wrapping up her pep talk to new staff members. "Just remember this," she said. "Always be sincere, whether you meant it or not."

And I bet her name is Suzie

A couple lived near the ocean and used to walk the beach a lot. One summer they noticed a girl who was at the beach pretty much every day. She wasn't unusual, nor was the travel bag she carried, except for one thing; she would approach people who were sitting on the beach, glance around furtively, then speak to them.

Generally the people would respond negatively and she would wander off, but occasionally someone would nod and there would be a quick exchange of money and something she carried in her bag. The couple assumed she was selling drugs, and debated calling the cops, but since they didn't know for sure they just continued to watch her.

After a couple of weeks the wife said, "Honey, have you ever noticed that she only goes up to people with boom boxes and other electronic devices?" He hadn't, and said so. Then she said, "Tomorrow I want you to get a towel and our big radio and go lie out on the beach. Then we can find out what she's really doing."

The plan went off without a hitch and the wife was almost hopping up and down with anticipation when she saw the girl talk to her husband and then leave. The man walked up the beach and met his wife at the road.

"Well, is she selling drugs?" she asked excitedly

"No, she's not," he said, enjoying this probably more than he should have.

"Well, What is it, then? What does she do?" his wife fairly shrieked.

The man grinned and said, "She's a battery salesperson."

"Batteries?" cried the wife.

"Yes," he replied. "She Sells C Cells By The Sea Shore!"

SALESMEN AND THEIR SPOUSES

The ultimate sales tool: the baseball bat

A group of travelling men seated in the smoker of a train approaching New York was joined by a drummer who said "Well, I've just shot off a wire telling my wife I'll be home in an hour, and she'll have a fine meal on the table all ready for me."

"I don't have to give mine that much notice," said one of the group. "I just call her up from the station, and by the time I get home she's all ready."

"Huh," sneered another of the group. "The first thing I do when I get off the train is to buy a good baseball bat. Then, I go home and ring the front bell. I run around to the back door quick and I haven't missed a bum in ten trips."

Something like Yogi's "deja vu all over again?"

Because they're on the road so much, salesmen often become virtual strangers to their families. As one salesman put it: "I'm away so much that half the time I can't even remember my own address. I have to telegraph my firm from time to time to find out where I live."

The other retorted, "At one time I was away so long that I actually forgot I was married, and, when I landed in a strange town, I fell in love with a beautiful woman and married her. Fortunately, when I introduced her to my boss, he informed me that she was my wife before."(*Brower, 1952)*

Watch whom you call "honey," honey

A young traveling salesman, whom we will call Smith, because that wasn't his real name (but easy to remember), was married a few weeks ago, and he arranged for his new bride-to-be to accompany him on his trip, which would serve as their honeymoon.

They arrived in a certain town that was known for its marvelous beehive industry. He mentioned the fact to his wife, telling her that at a certain hotel they served honey at every meal, and, as it was the hotel he usually patronized, he felt sure of excellent service. They arrived at the hotel just in time for tea. Smith proudly escorted his wife to a table in the dining room, and then, after an admiring glance at her, looked quizzically about, noticing that there was not any honey on the table. Rather surprised, Smith called a waiter.

"See here," he said, "where's my honey?"

The waiter, a bit bewildered, seemed at a loss as to what to say, but finally leaned forward, and in a stage whisper, said, "Sorry, Mr. Smith, but she was discharged for going out with too many of the traveling salesmen." (*Anecdota Americana,* 1934)

But well taken care of

First traveling man: "And what is your home state?"

Second traveling man, with a sigh: "Very poor. My wife and I have nine children and we live next to a fire house." (*Capt. Billy's Whiz Bang*, August, 1922)

Knock, knock, who's there?

The traveling salesman finally made the big step. He and his bride arrived at the hotel. While the husband was unpacking, the wife decided to go down into the lobby for a pack of cigarettes. She returned to the floor on which their room was located and knocked on the door. There was no answer.

"Honey, she cooed, "let me in." Still no answer. "Honey, honey!" she cried, let me in. "Honey, honey, honey, please open the door!," she nearly shouted.

From the precincts of the room came a deep bass voice: "Madam," it said, "this is not a beehive. It's a bathroom."

Must have been a couple of different storks

A traveling salesman returned home after a nine months' trip to find himself the father of twins. He looked amazed and perplexed. "But doctor," he protested, "I remember that I was only one night home when I was here last." *(Anecdota Americana, 1934)*

Just turn the other cheek

The salesman's wife was suing for divorce. Her reason: suspected infidelity. When the judge asked her to explain, she said: "Every time he comes home after one of those long trips of his, he pinches my cheek and says 'haven't we met somewhere before'?" *(Brower, 1952)*

An epitaph: Phipps & Chips

Here lies a salesman
Named Phipps,
Who married on
One of his trips
A widow named Block.
Then he died from
the shock
When he saw there
Were six little
Chips. *(Capt. Billy's Whiz Bang,* Aug., 1934)

What a doggone story!

The salesman had been on the road for three months. He finally arrived at his farm home and found his brother waiting for him at the station. “I’ve been away for a long time, Jack,” said the salesman. “Anything happen since I’ve been away?”

“Nope,” was the reply, ”nothing at all.”

“Nothing”” queried the salesman. “Surely something must have happened in three months.”

“Well,” said the brother, scratching his head, “there was one thing. The dog died.”

“Poor old Rover,” said the salesman. “How did he die?”

“From eating burnt horse meat,” was the answer

“Burnt horse meat?” asked the astonished salesman. “Where on earth did he ever get burnt horse meat?”

“When the barn burned down,” replied the brother.

“The barn burned down! How did that happen?” asked the salesman.

“Oh, it caught fire from the house,” said the brother.

“How did the house catch fire?” questioned the amazed salesman.

“One of the candles on the coffin tipped over,” was the reply.

“Coffin? What coffin? Who died?”

“Your mother-in-law,” answered the brother.

“What happened to her?” gasped the salesman. “She was in the best of health.”

“She died of the shock,” was the retort.

“What shock?” the traveling salesman whispered.

“When your wife ran away with the hired man,” responded the brother.

But nothing happened—except the dog died. *(Brower, 1952)*

TRAINS, TRACKS AND ROADS

Faster than a speeding slug

The drummer asked the conductor what the delay was.

“A cow on the track,” he replied.

“I thought that cow was chased off an hour ago.”

“Yes, but we caught up with it again.”

Just say what you mean

"May I have this seat? She asked of the genteel looking man whose baggage was occupying it.

"I don't know, ma'am," he answered, "it belongs to the railroad, you know; but I'll see the conductor, maybe he will give it to you."

She grew purple and said: "You don't understand me. I mean, can I take it?"

"Well, I don't know that either. You see it is fastened very firmly to the car floor, and would be troublesome to get up—however, I'll have a carpenter to come on board at the next station, and ask his advice."

"I don't want to take the old thing," she howled. "Is this your trap on it?"

"No'm, " blandly answered the drummer; "it belongs to the firm I travel for."

"Well, can I sit down here?" she finally screamed, shifting from one foot to the other.

"I don't know, ma'am, you are the best judge of your physical powers."

"And where do you travel from"" she yelled.

"Chicago," he replied.

"That settles it," she said meekly. "Will you please move your valise and permit me to occupy a small portion of your seat?"

"Certainly," he replied, "why didn't you say that at first?"

The train sped on, while he sat counting his expenses, and she wondering if Chicago's "cheek" had any equal under the sun. (*Atlanta Constitution*).

These guys know their ABC's

A commercial traveler in a railway carriage was endeavoring, with considerable earnestness, to impress some argument upon a fellow passenger who was seated opposite to him and who appeared rather dull of comprehension. At length, being slightly irritated, he exclaimed in a louder tone: "Why, sir, its as plain as A B C!"

"That may be," replied the other, with unexpected alacrity, "but I am D E F." (*Fisher's Almanac*, 1885)

A lamentable tale of the plastered drummer

Mr. and Mrs. Whiffin were on the way to the Hot Springs where he intended to get relief from his rheumatism in the baths. At a way station a drunken traveling man boarded the train and was put to bed in the berth next to Mr. and Mrs. W. by the porter. Shortly after, Mr. W. woke up with a dreadful stitch in his side. Like a good, dutiful wife, Mrs. W. arose and went to the lavatory to make a strong, extra strong, mustard plaster with which to relieve the pain of her liege lord.

On her return she pulled the wrong curtain aside and placed the plaster upon the stomach of the senseless drunken drummer. Then she went to the lavatory, washed her hands, and returned to her berth, getting into the right section, and finding Mr. W. asleep.

Finally a loud groan was heard, then these words: "Oh, my stomach, my s-t-o-m-a-c-h, oh-h-h!" This was followed by "I'll never touch another drop as long as I live. Oh, it's burning a hole in me, oh-h-h!"

By this time heads were peeping out from behind curtains, and the porter was on his way to the traveling man's berth. Of a sudden out came the bed clothes from the T.M.'s berth, and a cry of "Oh, my, there is my stomach! I'm dead!" The exclamation was topped off by the mustard plaster being thrown out on the aisle of the car. The porter then grabbed the drummer and shook him until awake.

During the first stages of sensibility he muttered: "Oh, my stomach is gone, gone!" *(St. Paul Pioneer Press)*

Those Frenchmen have "de-gall"

Peddler Schmidt recently returned from a motor tour to Florida and was discussing highway improvements in various states while loafing in the corner grocery store the other evening. The peddler evidently was not very familiar with the highway marking system in vogue in the United States. He insisted that the motor roads constructed by Lincoln, Jefferson and Mr. Dixie were the best ones on his recent tour.

"These men were all good road builders," insisted Schmidt, "but there is a damned Frenchman by the name of "Detour" who has built some of the rottenest roads I ever saw in my life. He should be fired from the construction gang." *(Capt. Billy's Whiz Bang,* May, 1920)

What's good for this goose is no sauce for the gander

"Is this seat engaged?" he asked of the prettiest girl in the car, and finding that it wasn't, he put his sample box in the rack and braced himself up for solid enjoyment.

"Pleasant day," said the girl, coming for him before he could get his tongue unkinked. "Most bewildering day, isn't it?"

"Y-yes, miss" stammered the drummer. He was in the habit of playing pitcher in this kind of a match, and the position of catcher didn't fit him as tight as his pantaloons.

"Nice weather for traveling," continued the girl, "much nicer than when it is cold. Are you perfectly comfortable?"

"Oh, yes, thanks," murmured the drummer.

"Glad of it," resumed the girl, cheerfully. "You don't look so. Let me put my shawl under your head, won't you? Hadn't you rather sit next to the window and have me describe the landscape to you?"

"No, please," he murmured, "I am doing well enough."

"Can I buy some peanuts or a book? Let me do something to make the trip happy! Suppose I slip my arm around your waist! Just lean forward a trifle, please, so that I can!"

"You'll—you'll have to excuse me," gasped the wretched drummer; "I don't think you really mean it."

"You look so tired," she pleaded; "wouldn't you like to rest your head on my shoulder? No one will notice. Just lay your head right down and I'll tell you stories."

"No, thanks! I won't today! I'm very comfortable," and the poor drummer looked around helplessly.

"Your scarf-pin is coming out. Let me fix it. There!" and she arrayed it deftly. "At the next station I'll get you a cup of tea and when we arrive at our destination you'll let me call on you?" And she smiled an anxious prayer into his pallid countenance.

"I think I'll go away and smoke," said the drummer, and hauled down his gripsack and made a bolt for the door, knee-deep in grins showered upon him by his fellow passengers

"Strange!" murmured the girl to a lady in front of her. "I only did with him just what he was making ready to do with me, and big and strong as he is, he couldn't stand it. I really think women have stronger stomachs than men; besides that, there isn't any smoking-car for them to fly to for refuge. I don't understand this thing."

But she settled back contentedly all the same; and at a convention of drummers, held in the smoker that next morning, it was unanimously resolved that the seat was engaged, as far as they were concerned, for the balance of the season. (George L. Marshall, 1891)

Two collar stays with a glass of water will work real wonders

One night this spring on a train coming east on the Erie road, the porter of a sleeping-car made the rounds of a half a dozen of the male sleepers to ask if they had anything with them to cure a case of colic for another traveler. A drummer for a city hardware house fumbled around in his coat and finally said: "Here's a box of soda-mints which may help him. He can use the whole box and be hanged to him, for he's no business to have colic!"

Nothing further was heard of the case until morning, when a strapping young man, with a far-West look to his hair, came into the sleeper with the mint box in his hand and inquired for the drummer, and said: "Took 'em all but one, and they smashed my colic right in the eye. How much to pay?"

"Nothing, sir. I'm only too glad to have been of service to you."

When the other had gone the drummer opened the box and we saw his hair trying to climb up

"Great Scott, boys; but what do you think?" he gasped.

"What is it?"

"I gave him the wrong box, and he's swallowed eleven bone collar buttons."—(M. Quad, in *New York Evening World*)

Still thinking about that poor fellow in Detroit

A drummer told a porter to take him at 5:30 a.m. and get him off the train in Detroit, even if he had to do it forcibly. "I might give you a struggle, because I like to sleep late." The next morning the drummer woke up at 9:00 and found himself still on the train. He stormed down the corridor to find a somewhat battered porter who was surprised to see him. "Good Lord, I wonder who I put off the train in Detroit?"

Battle scars

"What's that scar on your face?" a friend asked the traveling salesman.

"Why, it's my birthmark," responded the salesman.

"Your birthmark?"

"Yes, replied the salesman. "Last year, on the way to Buffalo, I crawled into the wrong berth."

This had him really steamin'

An elderly traveling man reached the depot just as his train was pulling out; so he ran down the track after it. Man and train disappeared around the curve. About ten minutes later, the salesman came walking back.

"Didn't catch her, did you, pop?" asked Station Agent McCormick.

"No, I didn't, but I made her puff, by heck." *(Capt. Billy's Whiz Bang, June 1924)*

Now, for the punch line

Have you heard about the traveling salesman who ended a train trip with a black eye? It seems that when the conductor asked him for his ticket, the salesman—a bit of a humorist—insisted that his face was his ticket. Naturally, the conductor punched it. *(Brower, 1952)*

A remarkable coincidence

The salesman awoke as the Pullman was approaching Chicago. He reached for his shoes which he had given the porter to be shined and discovered that one was black and the other was brown. He called the porter's attention to the mix-up. "You know, sir," declared the porter, "this is the second time that's happened to me this morning."

ONE LINERS

I'd like to say that our sales department has had the best year in its history. Wow, would I like to say that!

A good salesman can convince his wife that polyester is the generic name for mink!

My brother, the salesman, was put on a starting salary recently. Unfortunately, the salary started but he didn't.

He's a great salesman. During the day he sold pension plans to kamikaze pilots!

One salesman said that he'd gotten three orders that week—get out, stay out, and don't come back!

We just got a painting of our sales department. It's a still life!

My brother is an independent salesman. He takes orders from no one.

Salesmanship is the fine art of getting your customers to pass the buck.

Selling is a lot like water skiing. If you don't keep moving, you're sunk.

A good salesman is someone who has found a cure for the common cold shoulder.

A good salesman should never overlook the proper use of flattery. You go from show and tell to snow and sell.

Is this man a salesman?! He could have convinced the captain of the *Titanic* that it was a submarine.

Beware of the salesman who buys shoes by the pair and pants by the dozen.

Do you ever get the feeling that your sales staff couldn't sell pickles in a maternity ward?

We had one salesman who couldn't sell Blue Cross to Humpty Dumpty.

He's the sort of salesman who doesn't need leads. People keep telling him where to go.

A sales manager has two objectives: to make sure today's sales are better than yesterday's—and worse than tomorrow's.

I just met the world's greatest salesman. He rang our bell and I said I couldn't buy anything because I already had a hard enough time keeping track of all my bills. So he sold me a four-drawer file.

I lose a little on each sale; but I make up for it in volume.

And he even asked them for their John Hancocks

"Is he a good salesman?"

"Good! Say, brother, this guy sold framed copies of the Declaration of Independence in England." *(Capt. Billy's Whiz Bang*, January, 1925)

RIDDLES

What does it take to be a real estate salesman? *Lots.*

How do a traveling salesman who has just mislaid his valise, a person who has just recovered from the flu and a discouraged down-and-outer all resemble one another? *They have all lost their grip.*

What's the main difference between a salesman and a gorilla? *The monkey has no tail at all. The salesman's tale is far from small.* (Brower, 1952)

How did the housewife finally get rid of the door-to-door salesman? *Mind over patter.* (Brower, 1952)

The Drummer

Who is it passes out the smokes
And tells his highly flavored jokes
To customers and other folks?
The Drummer
Who is fills the merchant's ear
With optimistic tales of cheer,
Then sells him goods to last a year?
The Drummer
Who, on the train seeks the seat
Beside the girl who looks so neat
And fills her head with nonsense sweet?
The Drummer
Who holds her hand with wistful look,
Gains her address by hook or crook
And notes it in his little book?
The Drummer
Who's ever willing to be kissed?
Who's ready with a hand for whist,
Or lead in prayer if you insist?
The Drummer
At end of trip, with saint-like face,
who meets his wife with fond embrace
And tells her 'Home's the only place'?
The Drummer
(William Walter Shaw, 1926)

DEFINITIONS

Salesman

1. An individual who needs to have the wind taken out of his sales.
2. A person with both feet on the ground who takes orders from a person with feet on the desk.

3. Getting orders from some people is like pulling teeth; salesmen have to give them a lot of gas.
4. A soft answer turneth away wrath, but hath little effect on a door-to-door salesman.

Knock at the Door: One never knows whether it's opportunity at the door or just another salesman.

Married man: One who makes a good salesman because he is used to taking orders.

Salesman's tongue: The smoothest running thing about a car.

Auctioneer: One who always looks forbidding when conducting sales. (*Evan Esar's Comic Dictionary, Evan Esar, 1943)*

THIS 'N THAT

"The Frying Pan" (lyrics), John Prine, *Diamonds in the Rough, 1972.*

Come home from work this evening
There was a note in the frying pan
It said fix your own supper babe
I run off with the Fuller brush man

Chorus:
And I miss the way she used to yell at me
The way she used to cuss and moan
And if I ever go out and get married again
I'll never leave my wife at home

Sat down at the table
Screamed, and I hollered and cried
And I commenced a carryin' on
Till I almost lost my mind

Repeat Chorus

If I ever see another salesman
Come a knockin' at my door
I'm gonna pick up a rock and hit him on the head
And knock him down on the floor

Repeat Chorus

These are real gems

Since early 20th century grocery product peddlers Frank Vernon Skiff and Frank P. Ross saw fit to name their venture The Jewel Tea Company, "chosen because in those days, anything special was called a 'jewel'," we thought it appropriate, with some assistance from "Capt. Billy," to resurrect suitable jewelry for our other professionals:

Golfers ... Links
Pugilists ... Rings
Detectives ... Watch
Criminals ... Chains
Shippers ... F.O.B.
Horsemen ... Studs
Dairymen ... Milky Quartz
Dance hall performers ... Rosy Quartz
Printers ... Agates
Novelist ... Aventurine
Surgeons ... Blood Stone
Baseball Players ... Diamonds
Beverage Marketers ... Sodalite
Firemen ... Dalmatian Stones
Weathermen ... Snow Flake Obsidian
Ghost Busters ... Jasper
The Confidence Man ... Pyrite, (Fool's Gold)

CHAPTER 5

Anecdotes

"Buying Cheap and Selling Dear"

Just as with the salesman humor, these anecdotes tell us much about the traveling salesman, and his ways, past and present. As the narratives are presented chronologically, one who reads them through, from beginning to end, will see certain themes and trends.

The stories begin and nearly end with very clever sales pitches in "An Early Patent Medicine Story" and "A Most Remarkable Sale" where the salesmen take advantage of a moment to make the sale of their lives (or the lives of others). Other narratives report the deceptions that traveling men have used to close their deals such as in "Witty Knavery" and "Business is Business."

But the clever salesman may also end up with the short end of the stick when confronted by an even more savvy and clever customer as "Sevenfold Restitution" reveals. In the end, that "clever" customer is no match for the experienced and trail-hardened Yankee peddler in "Razor and Strop."

Several of the pieces suggest that salesman and customer are wrapped up together in a kind of game where both loser and winner enjoy the exchange, especially when the Yankee peddler is confronted by a Kentucky Jonathan in "Kentucky Hams vs. Yankee Nutmegs."

Both "Aladdin the Yankee" and "The real-life death of a salesman" raise interesting questions about how salesmen and their associates and friends witness the double-edged sword of triumph and tragedy.

Finally, two narratives—"Dip, dip, dip, dip …," and "The Man Nobody Knows"—provide us with three succinct recommendations for success: persistence, organizational skills, and "a superiority to personal resentment and small annoyances which is one of the surest signs of greatness."

An Early Patent Medicine Story: "An Extraordinary Medicine and Escape from Torture"

In the expedition against Fort du Quesne, now Pittsburgh, in 1758, under the command of General Forbes, several soldiers belonging to Montgomery's highlanders and other regiments, fell into the hands of the Indians, being taken in ambush.

Allan Macpherson, one of the Highland soldiers, witnessing the horrid fate of several of his fellow prisoners, who had expired under the most excruciating tortures, and observing that they were about to perpetrate the same barbarities upon himself, made signs that he had something to communicate. An interpreter was brought.

Macpherson told him that, provided his life was spared for a few minutes, he would communicate the secret of an extraordinary medicine, which, if applied to the skin, would cause it to resist the strongest blow of a tomahawk or sword; and that if they would allow him to go to the woods, with a guard, to collect the proper plants, he would prepare it, and allow the experiment to be tried on his own neck by the strongest and most active warrior among them. This story being repeated by the interpreter to the Indians, obtained full faith from their superstitious credulity, and the request of the Highlander was instantly granted.

Being sent into the woods he soon returned with such plants as he chose to pick up, and having boiled them, he rubbed his neck with the juice, and laying his head upon a log, desired the strongest man among them to strike with all his force at his neck with his tomahawk, when he would find he could not make the smallest impression.

An Indian then leveled a blow with all his might, and cut with such force that the head flew off to the distance of several feet. The Indians were fixed in amazement at their own credulity, and the address with which the prisoner had escaped the lingering death prepared for him; but instead of being enraged at this escape of their victim, they were so pleased with his ingenuity, that they refrained from inflicting further cruelties on the remaining prisoners.[1]

Keep to the Point

A certain English philosopher having asserted, in opposition to Dr. Franklin, that blunt conductors for lightning were the only safe ones, the King of Great Britain during the revolutionary war, caused the sharp conductors of his palace to be changed, and blunt ones to be put in their places, as though he disdained to owe this safety to the invention of an enemy. This he persisted in, although the royal society publickly condemned the pretended improvement. This anecdote produced the following neat and sarcastic epigram:

While you, great George, for safety hunt,
And sharp conductors change for blunt,
The nation's out of joint.
Franklin a wiser course pursues,
And all your thunder fearless views,
By keeping to the point.[2]

Witty Knavery

A Yankee lately brought into Boston a load of miserable water-soaked birch wood. A gentleman, after asking his price, said "What kind of wood do you call this, my friend?"

"It is excellent wood," replied the other, "for two reasons; it kindles quick, and burns a great while. They call it knot walnut."

On burning the wood, the gentleman found he had been shamefully deceived; and meeting the man in the market, not long after, he said to him, "How could you do such a knavish trick as to sell me that wood for walnut?"

"I deny the charge," replied the seller of wood. "I told you it was *not* walnut."

"You told me it was excellent wood, however."

"I told you it was excellent for two things: for kindling quick, and lasting long. Nobody will deny that birch bark catches fire quick, and if you have not found it long enough in burning out, I am mistaken."[3]

Aladdin the Yankee

When we go out on Saturday afternoon to moralize and see new houses, we usually take our young ones by Aladdin's palace. Aladdin was a Yankee. He started life by swapping jack-knives, then putting the halves of broken marbles together and passing them off for whole ones. When he gathered some brass, he went to school all the summer to learn the golden arithmetic—addition to himself, and subtraction from his neighbor.

At an early age Aladdin was considered to be good at a bargain—which meant the he could always succeed in changing a worse for the better—always keeping the blind side of a horse to the wall when he had to sell it; and the village said that certainly Aladdin would succeed. When he left, "he will be rich" said the village, with more approval than it would say, "he would be generous and true."

To Aladdin the world was but a market, in which to buy cheap and sell dear. For him there was no beauty, no history, no piety, no heroism. Vainly the stars shone over him; vainly the south wind blew. In the wake of the great ship Argo, in which Jason and his companions sailed for the Golden Fleece, over the gleaming Mediterranean—where the ships of Tyre, Rome, and the Crusaders have been before him—through the Pillars of Hercules, through which Columbus sailed to find fame in a new world—now sails Aladdin to find fortune. To him all lands are alike. No Homer sang for him in the Aegean; he only curses the wind that will not blow him into Odessa. No sirens sing for him, but he loves the huge oath of the lively boatswain.

With the Bible in his hand and a quid of tobacco in his mouth, he goes about the holy places in Jerusalem and "calculates" their exact site. He sees the land of the Rameses and Ptolemies; and the reverent echoes of the Lybian desert. Whose echoes have slumbered since they were tramped over by Alexander's army, are now awakened by the shrill whistle of Old Dan Tucker. He insults the Grand Llama, hobnobs with the Grand Mogul, turns his back upon emperors, and takes a pinch out of the Pope's sniff-box. He chews with the Arabs, smokes opium with the Turks, and rides for a bride with the Calmuck Tartars.

Aladdin comes home again, and the admiring village points him out to the younger generation as a successful man. "My son" does see, and beholds him owning millions of dollars—of all societies of which he is not president, a director. His name is as good as gold—he has bought pictures and statues—he has also bought a Mrs. Aladdin and housed her in luxury; but he picks his mouth with a silver fork.

He has a home for a poet, but he makes it his boast that he reads nothing but his newspapers. He goes to church twice on Sundays, and only wakes up when the preacher denounces the sinner of Sodom and Gomorrah, and those "tough old Jews" of Jerusalem. His head is bald and shiny with the sermons which hit and glanced off. He clasps his hands in prayer, but forgets to open them when the poor-box is passed around; and he goes home like a successful man, thanking God that he is not as other men are. And after dinner he sits before the fire in his easy chair, lights a cigar, and looks languidly at Mrs. Aladdin through the thick smoke.

By and by, old Aladdin dies. The conventional virtues are told over as the mourning carriages are called out. The papers regret they are called upon to deplore the loss of a revered parent, generous friend, public-spirited citizen, and pious man; and the precocious swapper of jackknives; and the model set up to the young generation, is laid in the dust.

Above his grave the stars he never saw now burn with a soft luster, which no lamp about a king's tomb can emulate; and the south wind, for whose breath upon his brow he was never grateful, strews his lonely last bed with anemones and violets that his heel crushed when living.

And we who are to be formed upon that model, carelessly remark, as we stir our toddies: "So old Aladdin is gone at last; and, by the way, how much did he leave?"[4]

Kentucky Hams vs. Yankee Nutmegs

The Kentucky nation has commenced a rivalship with the Yankee land, in the manufacture of wooden eatables. A merchant in our town of Port Gibson, Mississippi, desirous of procuring a lot of choice bacon hams, requested his agent at the Gulf to make the purchase for him from the boats passing down the Mississippi.

After many fruitless inquiries of the passing craft, he met with a Kentucky Jonathan, whose loading was composed of the nicest and choicest hams, all canvassed; and the one which was shown as a sample, looked so well, and tasted so delightfully, that the confiding agent made the purchase on the spot.—The new Jonathan had such an innocent, unsuspected and unsuspecting countenance too—giving forth no scintillations of vivacity, nor evidencing the owner to possess 'brains above an oyster-shell,' on any other subject than that of curing bacon—the art of which appeared to be impressed on the brain, as drippings wear the rock, or the knowledge of law and physic is made unavailable by some members of those honorable professions. Who would suspect him of perpetrating a miscellaneous or original act? Straws shew which way the wind blows: but the human countenance presents a mysterious enigma to the reader.

The hams, when opened, proved to be wood, neatly turned in the shape of a hog's hind leg; and the Kentuckian shewed that he was 'up to a trick or two.' All will agree that he was 'pretty tolerable cute.'[5]

If the Truth Be Known

I'd been on a trip ten months (about that)
When I returned to find my Mary true.
And though I questioned her, I doubted not,
T'was unnecessary so to do.
T'was in the chimney corner, we were sitting.
"Mary," said I, "have you been always true?"
"Well frankly," she said, just pausing in her knitting

"I don't think I've unfaithful been to you,
But since you've been gone I'll tell you what
I've done, then say if I've been true or not.
"When first you went away, my grief was uncontrollable,
Alone I moaned my miserable lot;
My friends all thought me inconsolable,
Till Captain Clifford came from Aldershot.
To flirt with him amused me while 'twas new—
But I don't count that unfaithfulness, do you?
"Charles Augustus Henderson lent me his horse;
My! How we rode and raced.
We scoured the downs, we rode to hounds,
And often was his arm around my waist,
That was to help me up or down; but who
Would count that unfaithfulness, do you?
"Next, young Frankie Pipps, just twenty-one,
We met at uncle's; 'twas at Christmas tide,
And 'neath the mistletoe, where lips meet lips,
He gave me his first kiss." (Here she sighed.)
"We were six weeks at uncle's—my! How time flew!
But I don't count that unfaithfulness, do you?
"You know Reggy Vere. My! How he sings!
We met, t'was at a picnic; ah, such weather.
And see, he gave me the first of these two rings,
When we were lost in Clifton's woods together.
What jolly times we had together, we two—
But I don't count that unfaithfulness, do you?
"And see, I have another ring. This plain gold band
that's shining here."
I took her hand, "Mary," said I, "can it be that you—"
Quoth she, "That I am Mrs. Vere.
I don't count that unfaithfulness, do you?"
"N-o," I replied, "for I'm married too."[6]

Sevenfold Restitution

The 1890's *Washington County Post* says that a man in a certain village, having had sanded sugar sold to him, inserted in the weekly paper the following: "Notice—I bought of a grocer in this village a quantity of sugar, from which I obtained one pound of sand. If the rascal who cheated me will send to my address seven pounds of good sugar (Scripture measure of restitution), I will be satisfied; if not, I shall expose him."

On the following day nine seven-pound packages of sugar were left at his residence from as many different dealers, each supposing himself the one intended.[7]

Mark Twain: The Lightning Rod Sale

After repeated visits by the lightning rod agent, Twain is sold 400-feet of "the best quality lightning zinc-plated, spiral twist rod system available that would stop a streak of lightning any time, no matter where it was bound, and render its errand harmless and its further progress apocryphal."

However, the agent is not yet satisfied that Twain will be completely protected and he urges Twain to acquire eight more rods of about 500 feet "of the stuff." Twain acquires this additional protection—but the agent is not yet done with him. After erecting the sixteen lightning rods on Twain's home, the agent suggests that even more are needed.

Twain responds: "Let us have peace!" shrieks Twain. "Put up a hundred and fifty! Put some on the kitchen! Put a dozen on the barn! Put a couple on the cow! Put one on the cook! Scatter them all over the persecuted place till it looks like a zinc-plated, spiral-twisted, silver-mounted cane-brake! Move! Use up all the material you can get your hands on; and when you run out of lightning-rods, put up ram-rods, cam-rods, stair-rods, piston-rods—anything that will pander to your dismal appetite for artificial scenery, and bring respite to my raging brain and healing to my lacerated soul!"

"Three Days Later. We are all about worn out. For four-and-twenty hours our bristling premises were the talk and wonder of the town. The theaters languished, for the happiest scenic inventions were tame and commonplace compared with my lightning-rods. Our street was blocked night and day with spectators, and among them were many came from the country to see.

"It was a blessed relief, on the second day, when a thunder-storm came up and the lightning began to 'go for' my house, as the historian Josephus quaintly phrases it. It cleared the galleries, so to speak. In five minutes there was not a spectator within half a mile of my place; but all the high houses about that distance away were full—windows, roof, and all. And well they might be; for all the falling stars and Fourth-of-July fireworks of a generation put down together and rained down simultaneously out of heaven in one brilliant shower upon one helpless roof would not have any advantage of the pyrotechnic display that was making my house so magnificently conspicuous in the general gloom of the storm.

"By actual count, the lightning struck at my establishment seven hundred and sixty-four times in forty minutes, but tripped on one of those faithful rods every time and slid down the spiral twist and shot into the earth before it probably had time to be surprised at the way the thing was done.

"And through all that bombardment, only one patch of slats was ripped up; and that was because, for a single instant, the rods in the vicinity were transporting all the lightning they could possibly accommodate.

"Well, nothing was ever seen like it since the world began. For one whole day and night not a member of my family stuck his head out of the window but he got the hair snatched off it as smooth as billiard-ball; and if the reader will believe me, not one of us ever dreamt of stirring abroad. But at last the awful siege came to an end, because there was absolutely no more electricity left in the clouds above us within grappling distance of my insatiable rods."

Following the storm, Twain has workmen tear down all of "terrific armament except just for three rods on the house, one on the kitchen and one on the barn."

Twain finishes his piece with an ad that he placed in the local magazine: "To Whom it May Concern- Parties having need of three thousand two hundred and eleven feet of the best quality zinc-plated spiral twist lightning-rod stuff, and sixteen hundred and thirty-one silver tipped points, all in tolerable repair (and, although much worn by use, still equal to any ordinary emergency), can hear of a bargain by addressing the publishers of this magazine." [8]

Beware These Swindles

It is the purpose of this volume to treat of that fairly numberless class of canvassers with whom the farmer, and towns-people most especially, are almost daily thrown into contact, and who, roaming from town to town, and house to house, have some article to dispose of which they will offer for sale at what may appear to be prices far below current rates.

These wares, generally novel in design, attractive in appearance, or seemingly valuable in application to the advertised end ... It is hardly necessary for us to say, in this connection, that the wares of these peripatetic salesmen are, for the major part, frauds, or, at least possess of such trifling merit as to be of no practical use.

In nearly every portion of the Eastern, Middle and Western States the people have been made to pay mighty tribute to the map, atlas and county history schemes. Then, in the wake of these have followed the garrulous subscription book agent, the cheeky and 'scientific' lightning-rod canvasser, the army of patent-right sellers, with everything under the sun; the fruit-tree sellers, with scrubby bush to be disposed of as valuable nursery stock; the cloth salesman, the jewelry fraud, the patent-medicine humbug—the legion of swindles dexterously disguised under high-sounding titles, and covered with the attract garb of novelty.[9]

Caught "De-fenceless"

Solomon Livitan, now state treasurer of Wisconsin and a Madison banker, was a frequent visitor at the Prairie House near Monroe and at other taverns in that region. As a former traveling man, while going from farmhouse to farmhouse and tavern to tavern many years ago, he had an amusing experience.

In haste to reduce distance he left the highway for a shorter route and as he climbed a high fence the topmost rail broke and left him high and dry, his pack on one side, himself on the other. His load was securely fastened to his back and he was unable extricate himself. The only recourse was to halloo. There was no answer and he was not able to wriggle out of his embarrassing situation.

Finally, along came a young man off to visit his sweetheart who saved the day. Levitan generously rewarded his rescuer with a pair of new suspenders.[10]

Razor and Strop

"What is the price of razor strops?" inquired my grandfather of a pedlar, whose wagon, loaded with Yankee notions, stood in front of our store.

"A dollar each Pomeroy's strops," responded the itinerant merchant.

"A dollar apiece," exclaimed my grandfather, "they will be sold for half the money before the year is out."

"If one of Pomeroy's strops is sold for fifty cents before the year is out, I'll make you a present of one," replied the pedlar.

"I'll purchase one on these conditions," said my grandfather. "Now, Ben, I want you to witness the contract," he added, addressing himself to Esquire Hoyt.

"All right," responded Ben.

"Yes," said the pedlar, "I'll do as I say, and there's no back out in me." My grandfather took the strop, and put it in his side coat-pocket.

Presently drawing it out and turning to Esquire Hoyt, he said, "Ben, I don't much like this strop, now I have bought it. How much will you give for it?"

"Well, I guess, seeing it's you, I'll give fifty cents," drawled the Squire, with a wicked twinkle in his eye, which said the strop and pedlar were both incontinently sold.

"You can take it. I guess I'll get along with my old one a spell longer," said my grandfather, giving the pedlar a knowing look.

The strop changed hands and the pedlar exclaimed, "I acknowledge, gentleman; what's to pay?" "Treat the company and confess you are taken in, or else give me a strop," replied my grandfather.

"I never will confess nor treat," said the pedlar, "but I'll give you a strop for your wit;" and suiting the action to the word, he handed a second strop to his customer. A hearty laugh ensued in which the pedlar joined.

"Some pretty sharp fellows here in Bethel," remarked a bystander, addressing the pedlar.

"Tolerable; but nothing to brag of," replied the pedlar. "I have made seventy-five cents by the operation."

"How is that?" was the inquiry. "I have received a dollar for two strops which only cost me twelve and a half cents each," replied the pedlar, "but having heard of the cute tricks of the Bethel chaps, I thought I would look out for them and fix my prices accordingly. I generally sell these strops at twenty-five cents each; but, gentlemen, if you want any more at fifty cents apiece I shall be happy to supply your whole village."

Our neighbors laughed out of the other side of their mouths; but no more strops were purchased."[11]

J.P. Johnston, 19th Century Auctioneer

My success as an auctioneer was assured from the result of my first sale. I soon learned that it required only hard study and close application to make it a profitable business.

I did not give up my furniture polish, but as soon as possible bought an extra suit of clothes, a silk hat and a wig with which to change my appearance from a polish-vender to an auctioneer. I would peddle from house to house during the day in a dark suit and Derby hat, with my hair clipped close to my head, while in the evening I would appear on the auction-wagon attired in a flashy, plaid suit, a blonde wig and silk hat. In no instance was my identify ever discovered.

We used to have great deal of sport at the hotels, where I invariably registered and represented myself as a polish vender, and never intimated that I was connected with the auction party.

As soon as the time drew near to open the sale I would go to my room, dress for the occasion and suddenly appear at the hotel office ready for business; and as soon as the wagon was driven to the door ready for the parade, I would climb in and perform my part of the programme.

I made auctioneering my constant study, jotting down every saying that suggested itself to me, and giving it a great deal of thought at odd times. In the morning, at noon, and while walking from house to house, I conjured up all sorts of expressions. Consequently I manufactured a large variety of comical descriptive talk on all lines of goods we handled, besides an endless variety of funny sayings and jokes with which to hold and entertain my audience .

Before quitting the business I was successful in acquiring a general line of talk on suspenders, shoe-laces, combs, brushes, handkerchiefs, hose, pocket-knives, razors, pencils, pins, stationery, towels, table-cloths, and in fact everything belonging to this line of goods, together with an endless variety of jokes and sayings used during and immediately after each sale.

My sales were made on what is termed the down-hill plan, or Dutch auction, instead of to the highest bidder, as is common in selling farm implements and stock. I would first describe the quality of the article for sale, and after placing its price as high as it usually sold at, would then run it down to our lowest bottom price, and as soon as a sale was made, proceed to duplicate and sell off as many of them as possible in a single run; and then introduce something else.

To give the reader a more definite knowledge of the manner of conducting this business and describing the goods, I will give an illustration on one or two articles, including a few sayings frequently used between sales. It should be borne in mind that as soon as I opened my sale I began talking at lightning speed, and talked incessantly from that moment till its final close, which usually lasted from two to four hours. I have talked six hours, incessantly, but it is very exhausting and wearing, and could not be kept up.

To hold the people and keep them buying, it was necessary to entertain them with a variety of talk. Whenever a sale was made, I would cry out at the top of my voice: 'Sold again;' and would not lose a chance then to add some joke or saying that would be likely to amuse the crowd, before offering another lot.

I will now illustrate a sale on soap:

> My friends, the next article I will offer for your inspection is the radical,' tragical,' incomprehensible compound extract of the double-distilled' rute-te-tute' toilet soap.
>
> T-a-l-k about your astronomical calculation and scientific investigation, but the man who invented this soap studied for one hundred years. As he d-o-v-e into the deep, d-a-r-k mysteries of chemical analysis, he solved the problem that n-o man born could be an honest Christian without the use of soap.
>
> Take a smell of it, gentlemen, eat a cake of it, and if you don't like it, spit it out. I'll guarantee it to remove tar, pitch, paint, oil or varnish from your clothing. It will remove stains from your conscience, pimples from your face, dandruff from your head, and whiskey from your stomach; it will enamel your teeth, strengthen your nerves, purify your blood, curl your hair, relax your muscles and put a smile on your face an inch and-a-half thick; time will never wear it away; it's a sure cure for bald heads, scald heads, bloody noses, chapped hands, or dirty feet.
>
> Now, gentlemen, I have here an extra fine toilet soap that you can't buy in your city for less than ten cents a cake. But I'm here my friends, to give you bargains. (then counting them out, one cake at a time): "I'll give you one cake for ten, two for twenty, three of 'em for thirty, four for forty, five for fifty and six for sixty cents. Yes, you lucky cusses, I'll see if there's a God in Israel. Here, I'll wrap them up for fifty-five—fifty—forty-five—forty—thirty-five—thirty. There! I hope never to see my Mary Ann or the back of my neck if a quarter of a dollar don't buy the whole lot. Remember, twenty-five cents; two dimes and a-half will neither make nor break you, buy you a farm, set

you up in business or take you out of the poor-house. Is there a gentleman in the crowd now who will take this lot for twenty-five cents?

(When some one cries out, 'I'll take 'em')

Take 'em, I should think you would take 'em. (*I took 'em too; but I took 'em when the man was asleep, or I never could sell 'em for the money).*

Will it make any difference to you, sir, if I give you six more cakes in the bargain? (throwing in six more.)

All right my friends. You can't give in vain to a good cause. Remember, God loveth a cheerful giver. Now gentlemen, who will have the next, last, and only remaining lot for the money? Here's one, another makes two, one more are three, another makes four, one more are five and one are six, and six more added make another dozen, the only remaining lot for the money. And sold again.

Not sold, but morally and Christianly. given away; where Christians dwell, blessings freely flow; I'm here to dispense blessings with a free and liberal hand. Ah, you lucky sinners, I have just one more lot—the last and only remaining one. Who'll have it? And sold again. The fountains of joy still come rushing along, the deeper we go the sweeter we get and the next song will be a dance. Well, dog my riggin,' if here ain't another dozen cakes. And who'll take them along for the same money? Sold again! Not sold, but given away. He that giveth to the poor lendeth to the Lord and when he dies he'll go to Georgetown by the short-line.

Well, there, gentlemen, I've soaped you to death. The next article I'll call your attention to is a fine Eagle rubber-tipped pencil with the lead running all the way through it and half way back again, and a pencil you can't buy in the regular way for less than ten cents. Now, gentlemen, after sharpening this pencil to a fine point, I propose to give you a specimen of my penmanship. I presume I'm the finest penman who ever visited your city.[12]

Business is Business ("or go figure")

"I calculate I couldn't drive a trade with you to-day?" said a true specimen of a Yankee pedlar, at the door of a merchant in St. Louis.

"I calculate you calculate about right, for you cannot," was the sneering reply.

"Well, I guess you needn't get huffy about it. Now here's a dozen real genuine razor strops, worth two dollars and a half; you may have 'em at two dollars."

"I tell you I don't want any of your trash, so you had better going."

"Well, now, I declare I'll bet you five dollars if you make me an offer for them strops, we'll have a trade yet."

"Done!" replied the merchant, placing the money in the hands of a bystander. The pedlar deposited the like sum; when the merchant offered him a couple of cents for his strops.

"They're yourn," said the Yankee, as he pocketed the stakes, but he added with an apparent honest, "I calculate a joke's a joke, and if you don't want them strops I'll trade back."

"You're not so bad a chap after all. Here are the strops—give me the money."

"There it is," said the Yankee as he received the strops, and passed over the couple of cents. "A trade's a trade, and now you're wide awake in earnest. I guess the next time you trade you'll do a little better than to buy razor strops."

And away he went with his strops and his wager, amid the shouts of the laughing crowd..[13]

An Insurance Agent's Story

"Oh, I guess we have our experiences," laughed the fire insurance agent. "We are just like others who have to deal with all kinds of people."

"Take the smart Alecs, for instance. They give us a whirl once in awhile, but we generally manage to get as good as a draw with them. It was only last fall that one of them came in and wanted me to insure his coal pile. Of course, I caught on at once, but I made out his policy and took his money.

"'In the spring he came around with a broad grin on his face and told me that the coal had been burned—in the furnace, of course. I solemnly informed him that we must decline to settle the loss. He said he would sue. I told him to blaze away, and I would have him arrested as an incendiary. That straightened his fact out, and it cost him a tidy little supper for a dozen of us just to insure our silence."[14]

The Man Nobody Knows: A Most Unusual Salesmanship Book

In 1924 author Bruce Barton penned what must be termed one of the most unusual salesmanship books ever written—*The Man Nobody Knows.*

Barton wrote about a man whom he considers a model for the modern salesmen. Barton describes the man, "though coming from the humblest of beginnings, as having extraordinary physical strength and mental skills. He was a very popular conversationalist and was probably the most invited dinner guest in the city." He established an organization that "conquered the world" and did it with "men from the bottom ranks of business."

Furthermore, Barton compares his model with other leaders in history who "have had that superiority to personal resentment and small annoyances which is one of the surest signs of greatness."[15]

Barton relates an example of "superiority to personal resentment" by Abraham Lincoln in the following anecdote.

> An important man left the White House in Washington for the War Office, with a letter from the President to the Secretary of War. In a very few minutes he was back in the White House again bursting with indignation.
>
> The President looked up in mild surprise. "Did you give the message to Stanton?" he asked. The other man nodded, too angry for words. "What did he do?"
>
> "He tore it up," exclaimed the outraged citizen, "and what's more, sir, he said you are a fool."
>
> The President rose slowly from the desk, stretching his long frame to its full height, and regarding the wrath of the other with a quizzical glance. "Did Stanton call me that?" he asked.

"He did, sir, and repeated it."

"Well," said the President with a dry laugh, "I reckon it must be true then, because Stanton is generally right."[16]

In the introduction to his book, Barton relates his early personal thoughts to "this man nobody knows". . . "Some day," said he, "someone will write a book about" this man. "Every business man will read it and send it to his partners and his salesmen. For it will tell the story of the founder of modern business. So the man waited for some one to write the book, but no one did.

"Instead, more books were published about the 'Lamb of God' who was weak and unhappy and glad to die. The man became impatient. One day he said, 'I believe I will try to write that book, myself.' And he did, writing the book about Jesus of Nazareth.[17]

Dip, Dip, Dip, Dip …

Colonel Remy tells this story.

After the fall of France, a significant fable was spread in hopeful whispers throughout the stricken country. In its heroic humor was proof of a deep and abiding faith in ultimate liberation by the stubborn people of that country.

The story related that in July, 1940, when England faced the enemy alone, Hitler invited Churchill to Paris for a secret conference. Churchill arrived by plane and was escorted to the Chateau of Fontainebleau, where Hitler and Mussolini awaited him at a tea table beside the famous carp pool.

The Fuhrer lost no time. "Here is what I've got to say to you, Churchill! England is finished. Sign this document admitting that England has lost the war, and all Europe will have peace tomorrow!"

"I regret that I cannot sign it," replied Churchill quietly. "I don't agree that we have lost the war."

"Ridiculous!" exclaimed Hitler, pounding the table. "Look at the evidence!"

Churchill sipped his tea. "In England," he said, "we often settle a difference of opinion by making a wager. Would you like to make one with me? The loser will agree that he has lost the war."

"What's the bet?" asked the Fuhrer, suspiciously.

"You see those big carp in the pool? Well, let's wager that the first to catch one without any of the usual fishing equipment will be declared winner of the war."

"It's a bet," snapped Hitler, who at once whipped out a revolver and emptied it at the nearest carp. But the water deflected the bullets and the carp swam on undisturbed.

"It's up to you, Musso!" growled Hitler. "They tell me you're a great swimmer—in you go."

The Duce shed his clothes and jumped into the pool; but try as he would, the carp slipped through his grasp. At last, exhausted, he clambered out empty-handed.

"It's your turn, Churchill" Hitler rasped. "Let's see what you can do."

Churchill calmly dipped his teaspoon into the pool and tossed the water over his shoulder. Then again. And again.

Hitler watched open-mouthed. "What on earth are you doing?" he demanded impatiently.

"It will take a long time," replied Churchill, keeping right on dipping, "but we are going to win the war!" [18]

The Real-Life Death of a Salesman

In 1949 Howard Fuller, son of Alfred Fuller, founder of the Fuller Brush Company, was asked to review a "new" play by Arthur Miller, *Death of A Salesman* for *Fortune* Magazine. At the time Howard was assuming more and more responsibility for operating the Fuller Brush Company.

"In peacetime," he wrote, "the professional salesman is the real hero of American society, the cutting edge of a free competitive economy … In a very real sense Willy (Willy Loman, the play's 'tragic' hero), with his slogans and enthusiasms, is symbolic of the true spirit of a large and important, and, one might say, a decisive segment of American life ... Selling is a tough business, exposing those who follow it as a trade to both physical and psychological stress.

"Enthusiasm is the driving force behind any human enterprise. No achievement is possible without it. It is like the fuel that drives an automobile ... but it can become a force for evil unless handled with intelligence. It can destroy and kill, as well as produce useful power.

"Under the guise of paternal affection, Willy would make Biff (his older of two sons) over into his own image and likeness by fair means or foul. It is for this that Willy blinds himself to the reality that Biff is essentially unsuited to play the role he has prescribed for him. It is for this that he gradually sacrifices his own career ... It is for this that Willy kills himself."

Howard concludes, "Just such conflicts between father and sons are all too common in real life."

Later, Alfred Fuller would reference his son's review in his 1960 book, *A Foot in the Door*, and mention a growing belligerence between his son and himself. Fuller the elder wonders about the cause of this belligerence and why Howard seemed so determined to "eradicate" his father's influence in the company. Perhaps, he suggests, that Howard was confessing to a Willy-Biff conflict with his own father in this review. And, as it turns out, Howard's automobile analogy and a force that "can destroy and kill" proved all too prophetic.

Just a year earlier, in 1959, Howard and his wife made a cross-country swing to visit many of his branch offices. Crossing Nevada a front tire of the car blew out. The car flipped, killing both Howard and Dora. The state police would later estimate the car's speed at 120 miles an hour at the time of the accident.

"I wish I knew," Alfred Fuller reflects, "I wish I knew why, for the first time, Dora went with him and shared his fate. I wish I understood why, if this end was in store for him, Howard was first permitted to overhaul the company completely in his own image, and drive it to a prosperity granted few industrial successes in this world."[19]

The Salesman Who Saved a President

In a strange twist of fate, a traveling salesman's serendipitous gift to a politician cleared the road for that politician to become an American president.

It all began in 1952 when Texas salesman Louis "Lou" Carrol read a story in the local newspaper that Senator Richard Nixon's wife, Pat, was looking for a puppy for their two daughters. As his cocker spaniel had recently given birth to a litter of puppies, Carrol telegrammed Nixon's office indicating that he had a puppy for Nixon and his family, if they were interested. A few days later, Carrol received a letter, responding that the puppy would be most welcome.

The puppy arrived in Washington just as a furor was arising out of press reports that Nixon was using an $18,000 political "slush fund" for personal purposes. At the time Nixon was running for vice president on the GOP ticket with Dwight Eisenhower. As a result of the revelation critics were calling for the vice-presidential candidate's resignation.

Later, Nixon would recall in his autobiography, that he considered the episode one of the six major crises of his career. Nixon decided to counter the accusations with a public broadcast, explaining the dull but true facts about the fund.

"I knew I had to go for broke. This broadcast must not just be good. It had to be a smash hit, one that really moved people ... one that would inspire them to an enthusiastic positive support."

With his wife Pat by his side, Nixon took his message to the airwaves on Sept. 23, 1952, arguing that he had used the disputed monies for political expenses only. Then Nixon introduced the puppy, "Checkers." He said a man down in Texas had sent the pooch. "And you know, the kids, like all kids, loved the dog. And I just want to say this right now, that regardless of what they say about it, we are going to keep it."

The public immediately responded to Nixon's message, sending the vice-presidential hopeful and his family loads of dog paraphernalia. The next day, Eisenhower met with Nixon and declared, "You're my boy."

Carrol would eventually move to Des Plaines, IL, where he built his career as a salesman. When he retired in 1996 he was a senior vice president for sales of Lawson Products. Carrol died in May, 2006.[20]

A Most Remarkable Sale

A very unusual and most remarkable insurance sale occurred in the mid-1970's high up in the Colorado Rockies.

An insurance agent and his wife were in a long line to board a tram that would carry them from one ski slope to another. Just before they boarded, the agent's wife pulled him from the line, as she needed to adjust a ski boot. They eventually got back in line and boarded the next available cable car. As they began their trip across the canyon, a single-engine airplane, flying low between the Colorado mountain peaks, clipped the cable carrying the cars. The cars ahead of the agent and his wife were catapulted into the canyon, killing their occupants. However, the agent's car was stuck between peaks and left dangling precariously above the valley below. While stranded in the tram, and prior to eventual rescue, the agent used the opportunity to sell a life insurance policy or two to the car's other occupants.[21]

The Fuller Brush Man and the Housewife

The following is an excerpt from a 2004 newspaper interview with a 34-year Fuller Brush veteran.

> *Interviewer:* "What about all those rumors and classic jokes about lonely housewives seducing door-to-door salesmen?"
>
> *Salesman:* "I don't know if I want to tell you this one, (he says coyly before closing the deal.) I was selling a beauty product to a lady with seven or eight kids. The woman took a whiff, dreamily sighed, 'Oh, that's so nice,' and fell down the stairs into my arms.
>
> "C'mon downstairs, I want to show you something,' she cooed as she attempted to lure me into a basement

bedroom. I was dumbfounded and ran out the door. Fearing the jilted woman might be angry enough to make me out to be the aggressor, I reported the incident to the police. Weeks later an amused cop flagged me down on the street and asked 'Are you the guy that woman tried to attack?' "[22]

GOYF!

Television direct response salesman Edward Valenti recommends the following GOYF ("get off your fax") message to prospects who don't return telephone calls. Valenti credits best friend Harvey Adelberg with the idea:

(Company Name) Fax
To: Person who doesn't call back
From: Tired of waiting
Subject: Soon to be fired

Message: Dear *Person Who Doesn't Call Back* (insert real name)
Subject: My proposal

As you know, I have tried numerous times to reach you on the phone. So, in an effort to get an answer on the proposal I sent you, could you please just check one of the boxes below and fax back to me? Thanks in advance.

P.S. My boss said my job is on the line if I don't get an answer because he/she thinks I'm playing golf instead of trying to reach you.

Check one of the choices below:

Dear Tired of Waiting:

I have been so swamped with work that I haven't even called my

(______) wife

(______) mistress

(_____) girlfriend

(_____) boyfriend

(_____) all of the above back.

So what does that tell you? I am interested, so keep trying.

(_____) Dear Tired of Waiting:

I am not busy. I am not returning your calls because I don't like you! In fact, I don't like your company, your wife, your kids, or your dog. By the way, as far as I'm concerned, you can gas up the dinghy and go fishing with Fredo, because you are dead to me! Do not try contacting me again.

Valenti indicates the above is just one suggestion, but that it "almost always gets a response—good or bad! We encourage you to be creative and do what works best and feels natural for you!" [23]

CHAPTER 6

Quotations by and about Salesmen

From Alessandra to Zigler

ADVICE

Alessandra, Tony: (Communications expert, speaker, author and producer of films including *The 10 qualities of Charismatic People)* "You can please all the people all the time ... people will teach you how they like to be treated, if you'll only listen to what they say and watch what they do."

Anonymous:

He who has a thing to sell
And goes and whispers in a well,
Is not so apt to get the dollars
As he who climbs a tree and hollers.

Anonymous: "The soft spoken salesman strikes the hardest bargain."

Anonymous: "Today's sales should be better than yesterday's—and worse than tomorrow's."

Arabic Proverb: "Live together like brothers and do business like strangers."

Ash, Mary Kay: (Founder, Mary Kay Cosmetics) "A mediocre idea that generates enthusiasm will go further than a great idea that inspires no one." ... "Aerodynamically, the bumblebee shouldn't be able to fly, but the bumblebee doesn't know it so it goes on flying anyway." ... "If you think you can, you can. And, if you think you can't, you're right." ... "People fail forward to success."

Ashe, Arthur: (Tennis champion) "You've got to get to the stage in life where going for it is more important than winning or losing."

Baber, Michael: (Business consultant/educator, author) "Sales champions sell something 'entirely' different, or in an 'entirely' different way, or in a 'far' better way than do other salespeople, by which they provide 'extraordinary' value to 'high potential' customer segments."

Bacon, Francis: (17th Century English statesman, essayist, and philosopher) "Time is the measure of business."

Baldwin, William H.: (President of the Boston Young Men's Christian Union, 1874) "The young man who has determined to make his mark as a Travelling Salesman, to be successful in the real and only true meaning of that word, who lays down as his first and imperative rule that principle, high toned character, faithfulness, truth, coupled with a keen sense of honor to his employer and to those with whom he may come in contact as buyers; with perseverance, patience, lively attention to duty, such a young man will have grand and ever opening and increasing opportunities which will all be to his interest and advancement as regards his business position and social standing, and with these a new stock of valuable information and profitable experience will be constantly presented to him."

On the greatest danger to which a traveling salesman is exposed: "Only yesterday afternoon I met one of our Boston business men who has for years sent out Travelling Salesmen into different sections of our Country; I asked him this question: What do you regard as the greatest danger to which the Travelling Salesman is exposed? He promptly, and with a decided emphasis, answered, 'the low and degraded of the female sex'." I earnestly beseech you, promptly turn away from any and every temptation to which you may be exposed in your social walks of life."

Beauvoir, Simone de: (French existentialist philosopher, writer) "Buying is a profound pleasure."

Becher, Barry & Edward Valenti: (The Ginsu Guys) "Get back to them or they'll get someone else."

Berle, Milton: (American comedian and television personality) "If opportunity doesn't knock, build a door."

Bettger, Frank: (Author of several books including *How I Raised Myself From Failure to Success in Selling*) "I no longer worry about being a brilliant conversationalist. I simply try to be a good listener. I notice that people who do that are usually welcome wherever they go."

Bible, Ecclesiastes 11:4,6: "If you wait for perfect conditions, you will never get anything done … Keep on sowing your seed, for you never know which will grow—perhaps it all will."

Blumkin, Rose: (Russian immigrant who founded the Nebraska Furniture Mart) "Sell cheap and tell the truth."

Bradbury, Ray: (Science fiction writer) "Life is trying things to see if they work."

Bush, Barbara: (Wife of President George H. W. Bush and mother of President George W. Bush) "You don't just luck into things … You build step by step, whether it's friendships or opportunity."

Cahan, Abraham: (Quote from main character in Cahan's 1917 book, *The Rise of David Levinsky*) "I developed into an excellent salesman. If I were asked to name some single element of my success on the road I should mention the enthusiasm with which I usually spoke of my merchandise. It was genuine, and it was contagious."

Canfield, Jack: (Motivational speaker, author, *Chicken Soup for the Soul*) "Get Started now. With each step you take you will grow stronger and stronger, more and more skilled, more and more self-confident, and more and more successful … But you have to take action to get it."

Carew, Jack: (Sales consultant and author of *You'll Never Get No for an Answer*) "You will be able to say you have done your best at selling when you satisfy your customers' needs on a steady and consistent basis. As a professional salesperson, you can't satisfy those needs unless you know what they are and appreciate the person who has them."

Carlson, Curtis Leroy: (Named one of the "100 Greatest Entrepreneurs of the Last Twenty-Five Years" by venture capitalist and author A. David Silver. Starting out as a salesman for P&G, Carlson eventually launched the very successful Gold Bond Stamp Company in 1938.) "You've got to be success-minded. You've got to feel that things are coming your way when you're out selling; otherwise, you won't be able to sell anything" . . . "I consider a goal as a journey rather than a destination. And each year I set a new goal."

Carnegie, Dale: (Speaker, author of several books including *How to Win Friends and Influence People*) "If you can't sleep, then get up and do something instead of lying there and worrying. It's the worry that gets you, not the loss of sleep." … "When dealing with people, let us remember we are not dealing with creatures of logic. We are dealing with creatures of emotion, creatures busting with prejudices and motivated by pride and vanity." … "You can make more friends in two months by becoming interested in other people than you can in two years by trying to get other people interested in you." … "Remember that a person's name is to that person the sweetest and most important sound in any language."

Carver, George Washington: (Great American educator, research scientist) "Start where you are. Work with what you have. Make something of it. Never be satisfied."

Chapman, Elwood N.: (Educator and author) "When you listen respectfully, help clients make a decision and then compliment them for making a good one; you help them feel better about themselves. This creates a better relationship between you and your customer."

Chinese Proverb: "A man without a smiling face must not open a shop."

Chinese Proverb: "Keep your broken arm inside your sleeve."

Chinese Proverb: "Fuel is not sold in a forest, nor fish on a lake."

Churchill, Winston: (English prime minister) "Nothing in life is so exhilarating as to be shot at with no result."

Cohen, Herb: (Author) "If you want to persuade people, show the immediate relevance and value of what you're saying in terms of meeting their needs and desires."

Dawson, Roger: (Author, *The 13 Secrets of Power Performance*) "Within each of us is a hidden store of energy. Energy we can release to compete in the marathon of life. Within each of us is a hidden store of courage. Courage to give us the strength to face any challenge. Within each of us is a hidden store of determination. Determination to keep us in the race when all seems lost."

de la Fontaine, Jean: (French poet) - "He told me never to sell the bear's skin before one has killed the bear."

Deming, W. Edwards: (Author) "It is not enough to just do your best or work hard. You must know what to work on."

de Montaigne, Michel: (French author) "One must always have one's boots on and ready to go." … "There are some defeats more triumphant than victories." … "Don't discuss yourself, for you are bound to lose; if you belittle yourself, you are believed; if you praise yourself, you are disbelieved."

Dickens, Charles: (English author)- "Here's the rule for bargains: 'Do other men, for they would do you.' That's the true business precept."

Eisenhower, Dwight: (WWII general and American President) "Leadership is the art of getting someone to do something you want done because they want to do it."

Emerson, Ralph Waldo: (19th Century American author)"The world makes way for the person who knows where they're going."

Esar, Evan: (American humorist) "In salesmanship, a foot in the door is worth two on the desk .... "Salesman's secret of success: Live well within your means, but dress far beyond your means." ... "Selling is easy, but only if you work hard at it."

Ford, Henry: (American industrialist) "Thinking first of money instead of work brings on fear of failure and this fear blocks every avenue of success."

Franklin, Benjamin: (Early American patriot, inventor, writer) "Do not squander time, that's the stuff life's made of."

Fromm, Erich: (Jewish-German-American social psychologist and humanistic philosopher) "Man does not only sell commodities, he sells himself and feels himself to be a commodity."

Fuller, Dr. Thomas: (17th Century British physician) "Get the facts, or the fact will get you. And when you get them, get them right, or they will get you wrong."

Gingrich, Newt: (American politician) Perseverance is the hard work you do after you get tired of doing the hard work you already did."

Girard, Joe: (Automobile salesman, author, motivational speaker) "The elevator to success is out of order, you'll have to use the stairs ... one step at a time."

Gustafson, Deil O.: (Real estate executive) "Inequality of knowledge is the key to the sale."

Hall, Kristyn: "Kids have more ideas because they play with toys. Playing with toys makes ideas come to you. It's fun, too."

Hannaford, E.: (1875 salesmanship author) "It is recorded of St. Augustine that, being asked, 'What is the first step in religion?' He replied, 'Humility.' 'The second step?' 'Humility.' 'The third step?' 'Humility!' If you should ask the progressive steps of success in canvassing, we should have to answer with similar iteration. Influence, Influence! Influence!! You can convince the most obstinate, mollify the most prejudiced and win the most crabbed, if you can only bring to bear enough influence of the right kind." ... "The philosophy of canvassing: First Step: Gaining a Hearing; Second Step: Creating a Desire; Third Step: Taking the Order."

Hawkins, Norval: (Early 20th Century Ford sales manager and motivational writer, speaker) "Too much emphasis cannot be laid on the fact that when you have sold a car to a customer your acquaintance and business relations with that customer have only just commenced—not ended."

Hayes, George M.: (19th Century drummer and author) Quoting his employer, "Any general advice I consider useless; you must learn by experience, but one point I want to press particularly on your mind: In making a new customer, try and read him through and through, but don't let him read you. Follow this rule, and act honestly and conscientiously ... Sell your goods on their merits, never misrepresent, and make the acquaintance of as few drummers as possible. Keep sober, be polite, economical and you will succeed. "

Heinz, Henry John: (Transformed early small vegetable-peddling business into international organization) "When once a salesman has established such relations between himself and the dealer that the merchant believes in him, almost any suggestion made by the salesman will be accepted by his customer as a good one, because he believes that the salesman is working for the interests of both."

Hess, Jr., Max: (Allentown, PA, department stores owner) "If the industrial history of America teaches us anything at all, it is that we achieve maximum production only when we strive for a specific goal."

Hill, Napoleon: (American author of one of the best-selling books of all time, *Think and Grow Rich*) "Do not wait; the time will never be 'just right.' Start where you stand, and work with whatever tools you may have at your command, and better tools will be found as you go along." ... "There is always room for those who can be relied upon to deliver the goods when they say they will." ..."Desire is the starting point of all achievement, not a hope, not a wish, but a keen pulsating desire which transcends everything."

Hugo, Victor: (19th Century French poet, novelist) "There's nothing more powerful than an idea whose time has come."

Iacocca, Lee: (American industrialist commonly known for his revival of the Chrysler brand in the 1980s) "So what do we do? Anything. Something. So long as we just don't sit there. If we screw it up, start over. Try something else. If we wait until we've satisfied all the uncertainties, it may be too late."

Indian Proverb: "Be the first at the feast, and last at the fight."

King, Martin Luther: (American civil rights leader) "If a man is called to be street sweeper, he should sweep streets even as Michelangelo painted or Beethoven composed music or Shakespeare wrote poetry. He should sweep streets so well that all the hosts of heaven and earth will pause and say, 'Here lived a great street sweeper who did his job well'"

Kipling, Rudyard: (19th Century English author and poet) "He travels the fastest who travels alone." … "I keep six honest serving men, they taught me all I knew: Where and What and When and Why and How and Who."

Kronenberger, Louis: (Drama critic) "Ours is the country where, in order to sell your product, you don't so much point out its merits as you first work like hell to sell yourself."

Krushchev, Nikita: (Mid-20th Century Russian leader) "When you are skinning your customers, you should leave some skin on to grow so that you can skin them again."

Lauder, Esteé: ("Cosmetic queen") "I never worked a day in my life without selling—and selling it hard."

LeBoeuf, Michael: (Speaker, author of *How to Win Customers and Keep Them for Life: Revised and Updated for the Digital Age*) "Treat your customers like lifetime partners." … "Waste your money and you're only out of money, but waste your time and you've lost a part of your life."

Lee, Gideon: (wealthy merchant and mayor of New York) "I had made a bargain with myself to labor each day a certain number of hours, and nothing but sickness and inability should make me break the contract."

Lec, Stanislaw J.:(Polish author of books of aphorisms) "Never lie when the truth is more profitable." … "If you don't believe in your product, or if you're not consistent and regular in the way you promote it, the odds of succeeding go way down. The primary function of the marketing plan is to ensure that you have the resources and the wherewithal to do what it takes to make your product work."

Letterman, Elmer G.: (Successful life Insurance salesman and author of *The Sales Begins When the Customer Says No*) "Luck is what happens when preparation meets opportunity." … "A man may fall many times, but he is not a failure until he starts saying somebody pushed him."

Lincoln, Abraham: "Public sentiment is everything. With it nothing can fail, without it, nothing can succeed." … "Whatever you are, be a good one."

Lyon, Alfred E.: (Street salesman and later, chairman, Philip Morris) "Remember, your customers don't buy your product. They buy you and they sell your product for you. If you've got a good, straight-forward look in you eye, if you make a good appearance, and if you make a courteous approach, dealers will buy your cigarettes."

MacArthur, Douglas: (WWII American general) "There is no security on this earth, only opportunity."

Mandino, Og: (Author of several books including the best selling *The Greatest Salesman in the World*) "I will act now. I will act now. I will act now. Henceforth, I will repeat these words each hour, each day, every day, until the words become as much a habit as my breathing, and the actions which follow become as instinctive as the blinking of my eyelids. With these words I can condition my mind to perform every action necessary for my success. I will act now. I will repeat these words again and again and again. I will walk where failures fear to walk. I will work when failures seek rest. I will act now for now is all I have. Tomorrow is the day reserved for the labor of the lazy. I am not lazy. Tomorrow is the day when the failure will succeed. I am not a failure. I will act now. Success will not wait. If I delay, success will become wed to another and lost to me forever. This is the time. This is the place. I am the person."

Maugham, Somerset: (English playwright, novelist) "Only the mediocre are always at their best."

McBride, Mary Margaret: (Radio broadcaster and columnist) If I have a formula or rule, it can be summed up in a single, too-familiar cliche: honesty is the best policy. This, undoubtedly is an over-simplification of a rather complicated relationship between my products, my sponsors, my listeners, and my radio program. I have a genuine affection and respect for all of these, and this big love-fest is what has hung the label of 'saleswoman' on me."

Overstreet, H.A.: (Author of *About Ourselves*) "Different is the salesman who shows respect for our intelligence, who tries to get us to express exactly what we ourselves wish, who listens to us as effectively as he talks to us; above all, who is cordial to us even after we have refused to sign."

Parker, Colonel Thomas: (American entertainment impresario, manager of Elvis Presley) "Don't try to explain it; just sell it."

Pasteur, Louis: (French chemist, best known for introduction of "pasteurization") "Chance favors the prepared mind."

Peale, Dr. Norman Vincent: (Clergyman, publisher of magazine *Guideposts,* and author of several books, including *The Power of Positive Think-*

ing) "Take the Bible quote, 'This one thing I do.' Now, this is a sound formula for doing a job systematically. As you dive into that pile of papers on your desk, complete each letter or memo in turn. Don't put any business aside and don't worry because you can't toss off the entire sheaf in 30 minutes. Do one thing at a time and do it well!" … "Formulate and stamp indelibly on your mind a mental picture of yourself as succeeding. Hold this picture tenaciously. Never permit it to fade. Your mind will seek to develop the picture. Do not build up obstacles in your imagination."

Powell, Colin: (American military leader and statesman) "There are no secrets to success; don't waste time looking for them. Success is the result of perfection, hard work, learning from failures, loyalty to those for whom you work, and persistence."

Proverb: "Better to wear out shoes than sheets."

Reilly, Tom: (Author, sales coach)

Have you hugged your customer lately?
Have you told 'em that you care?
Have you reached out boldly …
And said, 'We know you're there'?

Rohn, Jim: (Speaker and author of 17 different books and audio and video programs including *The Power of Ambition* and *Developing an Unshakable Character*) "Give to yourself the gift of patience, the virtue of reason, the value of knowledge, and the influence of faith in your own ability to dream about and achieve worthy rewards."

Roosevelt, Eleanor: (Wife of President Franklin Roosevelt and an activist political leader) "When you cease to make a contribution, you begin to die."

Roosevelt, Theodore: (26th President of the U.S.) "Far better it is to dare mighty things, to win glorious triumphs, even though checkered by failure, than to take rank with those poor spirits who neither enjoy much nor suffer much, because they live in the gray twilight that knows not victory nor defeat."

Rusk, Dean: (Secretary of State under Presidents Kennedy and Lyndon Johnson) "One of the best ways to persuade others is with your ears—by listening to them."

Saki: (Pen name of 19th Century British author) "In baiting a mousetrap with cheese, always leave room for the mouse."

Salk, M.D., Jonas: (Developed polio vaccine) "The reward for work well done is the opportunity to do more."

Saunders, Richard: "The lead dog gets the best view. The rest of the dogs' view is butt ugly. Of course, the lead dog is also the first to fall into the ravine."

Schwab, Charles R.: (Founder, chairman of the board, and co-CEO of the Charles Schwab Corporation) "I quickly learned that if I kept at it and plowed right through the rejections I would eventually get somebody to buy my wares."

Shakespeare, William: "Sell when you can, you are not for all markets."

Slick, Sam: (Character created by author Thomas Chandler Haliburton) "Don't stand shivering on the bank; plunge in at once and have it over."

Stein, Dave: (Sales trainer and author) "Winners are accountable. Mistakes may be made and deadlines missed, but winners take responsibility and tell why it has happened, what they are going to do about it, and why it will not happen again."

Stein, Gertrude: (American writer) "Money is always there but the pockets change."

Stone, W. Clement: (Insurance executive, philanthropist, and self-help book author) "There is little difference in people, but that little difference makes a big difference. That little difference is attitude. The big difference is whether it is positive or negative." … "You are a product of your environment. So choose the environment that will best develop you toward your objective. Analyze your life in terms of its environment. Are the things around you helping you toward success—or are they holding you back?" … "We have a problem. 'Congratulations'. But, it's a tough problem.'Then, double congratulations'."

Strauss, Levi: (Creator of the first company to manufacture blue jeans) "My happiness lies in my routine work … I do not think large fortunes cause happiness to their owners, for immediately those who possess them become slaves to their wealth. They must devote their lives to caring for their possessions. I don't think money brings friends to its owner. In fact, often the result is quite contrary."

Syrus, Publilius: (1st Century B.C. Latin writer of maxims) "You need not hang up the ivy branch over the wine that will sell."

Thayer, Wm. M.: (Author of 1897 book *Onward to Fame and Fortune or Climbing Life's Ladder*) "A good companion is better than a fortune, for a fortune cannot purchase those elements of character which make companionship a blessing. The best companion is one who is wiser and better than ourselves, for we are inspired by his wisdom and virtue to nobler deeds."

Tilton, George R.: (Writer and geological sciences faculty research lecturer, U. of C., Santa Barbara) "Success is never final and failure never fatal. It's courage that counts." *(Quote is also credited to Winston Churchill)*

Truman, Harry: (33rd President of the U.S.) "If you can't convince 'em, confuse 'em."

Voltaire: (18th Century French philosopher) "Judge a person by their questions, rather than their answers."

Wagman, Michael: (Author) "Years ago when Ken Stabler was a quarterback for the Raiders, a newspaperman said: 'Ken, I want to read you something Jack London wrote: *I would rather be ashes than dust. I would rather that my spark burn out in a brilliant blaze than be stifled by dry rot. I would rather be a superb meteor, every atom of me a magnificent glow, than a sleepy crumbling planet. For the proper function of man is to live, not exist. I shall not waste my days in trying to prolong them. I shall use my time.* What does that mean to you, Kenny?' Without hesitation, Stabler said: 'Throw deep'!"

Waitley, Denis: (Keynote lecturer, productivity consultant, and author of several books including *Seeds of Greatness*) "The winners in life think constantly in terms of I can, I will and I am. Losers, on the other hand, concentrate their waking thoughts on what they should have done, or what they don't do."

Walker, Sarah Breedlove: (Successful 19th Century African American business and saleswoman) "In an intelligent and emphatic way, watch his or her face, note what statements impress most. And then drive the nail home, always remembering you are there to sell."

Watson, Thomas J.: (Early president of IBM) "A manager is an assistant to his men." … "the way to succeed is to double your error rate." … "Good design is good business."

Weldon, Joel: (Speaker, sales consultant, seminar leader, and known for his registered trademark, a heavy 8-ounce can that says: "Success comes in can's, not in cannot's") "It's not what happens to you, it's how you respond! It's all up to you! Control the controllables! Forget the excuses, and take action!"

Wheeler, Elmer: (Mid-20th Century salesman and author whose "Wheeler Institute of Words" developed a "best practices" of selling by testing a variety of words in over 19 million selling situations) "Don't sell the steak; sell the sizzle. It is the sizzle that sells the steak and not the cow, although the cow is, of course, mighty important."

Wilson, Earl: (First African American pitcher for the Boston Red Sox in 1959, considered one of baseball's greatest power-hitting pitchers in major league history) "To sell something, tell a woman it's a bargain; tell a man it's deductible." ... "One way to get high blood pressure is to go mountain climbing over molehills." ... "Success is simply a matter of luck. Ask any failure."

Wooden, Joshua: (Father of basketball coach Johnny Wooden) "Make each day your masterpiece."

Zigler, Hillary Hinton: "Zig" (American author, salesperson and motivational speaker) "I believe that persistent effort, supported by a character-based foundation, will enable you to get more of the things money will buy and all of the things money won't buy."

SELLING TIPS

Cox, Jeff: (Sales and marketing author) "Silence has been used for centuries as a closing technique. The game is simple. After asking a closing question, say nothing—because the person who speaks next loses."

Duncan, Todd: (Author of *Sales Motivation* and *Simple Truths of Selling*) "The 10 Fatal Mistakes Salespeople Make & How to Avoid Them "1. Relying on 'You can do it" propaganda to maintain your sales motivation; 2. Trying to sell before training to sell; 3. Treating the symptoms but not the sickness of poor selling efforts; 4. Building a business-based life instead of a life-based business; 5. Taking Lone Ranger actions instead of using team-connected strategies; 6. Selling your product before knowing your customer; 7. Making unplanned calls on unknown customers; 8. Seeking your customers' business before earning your customers' trust; 9. Focusing on surface profitability instead of client satisfaction; 10. Losing your sales edge by neglecting your growth curve."

Farley, James A.: (Mid-1900's figure who successfully sold people, e.g. 1932 Presidential hopeful FDR, politics, building supplies, and soft drinks. e.g. Coca-Cola) "Essentially ... successful selling is ... giving one's self the benefit of the doubt by going to see every possible prospect, however tough the situation may seem. You never know what unsuspected forces may be at work in your favor which could throw the business your way."

Feldman, Ben: (Considered by some to be the most successful life insurance salesman of all time. Agent for New York Life, East Liverpool, OH, working in the mid- to late-1900s) "I'm always trying to find new fundamental ideas—ideas that result in big sales ... I may take a little something from you. And from you. And from you. I'll beg it, I'll borrow it,

I'll steal it, and I'll try to make it my own. I have gleaned my ideas from the minds of many men—but in return, I'll share any ideas I have with you. If you have an idea and I have an idea, and we trade ideas, no one has lost! Now we each have two ideas!" ... "On cold calls, I just walk in—and my first barrier is usually the switchboard operator or the receptionist. Face to face, the odds are I'll get by! I'm very frank, very open. I just say I want to meet the boss, whoever that might be. (And you'd better know the boss's name!) The receptionist ordinarily announces me, but it's a cold call, and the odds are the boss doesn't want to see me. I get thrown out of more places! As many places as anyone. I don't mean physically. There are so many ways of saying, 'No.' The boss probably won't see me the first time. That isn't so bad. Why? Because I'm coming back, and when I come back I'm no longer a stranger. I've been there before."

Fuller, Alfred: (Founder of Fuller Brush Company) "I discovered the basic truth on which the Fuller Brush Company was to be founded. Previously I had imagined the salesman as a talker who could charm a doorknob into buying brass polish. Now I know that such eloquence was a deterrent rather than an aid; that the product must sell itself. Whenever a housewife saw that I had a superior brush or mop which she needed, at a price she could pay, she bought it. The trick was not to make her buy, but to show her what the brush could do. This required actions rather than words." ... "The successful seller must feel some commitment that his product offers mankind as much altruistic benefit as it yields the seller in money. The salesman is an idealist and an artist; in that respect he differs from the huckster, who is just out for profit."

Gitomer, Jeffrey: (Salesmanship author, speaker) "If you cannot distinguish yourself from the competition, you will only sell based on price ... All things being equal, people want to do business with their friends. All things being not quite so equal, people STILL want to do business with their friends."

Hilton, Conrad N.: (Hotel chain founder) " I learned what I think is fundamental in successful selling. It is simply that most 'no' answers are not nearly as final as they sound in the saying. With a new approach, a good percentage of them can be veered in the direction of 'yes.' To me the fascination of any deal is the fact that you never know what may make a man change his mind. You figure out one approach and fail, and then you think of another. Often it is the unexpected that turns the tide."

Hopkins, Tom: (Sales trainer and author of *How to Master the Art of Selling*) "'By the way' are three of the most important words in any attempt to persuade or convince another person. Use these words to change gears—to move on to the next topic. Don't just keep talking. Take a conscious, purposeful step back into your presentation." . ."Every evening, write down the six most important things that you must do the next day. Then while you sleep your subconscious will work on the best ways for you to accomplish them. Your next day will go much more smoothly."

Ives, Charles: (Early 20th Century American insurance salesman and music composer) On selling life insurance: "Don't try to make too many points—no matter how good your arguments may be. Always be on the lookout for a chance to close in, get the application or arrange a medical examination. In this connection, put what you have to say in the form of a statement, not a question. There comes a time … when he must chance offending the prospect and losing out altogether, by 'taking the bull by the horns' and 'by going to the mat hard' … If you cannot interest the prospect … try not to leave his office without getting some information for future reference. At least get the date of birth … If you cannot interest the head man, make him at least admit that your plan in principle is valuable … It is not a bad plan to carry a specimen-bottle with you."

Letterman, Elmer G.: (Insurance salesman, representing 32 leading insurance firms in the 1950s and sold about $100 million in group policies annually.) Letterman's *Seven rules for the Salesman*: 1) "Don't wait for people to come to you. Always take the initiative in making acquaintances. 2) Carry something with you that will develop curiosity—take my watch for instance; it has a glass case which makes visible the movements. Properly dangled it is an eye catcher and an opening wedge subject. 3) Don't sell cold statistics; sell ideas. 4) Be enthusiastic. Nobody will believe in our product unless you show that you do. 5) Do favors, and pay particular attention to the kind of small favor that shows your thoughtfulness. 6) Ask favors that require little trouble, but build up the other fellow's self-esteem. 7) Give your client as much attention after you've sold him as before."

Levitt, Larry: (VP communications and online information and editor-in-chief, Kaisernetwork.org for the Henry J. Kaiser Family Foundation) "When my client gives me an absolute no, I blow a whistle and announce, 'The second half is just beginning'."

Mackay, Harvey: (Motivational speaker, author of several books including *Pushing the Envelope: All the Way to the Top*) "Put into practice a plan to become the sole source of supply to your largest customers. The most important element of your plan is to treat your customers as though you were their most dedicated employee and consultant, ready to serve them in every way so they feel your company is practically a division of their company."

Motley, Arthur H.: (Fuller Brush man, cough syrup salesman, advertising space salesman, eventually becoming publisher of *Parade Magazine*) "A simple 15-word sales course: Know your product. See a lot of people. Ask all to buy. Use common sense." … "You can't sell peanuts at a funeral, but they go great at the circus!"

Peppers, Don: (Business development executive and author) "First crash the gate, then be nice to the security guard."

Phillips, Wendell: (19th Century Native American abolitionist, orator) "Many know how to flatter, few know how to praise." … "What is defeat? Nothing but education. Nothing but the first step to something better."

Popeil, Ron: (Inventor and on-air salesman for his Ronco products) "I would like to leave you now with my best three words of advice: Work for yourself … If you're a good salesperson, you can make more money in one month selling a product that you make or market than you can in a year working for an employer." … "Have a quality product, believe in it thoroughly, and go out and sell it. And don't forget: Make sure it's a great gift." … "My philosophy is when you snooze, you lose. If you have a great idea, at least take the chance and put your best foot forward."

Schiffman, Steve: (Sales consultant and author of *Cold Calling Techniques that Really Work*) "Selling is nothing more than asking people: what they do; how they do it; when they do it; who they do it with; why they do it that way; and then helping them do it better." … "The golden rule for closing a sale: "Be patient. Wait for the answer to the question, 'what do you think'?"

von Goethe, Johann Wolfgang: (18th-19th Century German poet, novelist, scientist and musician) "Try novelties for salesmen's bait. For novelty wins everyone."

Watson, Thomas J.: (Began work in 1893 as a salesman for National Cash Register, eventually becoming chairman, IBM): "Pack your today's with effort—extra effort! Your tomorrows will take care of themselves. They will also take good care of you and your family." … "It is worth any salesman's thinking time to figure out ways to work a 'why' into interviews. By the very sincerity of listening to a prospect's reasons for not buying you bring the sales call to its most perfect form—two men talking with each other in a friendly relaxed way." … "One of the best salesmen I ever met in my life worked provincial territory, and he always had a big record. When he was asked how he did it, he said, 'When I get into a town, I unhitch!' He meant, of course, that when he reached a town he stayed there until he finished the job, until he had talked to every prospect" … "Whenever an individual or a business decides that success has been attained, progress stops."

Wilson, President Woodrow: (Delivered at Detroit, July 10, 1916, the first World's Salesman Congress) "Lift your eyes to the horizon of business. Do not look too close at the little processes with which you are concerned, but let your thoughts and your imaginations run abroad throughout the whole world. And with the inspiration of the thought that you are Americans and are meant to carry liberty and justice and the principles of humanity wherever you go, go out and sell goods that will make the world more comfortable and more happy, and convert them to the principles of America."

ANONYMOUS APHORISMS

A salesman is one who sells goods that won't come back to customers who will.

A salesman is the high priest of profits.

A salesman is someone who it is always a pleasure to bid goodbye to.

Good salesmanship will find a cure for the common cold shoulder.

Selling is easy if you work hard enough at it.

Cash can buy, but it takes enthusiasm to sell.

The object of a salesman is not to make sales, but to make customers.

It takes less effort to keep an old customer satisfied than to get a new customer interested.

Salesmanship means transferring a conviction from the seller to a buyer.

A salesman who covers a chair instead of his territory will always be on the bottom.

The law of diminishing returns catches up with the salesman who rests on his laurels.

When we think an unreasonable price when we are to buy, we think just and equitable when we are to sell.

Samson was a piker; he killed only a thousand men with the jawbone of an ass. Every hour in the day ten thousand sales are killed with the same weapon.

Insurance broker's axiom: No one has the endurance, Like the man who sells insurance.

CHARACTERIZATIONS (ATTRIBUTED)

Alcott, Amos Bronson: (19th Century American teacher, writer and father of novelist Louisa May Alcott) "Prudence is the footprint of wisdom."

Barnum, P.T.: (19th Century American promoter and showman) "Advertising is to a genuine article what manure is to land—it largely increases the product." And about Christoforo, an early 19th Century Italian "quack doctor," Barnum said: "He understood human nature … its superstitions, tastes, changefulness and love of display and excitement. He has done no harm, and given as much amusement as he has been paid for … I dare say his death … will cause more sensation and evoke more tears than that of any better physician in Tuscany."

Baudelaire, Charles: (19th Century French poet) "For the merchant, even honesty is a financial speculation."

Beecher, Henry Ward: (Prominent 19th Century American clergyman, social reformer, abolitionist, and speaker) "Men go shopping just as men go out fishing or hunting, to see how large a fish may be caught with the smallest hook." … "How many pretenses men that sell goods weave! What poor articles, with what a good face, do they palm off on their customers." … "No matter who reigns, the merchant reigns." … "The commerce of the world is conducted by the strong, and usually it operates against the weak."

Bible, Proverbs 11:1: "A false balance is abomination to the Lord, but a just weight is his delight."

Bierce, Ambrose: (19th Century editorialist, journalist, short-story writer and satirist) Definition of auctioneer, "The man who proclaims with a hammer that he has picked a pocket with his tongue."

Brower, Charles: (Explorer, writer) "There is no such thing as 'soft sell' and 'hard sell.' There is only 'smart sell' and 'stupid sell'."

Confucius: (Early Chinese philosopher) "The superior man understands what is right. The inferior man understands what will sell."

Covey, Stephen R.: (Leadership and sales consultant, author of *The 7 Habits of Highly Effective People*)"The main thing is to keep the main thing the main thing."

de Tocqueville, Alexis: (French author of *Democracy in America*, observations of U.S. travels in 1831) "In democracies, nothing is more great or more brilliant than commerce: it attracts the attention of the public, and fills the imagination of the multitude; all energetic passions are directed toward it."

Dyer, Dr. Wayne: (Motivational speaker, author of books, audio cassettes) "You're the creator of your thought, which means that in some metaphysical way, you're the creator of your life."

Esar, Evan: "A soft answer turneth away wrath, but not the door-to-door salesman." … "A man never knows how many friends he hasn't got until he tries to sell them something." … "There are two kinds of businessmen: one kind is selling out and other is out selling." … "He who sells what isn't his'n, must buy it back or go to prison." … "Doing business without advertising is like winking at a girl in the dark; you know what you are doing but nobody else does." … "Stopping your advertising to save money is like stopping your watch to save time."

Fogleman, H.L.: (Master salesman writing in premier issue of *Opportunity* magazine, June, 1923) "Every normal being is a Salesman. The Minister, the Doctor, the Lawyer—selling their knowledge of Religion, of Medicine, of Law. The President of the United States is a salesman—selling his time, his talent, his ability—trying to persuade the people of this Country to think as he thinks and get them to do as wants them to do."

Franklin, Benjamin: "He that speaks ill of the mare will buy her."

Fuller, Edmund: (Author) "Sales resistance is the triumph of mind over patter."

Fuller, Thomas: (17th Century churchman and historian) "The usual trade and commerce is cheating all round by consent."

Galbraith, John Kenneth: (American economist) "Production only fills a void that it has itself created."

Gandhi, Mohandas K: (Early 20th Century India leader) "It is difficult but not impossible to conduct strictly honest business. What is true is that honesty is incompatible with the amassing of a large fortune."

Glasgow, Arnold H.: (Psychologist, writer) "Salesmanship consists of transferring a conviction by a seller to a buyer."

Goldsmith, Oliver: (18th Century Irish writer, poet and physician) "Honour sinks where commerce long prevails."

Halifax, Lord: (1935 English war secretary and leader of the House of Lords) "There is hardly any man so strict as not to vary a little from truth when he is to make an excuse."

Hammett, Dashiell: (American author of "hardboiled" detective novels and short stories) "The cheaper the crook, the gaudier the patter."

Hawkins, Norval: (Author of the 1922 book, *The Selling Process*) "A man who saves his employer money in the office or the factory is not so well paid for his services as is the salesman who increases his employer's volume of business with a corresponding increase in profits. A man loses his purse and you find it. He thanks you sincerely, and rather grudgingly gives you a small reward. You show the man how to make exactly the same amount of money that was in his purse, and he'll hunt you up to pay you a quarter or a third or half of his profits. Human nature doesn't believe a penny saved is the same as a penny earned." . . . "Who of us who have chosen to live among the mountains of Salesmanship would be content to dwell on the Dead Sea level of men in other vocations?"

Herbert, George: (17th Century Welsh poet, orator and priest) "The buyer needs a hundred eyes, the seller not one."

Hill, Napoleon: (American author of *Think and Grow Rich*) "The ladder of success is never crowded at the top."

Hubbard, Frank McKinney: (Indianapolis cartoonist, humorist and journalist, better known by his pen name "Kin" Hubbard and for his alter ego cartoon character, "Abe Martin") "There's no way to recondition a welcome when it's worn out." ..."We may not know when we're well off, but investment salesmen get on it somehow."

Jefferson, President Thomas: (3rd President of the U.S.) "Merchants have no country. The mere spot they stand on does not constitute so strong an attachment as that from which they draw their gains."

Johnson, Dr. Kerry: (Keynote speaker, author) "Top producers constantly look for new business. Very few rest on the security of prospects calling in to get a price quote. Nearly every big producer possesses an ego that suggests effortless success. But when you force them to be honest, they always act scared stiff that they will not be in business next year."

Kafka, Franz: (From his 1912 short story, *The Metamorphosis*) "As Gregor Samsa awoke one morning from uneasy dreams he found himself transformed on his bed into a gigantic insect ... What has happened to me, he thought. It was no dream. His room, a regular human bedroom, only rather too small, lay quiet between the four familiar walls. Above the table on which a collection of cloth samples was unpacked and spread out—Samsa was a commercial traveler—hung the picture which he had recently cut out of an illustrated magazine and put into a pretty gilt frame. It showed a lady, with a fur cap on and a fur stole, sitting upright and holding out to the spectator a huge fur muff into which the whole of her forearm had vanished."

Larkin, Jonathan: (English playwright) "Friendliness stops as soon as the sale is made."

Lewis, Sinclair: (Early 20th Century American novelist) "His name was George F. Babbitt … he was nimble in the calling of selling houses for more than people could afford to pay."

Maltz, Dr. Maxwell: (Author, *Psycho-Cybernetics*) "You came into this world to succeed, not to fail."

Maxwell, William: (Early 20th Century author of *If I were Twenty-One*) "With certain exceptions the business of this country rests largely upon a demand which is artificially stimulated by salesmanship. But for the stimulus of salesmanship that forces upon us new fashions in wearing apparel, half the cotton fields would be fallow ground and half the silkworms and sheep would be out of work. But for the salesmanship that forces on us new kinds of mechanical devices, half of the mines would be closed and half of the furnaces would be cold. But for the feverish business activity that salesmanship inspires, half of the freight cars would be rusting and rotting in railroad switch yards."

Mencken, H.L.: (American author, scholar, journalist) "It takes no more actual sagacity to carry on the everyday hawking and haggling of the world, or to ladle out its normal doses of bad medicine and worse law, than it takes to operate a taxicab or fry a pan of fish."

Miller, Arthur: (From his play *Death of a Salesman*) "For a salesman, there is no rock bottom to the life. He don't put a bolt to a nut. He don't tell you the law or give you medicine. He's a man way out there in the blue, riding on a smile and a shoeshine. And when they start not smiling back—that's an earthquake. And then you get yourself a couple of spots on your hat and you're finished. Nobody dast blame this man. A salesman is got a dream, boy. It come with the territory."

Moody, Walter D.: (Early 20th Century author) About the *Right Kind of Salesman*: "In place of being a knocker, he is a booster; in place of being an order-taker, he is a business-getter; in place of being fussy or overanxious, he is composed, but aggressive; in place of being a a wheelbarrow, he is a Great Mogul; in place of being a know-it-all, he is keen and dignified; in place of being quick tempered, he is self-poised and genial;

in place of being a sky-rocket, he is a wear-weller; in place of being all head and no soul, he is a mixture of both; in place of being an old-timer or a down-and-outer, he is an up-and-inner."

Nightingale, Earl: (Motivational speaker, sales consultant, radio personality) "We can let circumstances rule us, or we can take charge and rule our lives from within."

Peters, Tom: (Speaker, corporate consultant, author) "It's a poor workman who blames his tools."

Popeil, Ron: "I pushed. I yelled. I hawked. And it worked. I was stuffing money into my pockets, more money than I had ever seen in my life. I didn't have to be poor the rest of my life. Through sales I could escape from the poverty and the miserable existence I had with my grandparents." … "What product do I wish I had invented? The Clapper … I'm disappointed I didn't come up with the great idea of a device that turned off lights, stereo, and the TV just by clapping your hands … The product was simple, entertaining, and it solved a problem." … "The line I want on my tombstone: 'The knife I'm demonstrating is so sharp, it will even cut a cow. And that's no bull."

Robbins, Anthony: (Sales consultant, seminar presenter, author of several books) "People are not lazy, they simply have impotent goals—that is, goals that do not inspire them."

Russian Proverb: "There are two fools in every market: one asks too little, one asks too much."

Shook, Robert L.: (Business writer, author of several books including *The Greatest Sales Stories Ever Told*) "Selling is a key part—an indispensable part of the free enterprise system. You, as a salesperson, occupy a special niche in this system. Without you and your fellow salesperson, our standard of living would be far different, and our system would probably collapse. To a very great extent, we owe our affluent way of life in the Western World to our salesmen, past and present, who move the goods and services from producers to users. Because of the salesperson, the wheels of industry are kept turning; income is created; and our standard of living flourishes."

Slobodkina, Esphyr: (Children's book author) From *Caps For Sale: A Tale of a Peddler, Some Monkeys and Their Monkey Business*: "'Caps! Caps for sale! Fifty cents a cap!' calls the peddler, walking up and down the streets. He balances a huge stack of caps on his head—gray, brown, blue, and red—all piled on his own checked cap."

Sprague, Jesse Rainsford: (From Oct. 5, 1929, *Saturday Evening Post* article) "The history of America is in effect a saga of salesmanship. Early pioneers who broke away from the settled life of the Atlantic Coast were traveling salesmen par excellence. They sold the Western country to the world as they went successively over the Alleghenies, the Mississippi, the Rockies; a continent was brought under civilization in a fraction of the time that such a task had ever been accomplished before."

Stevenson, Robert Louis: (19th Century Scottish novelist, poet) "Everyone lives by selling something."

Thoreau, Henry David: (19th Century American author, poet, and philosopher) "Through want of enterprise and faith men are where they are, buying and selling, and spending their lives like serfs."

Tracy, Brian: (Motivational speaker, seminar leader, sales consultant) "More people are becoming successful at a faster rate than at any other time in history. There have never been more opportunities for you to turn your dreams into reality than there are right now."

Van Andel, Jay: (co-founder of Amway) "No matter what government may do to hinder their essential work, entrepreneurs will always be there. And as long as entrepreneurs are with us, and they live moral lives, there is hope."

Van Horne, Sir William Cornelius: (Early 20th Century president and chairman of the board of the Canadian Pacific Railway) "The biggest things are the easiest to do because there's less competition."

Willson, Meredith: (Author and composer of 1957 musical *The Music Man*) From *The Music Man,* conversation between salesmen on a train: "You can talk all you wanna, but it's different than it was." … "No it ain't! But you gotta know the territory!" … "Why it's the Model T Ford made the trouble, made the people wanna go, wanna git up and go!" … "Yes, sir! Yes, sir! Who's gonna patronize a little bitty 2x4 kinda store anymore?"

Wordsworth, William: (19th Century English poet) "The world is too much with us: late and soon/ Getting and spending, we lay waste our powers:/ Little we see in Nature that is ours; / We have given our hearts away, a sordid boon."

Zigler, Zig: "The cathedral of success is built on the foundation of failure."

THE LAST WORD

Perret, Gene: (American humorist) "I like to meet a good salesman. It's how I got my set of electric forks." ... "We need salesmanship in the world. The only thing that sells itself is illegal and leans against a lamp-post." ... "A cold call is contacting someone you never heard of and trying to sell him something he never of. Often he calls you names you never heard of ... and never want to hear again." ... "I knew a great salesman who once sold a refrigerator to an Eskimo. He told him it was a doghouse for his pet penguin." ... "One salesman firmly believed that if he could sell two of an item, he could just as easily sell three. It nearly killed him. He worked in a shoe store."

Prochnow, Herbert V.: (Author of *1000 Tips and Quips for Speakers and Toastmasters*) "The best salesman we ever heard of was the one who sold two milking machines to a farmer who had only one cow. Then this salesman helped finance the deal by taking the cow as down payment on the two milking machines."

Twain, Mark: (American humorist and author) "The preacher's voice was beautiful. He told us about sufferings of the natives, and he pleaded for help with such moving simplicity that I mentally doubled the fifty cents I had intended to put into the plate. He described the pitiful misery of those savages so vividly that the dollar I had in mind gradually rose to five. Then, that preacher continued, and I felt that all the cash I carried on me would be insufficient, and I decided to write a large check. Then he went on, and on, and on and on about the dreadful state of those natives and I abandoned the idea of the check. And he went on. And I got back to the five dollars. And he went on, and I got back to four, two, one. And he still went on. And when the plate came around, I took ten cents out of it."

CHAPTER 7

The Quaint Characters of A.M. Jones, Colporteur

By A.M. Jones
Adapted for the stage by Ron Solberg

I. Introduction: In A.M.'s own words

II. They Gits All the Money
Jones • Lady

III. We Don't Want To Go Thar
Jones • Little Girl

IV. A Good Ole Man
Jones • Old Lady • Old Man • Preacher 1 • Preacher 2

V. Shout Hallelujah
Jones • Good Brother

VI. A Member of the Floor
Jones • Elderly Lady • Young Lady

VII. Looney's Tavern
Jones • Old Gent

VIII. The Remedy
Jones • Woman • Husband • Wife • Doctor

IX. Circus, Circus
Jones • Bishop Andrew • Editor

X. If It's Round, It Can't Be Square
Jones • Old Man • Young Gentleman

XI. The Venerable Divine
Jones • Aged Minister

XII. The Truth, The Light, The Directions
Jones • Housewife

Note: If specific sketches are eliminated for presentation, number IX should be maintained if XI is used, since XI makes reference to an incident in the earlier sketch.

I. Introduction

While doing some research at Chicago's Newberry Library on "The American Traveling Salesman at the Turn of the Century" for an instructional unit in American studies, I uncovered a wonderful little book, *Quaint Characters or Colportage Sketches.* Written in 1891 by A.M. Jones, it's a kind of journal by Jones who was a Bible salesman in rural Alabama. Colportage, or colporteur, are words, rarely used today, that refer to someone who carries what he sells on his back or around his neck—thus a peddler of religious tracts, or more specifically, Bibles. As I read through the aging and very fragile volume, I became taken with Jones' colorful and sensitive rendering of his encounters and his times. So much so, that I immediately envisioned his experiences as short dramatic vignettes. With thanks and appreciation to Mr. Jones, I offer up the play. Although I have adapted Jones' work to stage—taking some liberties with characters, language and sequence of events—most of the words and incidents are still his as he used and reported them more than a century ago. I was pleased and proud to be able to premier this play for our playreading friends on Saturday, March 9, 2002. I hope you enjoy the rendering of these eyewitness accounts of A.M. Jones as much as I did when I first read them 111 years later.

In Jones' own words . . .

These Sketches are only a few of the incidents and events which occurred in my travels during a period of five consecutive years, while canvassing, for the American Bible Society, twenty-one counties of the State of Alabama. They were written for my own amusement, and published in the *New Orleans Christian Advocate,* in 1881 and 1882.

To My Devoted Wife, Mrs. Fannie Ophelia Jones, who so patiently endured my absence, and so lovingly cared for the children, during those memorable five years, this little volume is most sincerely inscribed by her grateful husband.

—A.M. Jones

II. They Gits All the Money

(Jones appears in front of a rail fence, gate, and a box of books sits on the ground next to him. A middle-aged woman is speaking to him.)

Lady: I tell you, sir, you are at the right place to sell a Bible. We has bin wantin' one for more nor two year. Jist look at the books—a whole box full, more than you can sell in a year! The store-keepers 'bout here never has sich a thing as a Bible or hymn-book, but you can always git plenty of meat, an' cloth, an' snuff, an' 'backer; an' some of um has whisky to make men drunk. They is might nice, an' I s'pose cheap enough, bit I like this best of all. What did you say is the least you will take for it? You must put it down might low, if we trade, for I tell yer I do n't give none of yer big price for things these days. We used to have plenty of money, an' could git any thing we wanted, before the people turned sich big fools an' got up that war. Since then money is might skerce. Don't know what folks want to have wars fur. They might knowed somebody would git kilt. Well, the rich folks lost the negroes anyhow for their smartness, and has to go to work like the rest of us. Did you say this is worth forty cents? Well, if that is the best you can do, I will take it; but you must let me read it two hours first.

Jones: *(To the audience)* These sentences were uttered in rapid succession by a lady who appeared to be forty-five years of age, medium height, slender form, with small, keen eyes, sharp nose, and thin lips. I was driving but one horse, and he was hot and tired, having traveled twenty miles during the day, and stopped at a score of houses. I looked at my watch. The sun was only an hour high, and I had eight long miles farther to go before resting for the night. I was already impatient, but as kindly as possible said:

"Madam, it will be dark in two hours, and I must go eight miles before stopping. It is impossible for you to read the book so long."

Lady: That is always the way. Some folks never has time for anything. It is a wonder they takes time to eat. Well, if you don't let me read it two hours, I won't buy it then, that's all.

Jones: Madam, how long have you been a widow?

Lady: I am not a widder at all, *(defiantly)* I thank yer, sir. My husband is on the plantation. We live out here in this little cabin for our health, but has good land an' every thin' else anybody wants down on the crick.

Jones: I intended no offense at all by the question, but thought you were a widow, and intended to give you a Bible and go on.

Lady: I am no beggar, I thank you, sir, and don't want you to give me a Bible. I am able to pay for one, if I want it. I like this one very well, and think I would buy it if you would let me read it two hours.

Jones: *(To the audience)* When she gave me time to speak again, I asked her why she wanted to read it two hours.

Lady: I want to see if it is like my old one.

Jones: Let me see your 'old one,' and I will tell you in a moment.

Lady: It is not here. I give it to my oldest darter when she moved to Texas two year ago.

Jones: Do you have no Bible at all?

Lady: No, we don't; if we had, I wouldn't be out here talkin' to you about your'n. What do you think a body would want with two Bibles?

Jones: As you have no Bible, I insist on you taking one, as it may be a long time before you have another opportunity.

Lady: I don't care; I won't buy anybody's Bible without readin' it two hours, bekase I said a long time ago I wouldn't, and I won't either.

This reconstructed 1830s country home resides on the grounds of the Crooked Creek Civil War Museum and Park in Winston County, AL. Fred and Mike Wise are the owners and proprietors of this privately-funded facility.

Jones: Why did you say that?

Lady: Well, I didn't want to tell you, bekase you may be one of them very men; but as you axed me, I will tell you.

Jones: You must talk fast, madam, because it is getting late, and I must be going.

Lady: Well, a Methodist man come to our house one day a long time ago, an' brought a Bible, an' he called it a Baptist Bible. He did it jist to make me an' my ole man mad, too. He said the Bible wouldn't prove the doctrine of the Baptist Church, an' the Baptists and the Campbellites made them one that would. When he read that book (I don't call it a Bible), an' laughed at us about it, I was so mad at them Yankee Baptists an' Campbellites that I could hardly see. They might know'd sensible people wouldn't have sich a book as that, an' call it a Bible.

Jones: *(To the audience)* In the midst of her talk, for there seemed to be no stopping-place, I ventured to ask if there were many changes in the Baptist Bible.

Lady: I tell you I don't call it a Bible. You never seed sich nonsense as that Methodist man read an' laughed at that day. He read about John the Immerser, an' being immersed in the Holy Ghost, an' all sich stuff as that. I axed him if there was any more sich books as that, an' he said, 'Lots of um.' He said they had lots of money, an' was makin'a aheap of 'um in New York, an' was going to send um all over the country. I said then I would never buy a Bible without readin' it two hours, an' I am going' to keep my word, an' you can't blame me, nuther. You say these Bibles were made in New York, an' they may be the same sort. How do I know, if I don't read it?

Jones: *(To the audience)* Her style was original, and conversation somewhat amusing; but a half-hour of my precious time was already gone, and it was highly important that I should be going. I said:

(Returning, in conversation to Lady)
"Madam, I assure you this Bible is not like the one you speak of. If I had time, you might read it as long as you please; but I cannot stay longer now. It is a very cheap book—only costs forty cents; take it, and if I should ever pass here again, and you don't like it, I will return your money."

Lady: You are always talkin' 'bout um bein' cheap. I would like to know what makes um cheaper than anybody else's Bibles.

Jones: *(To the audience)* Not having time to explain at length, I simple stated that good men gave their money to make them, and they were sent to the people at the cost of publication.

Lady: Yes, *(in a whining tone)* that's the way of it. Good men sends um to us, but them who brings um they gits all the money.

Jones: *(To the audience)* Having exhausted my skill, and utterly failed to supply her with the Holy Scriptures, I had no more time to spare, and moved on. The roads being level and good, by a half-hour after dark I had made the eight miles, and self and horse, both tired and hungry, were in comfortable quarters for the night.

III. We Don't Want to Go Thar

(Jones enters the stage and stands before a fence gate, much like the one in the last scene.)

Jones: Halloo. Halloo. Halloo. Anyone home?

Jones: *(To the audience)* After the third or fourth halloo at the gate, in front of a small log-house, a little girl of about 7 or 8 years comes out, clutching a rag doll.

Jones: *(Turning to the girl)* Who lives here?

Little Girl: Daddy.

Jones: Where is your daddy?

Little Girl: In the new ground.

Jones: Where is the new ground?

Little Girl: Right down thar. *(Pointing stage left)*

Jones: *(Aside to audience)* She points toward brush-heaps and fresh-cut timber. Her father could neither be seen nor heard.

Jones: Is your mother at home?

Little Girl: Yes.

Jones: Will she come to the door?

Little Girl: No.

Jones: Ask her to do so.

Little Girl: *(Immediately)* She says she won't.

Jones: Is she sick?

Little Girl: No.

Jones: Tell her to come to the door; I want to speak to her.

Little Girl: She says she won't.

Jones: Does she want a Bible?

Little Girl: I don't know.

Jones: Ask her.

Little Girl: She says she don't.

Jones: Does she have a Bible?

Little Girl: I don't know.

Jones: *(A little impatiently)* Will you ask her?

Little Girl: She says she don't want any.

Jones: Can she read?

Little Girl: I don't know.

Jones: Ask her if she can read.

Little Girl: She says no.

Jones: Can your daddy read?

Little Girl: I don't know.

Jones: Ask your mother if he can read.

Little Girl: She says she believes so.

Jones: *(Somewhat irritated)* Can you read?

Little Girl: No.

Jones: Did you ever go to school?

Little Girl: No.

Jones: Do you want to go to school?

Little Girl: No.

Jones: Don't you want to learn to read?

Little Girl: No.

Jones: Do you ever go to church?

Little Girl: No.

Jones: Does your daddy go to church?

Little Girl: I don't know.

Jones: Don't you want to learn to read the Bible, be good, and get to heaven after awhile?

Little Girl: No.

Jones: *(Finally exasperated)* Don't you want to go to heaven when you die?

Jones: *(Aside to audience)* The little girl was silent, but a fat boy about eleven years, who in the meantime had seated himself on the door-step cried out,

(A young voice from off stage yells, "No, we don't want to go thar!")

By this time I was embarrassed, confused, and unconsciously looked around to see if anyone was near, witnessing my defeat. Not knowing what else to say or do, I said …

Jones: *(Turning to little girl)* Sis, if you will come I will give you a Testament.

Jones: *(Aside to audience)* After a moment's hesitation, she came in a run … *(little girl runs to Jones and grabs book from him while Jones continues)*

… snatched the book out of my hand, darted back into the house, and shut the door.

(Jones looks back as a door slams, shrugging shoulders, shaking head)

(Back to audience) I never learned anything of the history of the family. My sympathy was excited on account of the condition of those unhappy children—the boy, a chubby, clever-looking little fellow, with sallow face, bare, fat feet, and long disordered hair; the girl, tiny and slender, with rather a pretty face, and large, soft blue eyes. Education and home training, no doubt, would have developed them into an intelligent useful man and a refined, noble woman.

IV. A Good Ole Man

Jones: *(To audience)* On the afternoon of a cold, rainy day in February, 1878, while canvassing one of those barren, desolate wire-grass regions in Northeastern Alabama, I began to cast about for horse-feed, and a place to spend the night. Some one informed me that an old Methodist man lived four or five miles to the west, with whom preachers had been known to stop.

I turned my horses in that direction, and urging them forward at full speed. *(Turning stage left, clicking his tongue, pretending to whip the reins)*

"Hey, Molly, Jolly. Git, you horses. Hai, hai."

In less than an hour we halted at the gate. " Woa, woa there." *(Pulling back on pretend reins)*

(Turning to face audience) A good woman, an old lady at least seventy-five years of age, appeared shortly. *(Old Lady enters)*

And, on learning who I was, and what I was doing, said:

Old Lady: Git down an' come in out of the rain; I'm glad to see you. No preachers hardly ever comes to our house these days. The old man is not at home. When he comes I know he'll be glad you've come.

Jones: *(To audience, rubbing hands together)* In a short time my horses were in good, dry stables, fed and made comfortable, and I was warming and drying myself by the luxurious fire, which the kind old lady had replenished with a good supply of pine-knots while waiting my return from the lot. *(Seats himself next to imaginary fire, continuing to speak to audience. Old Lady seats herself as Jones speaks)*

Two hours expired before the old gentleman came, during which time this mother in Israel entertained me by relating the following interesting narrative. *(Turns back to Old Lady who has begun story)*

Old Lady: I was a young girl when I got religion an' jined the Church, away back in the old State. I have bin a Methodist more nor fifty years… which is a long time. When me an' the old man was married—I call him the "old man," but he was not old then, though—he was mighty wild an' wicked.

Old Lady: After we was married awhile, an' was keepin' house by ourselves, I axed him one Sunday mornin' if he was goin' to meetin,'

(Old Man enters. Stage lights darken over Jones with lights now on Old Lady and Old Man speaking with one another.)

Old Man: No, I'm goin' somewhar else.

Old Lady: *(To audience)*I wanted to go, an' tol him so. An' he got real mad:

Old Man: I don't know what you wan to go to the meetin' for; it don do no body no good.

Old Lady: I'm a member of the Church, an' want to go. *(Turning to audience, frowning, shaking head)*

Then he cursed an' said a heap of ugly words.

Old Man: If your goin' to live with me, you'll have to quit all sich foolishness as that.

A. J. Showalter's famous gospel piece, "Leaning on the Everlasting Arms," was created in 1887 for two of the hymn writer's Alabama music students who had lost their spouses. The song book is open to the hymn on an old-time pump organ in the home of Ray and Ann Hill, current proprietors of the Oden House Bed and Breakfast in Hartselle. The home was originally owned by a Mr. Andrew Augustus Oden. The home served as a temporary studio/ residence for Showalter when he wrote the music. It is very likely that both A.M. and "the good ole man" were quite familiar with the music. The song was sung in the 1943 movie The Human Comedy, *starring Mickey Rooney. It was nominated for Academy Awards in five categories including Best Picture and Best Actor. William Saroyan won Best Original Story for the film.*

Old Lady: *(Aside to audience)* Then he went off an' …

(Old Man leaves) staid all day. I staid at home all day by myself an' cried, an' was sorry we was married. But I'm not sorry now, though … *(Old Man slowly returns, sits down)*

Old Lady: *(Turning to Old Man)* A long time after that I told him one day, "I wan' a Bible," *(Turning to audience)* an' he got mad an' cursed, an' said:

Old Man: The Bible is a bad book. It make folks crazy. I won have one about the house. *(Old Man walks off in a huff)*

Old Lady: *(Rubbing eyes, turning to audience)* An' I want off an' cried, an' dint say another word, beca'se I knowed it wouldn't do no good. A long time after that, when we had two or three children—I most forgot which—a man come along one day who was a preacher.

(A man dressed in dark, "preacher-like" clothing enters)

Preacher: I'm huntin' up the people an' supplyin' them with Bibles. Do you want one?"

Old Lady: *(To audience)* I hated to tell him the old man dint want a Bible.

(Turning to preacher) The old man is not at home, an' I don have no money to pay for it.

Preacher: I will give you one, if you would read it, an' tell your husband to read it too.

(Preacher hands Bible to Old Lady, embraces her briefly and bids her a "goodbye" as he walks off.)

Old Lady: *(To audience, gently caressing Bible)* I was might proud of my Bible at first; it was so nice and purty,

(Hesitating, Old Lady seats herself and continues …) an' I read a right smart in it that day.

(Looks up) But I thought after awhile the old man would be mad. Then I was sorry I took it, beca'se I always tried to please him about every thing. So, when the old man come home that night,

(Old Man enters, seating himself) an' the children all went to sleep, I thought it was best to tell him all about it.

I got this new Bible, an' I'm mighty proud of it. Here, look at what I got.

(Aside to audience) An' he got real mad an' cursed, an' axed me how I got it.

(To Old Man) A preacher who came by just gave it to me to read.

(Aside to audience, as Old Man, stands, grabs Bible) He got madder still, an' snatched it out of my hand, an' went to fling it in the fire. But I couldn't stand that. An' I knowed I was wicked again, cuz I was mad too,

(Turning to Old Man, standing, grabbing back Bible) an' jerked it away from him. You don't burn up my Bible. It's mine.

(Embracing the Bible) An' it dint cost you any thin.'

(To audience) I was might sorry I did that way, an' talked cross to him, but somehow I cun't help it when he went to burn up the Bible. Then he said,

Old Man: You had better keep it out of my sight, an' if that preacher comes along here again, leavin' sich books at my house, I will take a stick to him. *(Old Man leaves)*

Old Lady: *(To audience)* But he won't do so now. I was mighty onhappy them days, an' cried a heap at night … I kept the Bible put away a long time, an' when the old man (I keep calling him the old man, but he was not old then, though) was gone,

(seating herself, opening up Bible) I read it most every day. When we had been married eight or ten years, the old man had not been to Church, an' one day one of our neighbor men come to our house an' told us a Universal preacher was goin' to preach at his house the next Sunday, an' wanted us to come an' hear him. I told him I wouldn't go to hear him, cuz all the Universal folks I ever saw was wicked, an' I reckon the preacher is wicked too. The old man said he would go, an' I dint say another word. I knowed the old man thought the preacher was wicked, but his preachin' would suit him.

When Sunday come, the old man went to hear the Universal preacher, an' when he come back he was in a mighty good humor. *(Old Man enters, happy, enthusiastic, with book)*

Old Man: That Universal preacher convinced me the Bible is right true an' Universal religion is the only true religion in the world. *(Turns away as Old Lady speaks to audience)*

Old Lady: *(To audience)* When the preacher come the next time, the old man went agin, an' when he come back he said

Old Man: *(Old Man turns around, speaking to Old Lady)* I heard a might good sermon, an' now am not afraid to die. The preacher proved from the Bible that there is no hell, an' when the Bible reads about hell it means the grave, an' when people die they all go to heaven, whether they are wicked or not.

Old Lady: *(To Old Man)* Do you b'lieve that?

Old Man: I knowed it so, *(Sits down, reading book)*

Old Lady: *(To audience while gesturing toward Old Man)* An' he kept on readin' a Universal book the preacher give him to read. I tell you all this made me might onhappy. When he kept on talkin' an' readin' out of the book, I said

(To Old Man) I tell you if you got me to b'lieve your Universal religion I would soon go to heaven.

Old Man: Go right off?

Old Lady: Yes, I wish I was thar now.

Old Man: What makes you want to go so soon?

Old Lady: I'm very onhappy in this world.

Old Man: What makes you so onhappy?

Old Lady: The plan truth. You will git drunk, an' git mad an' curse an' abuse my Church, an' our little boys will soon be mend, an' they will learn to be wicked like you. You know I am onhappy, an' if I b'lieved in your Universal religion, I would end my life an' go home to heaven, where I could be happy."

(To audience) When I quit talkin,' the old man (I keep calling him the old man, but he was not old then, though) dint say a word, an' when I looked around …

(She turns around briefly to Old Man, then turns to audience) he looked so sorry that I begun to cry, an' I cried a long time after he went to bed.

(Old Man leaves, Old Woman sits down, wiping her eyes) After that night the old man never said any more about Universal religion, an' never read the book any more, an' never went to hear the preacher preach again. an' that's bin most fifty years ago.

(At this the old lady dries the tears from her face with her apron, and continues, speaking to the audience):

Old Lady: A month or two after I talked to the old man so plain, the new preacher come on the circuit an' went all round to every house an' read the Bible an' prayed.

(Old Man enters, followed by New Preacher) When he come to our house, I was afraid the old man would say something bad to him, but he dint, though.

New Preacher: I bin sent to preach to you, an' wanted to see everybody in the neighborhood before I preached.

Old Lady: *(Facing audience)* Then he read the Bible an' prayed before he started, an' axed us to come to hear him preach. The old man dint git mad a bit, an' I knowed he was gittin' better.

(Old Man and New Preacher walk off together)

When the day for preachin' come, the old man said he would go to Church with me if I want him to go; an' I knowed I was goin' to cry, an' went off in the other room, an' staid a long time, beca'se I dint want him to see me cry, an' I knowed he was gittin' better. The new preacher preached a might good sermon that day about Jesus comin' in the world to save sinners. I knowed the old man had bin a mighty bad sinner, but prayed that he might be saved, too

The next Sunday, the old man did not go off some place whar he always did, an' I was so glad. After dinner, though, he went out an' was gone a long time, an' when he come back I seed he had somethin' in his hand on the other side he dint want me to see. *(Old Man enters carrying book in hand opposite audience, placing book on a shelf)*

I dint let on, but when he went to the book-shelf, *(looking back briefly)*

I knowed it was my Bible which he had bin readin.' Later that week after I cleaned up my things after supper, an' went in the house, the old man was settin' there readin,'

(Old Man is sitting down now and reading from his Bible)

and dint care if I did see him. So he read a long time. An' when the children were all put to bed, an' asleep, he said:

Old Man: I have bin a mighty bad man, an' am sorry for it now, an' going' to do better. When I wanted to burn up this Bible, an' talked about Universal religion, I knowed it was wicked, an' I don't know what made me do that way. I am goin' to be a better man, an' jine the Church the next meetin'day.

(Old Man bows head, wiping tears)

Old Lady: Then he couldn't say any thing more, and we both cried a long time.

(Old Lady embraces husband, then sits down, sobbing in hands; stage lights up on Jones, who is still seated in chair, speaking aside to audience as he glances some at Old Lady)

Jones: This scene, almost fifty years ago, came up so fresh and so vividly before this good woman's recollection that she buried her face in her hands and sobbed aloud. The simple narrative, told with so much feeling, touched my heart, and caused me time and again, to apply my handkerchief to my eyes. Having recovered her voice, and drying her face again with her apron, she proceeded:

Old Lady: The next meetin' day the old man jined the Church, an' ever since then has bin one of the best men you ever saw. An' when he comes home to-night, an' you see him, you'll say he's a good old man.

(Old Lady walks off, coming back with some dishes to set the table; lights go down on Old Lady; Jones steps forward with Bible in hand, speaking to audience)

Jones: It was now time to spread the table, and the good old woman could talk no longer. I was anxious to see the old gentleman, who soon came, and expressed himself as being very glad to see me at his house. After an hour's conversation and prayers, I retired to rest, with the full assurance that those two old people were ripe for heaven.

What a treasure the Bible is! What a blessing to our race! Folks, read your Bible, and see that each of your children has a copy.

Preachers such as A.M. would have found themselves seated in one of two rocking chairs, like these, on a stage in front of an attentive audience awaiting "the word." This open-air 1897 "Tabernacle" in Hartselle, with original furnishings, is still used today for camp and revival meetings.

V. Shout Hallelujah

Jones: *(Light down on a few chairs sitting at an angle, with people sitting in them, facing a podium, stage right. Lights up on Jones, stage front, begins speaking to the audience, eventually turning and walking to podium.)*

While canvassing a community of clever people, I was induced by kind brethren to publish an appointment, and preach for them at night.

(Church music begins, a few voices, then more join in)

At the hour for service a small congregation was assembled, and as I passed up the aisle, a brother in the amen-corner raised an old familiar missionary hymn, to which ten or a dozen other voices were immediately united in sacred song.

(Jones is now at the podium, seeing the animated "brother" who is seated, front, near the podium)

Supposing the good brother had fully divined my mission, and was preparing the congregation for the collection, I felt much encouraged.

(As Jones continues, music trails off)

During the opening hymn and prayer he was loud in song, and vehement in amen. His attention seemed to be keenly alive to the reading of the text and the introduction to the sermon. As I advanced in my discourse, this singing brother became absorbed, then enrapped, *(Good Brother becomes agitated, groans, sighs, says "Amen.")* groans, sighs, rubs his hands, until finally, as if unable longer to restrain his pent up feelings of joy, he gave vent to the most exultant expressions of halleluiahs to the glory of God:

Good Brother: Hallelujah! *(louder)* Hallelujah! *(louder still, now standing)* Hallelujah!

Jones: While my closing prayer was being offered, this shouting brother actually filled the house with violent praise.

Good Brother: Oh, hallelujah! Hallelujah, brother! Hallelujah!

Jones: When the time came to make my Bible talk and lift the collection, I had to wait at least two minutes for him to become quiet.

Good Brother: Hallelujah! Hallelujah! Oh, hallelujah!

Jones: And after beginning I was frequently …

Good Brother: Hallelujah!

Jones: …disturbed by his responses and fits of rejoicing. I spoke of the American Bible Society, and he thanked God for the existence of such a noble institution.

Good Brother: Thank you, God, for the existence of such a noble institution.

Jones: I spoke of the cheapness of the Bible.

Good Brother: Praise the Lord! It is within the reach of all the people.

Jones: I spoke of giving Bibles to the poor.

Good Brother: Bless the Lord. The poor can have the Holy Scriptures without money and without price.

Jones: I gave reasons why the Bible had become so cheap, and spoke of good men now in heaven who had been a benediction to their race by giving their money to publish and circulate the sacred Scriptures.

Good Brother: Glory to God that such men ever lived in the world!

Jones: I had a right to believe that there was at least one man in the congregation who would give a liberal contribution to a cause in which he gloried so much.

Good Brother: Glory, hallelujah.

Jones: Brethren, it is my duty before closing this meeting to ask you to aid in this great work…

Good Brother: Yes, hallelujah, yes …

Jones: …with a collection.

Good Brother: Halle …

Jones: The brother had been shouting and rejoicing almost from the beginning. But, alas, the word 'collection,' in connection with the great cause over which he had been rejoicing, had been uttered, and his religious fervor was suddenly checked. He instantly became as quiet as the grave; you could not hear him breathe. Being the nearest man to me in the house, I was almost compelled to approach him first.

(Jones moves to the "Good Brother" with a collection plate in his hand. He places his hand on the brother's shoulder)

On coming near him, I beheld a pitiable object. Only a moment ago so triumphant, so victorious, such a brave soldier of the Cross, but now a skulking coward, showing the white feather in the midst of the Lord's battle. In my heart, I pitied the poor fellow, but could not spare him. I said: "My brother, how much will you give to this cause?"

His face was buried in his hands. He could not see me. I had heard him so much and so long that evening, and resolved now that he should hear me. Placing my hand upon his shoulder, I said again, "My brother, how much will you give to this cause?" His lips moved not, and without looking up, he gave a feeble shake of the head. "You will certainly give something. You love God; you love the Bible—it makes you happy. Give me something, that others may have this great blessing as well as yourself. Then, in a very soft whisper, he replied,

This 1875 residence of a "well-to-do" doctor, Aldo Weiss, is representative of the kind of home that A.M. would have seen as he approached the "residence of a well-to-do farmer." Weiss, a resident of Cullman, AL, billed himself as "Practical Physician and Accoucheur." (Accoucheur, little-used today, means midwife or obstetrician.) In addition to his residence, Weiss used the house as his office. The house was often called "The Goat House" because Weiss housed his goats in the cellar. (Information from Gay Voss, Cullman County Museum.)

Good Brother: Put me down ten cents.

Jones: *(Jones walks to stage front, addressing audience)* Others gave a fair collection, and when the congregation was dismissed it seemed to me that the shouting brother was ashamed that he had ever shouted before in his life. I saw him afterward, but the ten cents was never paid.

Shouting is all a great many Church members ever do for the kingdom of Christ. It is so easy for some people to shout, and so hard for them to give.

VI. A Member of the Floor

(Jones is stage front, addressing audience. Lights down behind him as he speaks. When the Elderly Lady begins to speak, lights up, revealing a woman with a wash load.)

Jones: It was a hot, sultry morning in August. My horses were making full speed over a beautiful level road, endeavoring to reach a protracted meeting ten miles ahead by eleven o'clock. The country had been canvassed, except the families on the road, and I was anxious to stop at every house, and reach the church by the appointed time. On hailing at the residence of a well-to-do farmer, with a large fenced-in front-yard, an elderly lady standing behind the fence window, very significantly asked …

Elderly Lady: And, what sir, is your business in these parts?

Jones: I forced a smile, and as pleasantly as possible said, "I come by to see if you wished a Bible."

Elderly Lady: We has two now. But how does you sell 'um?

Jones: Almost for nothin'; come out and see 'em.

Elderly Lady: I'll be thar in a minute.

(As she walks off the stage with the clothes basket, a much younger woman, wearing a bonnet, walks on stage, passing her, with a broom in hand)

Jones: Just at that time one young lady, who was sweeping the yard, came round in front. Addressing her, I said, "Do you have a Bible of your own?"

Young Lady: We have Bibles enough, sir.

Jones: Yes, but don't you want one of your own?

Young Lady: No. Members of the floor has no use for Bibles.

Jones: *(Aside to audience, then turning to young lady)* Not understanding her meaning, and being a little confused, I exclaimed, "Members of what?"

Young Lady: *(Very cooly)* Members of the floor!

Jones: *(To the audience)* After a moment's silence, though, the mind was exceedingly active, and I divined her meaning, and said, *(turning to young lady)* "You dance?"

Young Lady: Yes, I do dance, and will dance whenever I git ready, and don't care who knows it.

Jones: You ought not to dance, but get a Bible, read it, be good, and get to heaven.

Young Lady: I love to dance, sir, and will dance whenever I please; but I don't go to church, like some folks, and stay a week—I believe in work, myself.

Jones: I know wicked men like to dance and go to balls and places of vice, but I'm sorry to hear a young lady say she loves to dance.

Young Lady: Well, I reckon, women enjoy it as well as men; don't they?

Jones: I suppose they do; but it is not proper for a lady to dance with wicked men, and you ought to quit it, get a Bible, and becomes religious.

(Aside to audience) At this she straightened herself up to full height, and seemed to grow at least two inches taller, and pointing her finger direct at my face, said,

Young Lady: I tell you, sir, I love to dance, and will dance whenever I please, and don't care who knows it; and if I do dance, and don't have one of your Bibles, I am just as good as them who goes about here sellin' things and tryin' to cheat the poor folks out of their work.

Jones: *(Turns away from the young lady, who walks briskly off the stage. In the meantime, the Old Lady returns)*

Having delivered this speech, she drew her sun-bonnet close about her face, turned away with the most supreme contempt, and made the dust fly. When the old lady made her appearance, she said,

Old Lady: My daughter a'ways says what she thinks; you need not mind her. The Bibles are nice an' cheap, but I got two a'ready, Sir. Don' need no more. *(Old Lady walks off as Jones moves to stage front, addressing audience)*

Jones: Having filled my mission at that house, I went on, reflecting. Even the most ignorant know the teachings of the Bible are incompatible with dancing.

VII. Looney's Tavern

(Stage center, Jones addresses audience)

Jones: While canvassing Winston county, Alabama, I heard frequent references made to Looney's Tavern. It is a noted place, the musterground of antebellum times, the seat of the justice's court, and voting precinct of the present day. Soon after I entered the county, an old gent, who was directing me to a certain house, said,

Old Gent: *(From the dark stage, behind Jones, an "elderly voice" says …*Jist a mile beant Looney's Tavern, take a right-hand.

Jones: I found the right, but the tavern was nowhere to be seen.

Traveling the same road on another occasion, I minutely looked in every direction, but failed to discover the ancient castle. My curiosity was excited, of course, as persons in referring to the tavern always spoke as though it was near the road. Fortunately, however, within a few hundred yards of the renowned spot, I came up on the old gent I'd seen earlier who gave me directions.

(Stage lights up behind Jones, revealing an elderly gentleman working hard on a bit of wood. He's sitting on an old stump. Jones continues his recitation to audience)

He was just a sittin' there on the side of the road whittlin' away on something. He kindly pointed out the mysterious building, and gave me its history. You may be as much astonished as I was when you learn that this far-famed tavern, at least seventy-five or a hundred years old, in good repair, stands in all its glory within fifty yards of the

Jasper and Decatur roads. A traveler might pass it fifty times, and if not pointed out, it would never attract his attention. It has a name and a history. But, truth is, the mysterious building and tavern was simply a stooping hickory-tree, and by no means the best specimen of that splendid wood.

(Jones moves over to old gent as he continues ...) The old gent tole me that forty-five or fifty years ago, Mr. Looney, a sportsman and hunter, one of the first settlers of North Alabama, located in the mountains on account of the game ... *(fades out as old gent fades in with story).*

Old Gent: At that time the country was new, and wild-turkeys and deer could be seen in droves, while wildcats, wolves, panthers, and bears abounded in the land. There were no roads in the mountains, except maybe the trails of wild beasts, and not a house within miles. Wild, indeed. The only sounds were the birds and ...

Jones: And about this Mr. Looney, Sir?

Old Gent: Yes, yes. let's see. *(scratching his head with the piece of wood he was whittling on)* While hunting, one cloudy day, Looney wanderin' farther than usual from his house, became bewildered and lost. The sun had gone down behind a bank of clouds, and twilight was rapidly castin' her misty curtains around him. Not knowin' which way to go, havin' lost the points of the compass, he had already despaired of reachin' his home that night, and cast about for a place of safety til mornin,' where he might be secure from those ravenous beasts—the wolves, panthers, bears, and wildcats. Those wildcats were somethin.' Yes, indeed. *(Shaking his head)* Did you hear 'bout the wildcat that broke into a church meetin' one mornin' and. . .

Jones: And what did Mr. Looney do?

Old Gent: Sure enuf. He made his way to a cool spring gushin' from a bluff, where he filled his thirst. He was meditatin' the propri'ty of takin' shelter under the rock, when all of a sudden he was rightly parlizd at the terrible discovery that a panther was on his track. You know about the 'dacity, activity, and strength of those wily monsters?

Jones: Yes, yes, so, what did he do, sir?

Old Gent: Well, he regarded his condition as exceedin' precarious. To shoot with an' degree of accur'cy was nye possible, as it was too dark to see the bead on his rifle. And not a moment was to be lost.

Jones: Did he run?

Old Gent: No sar. His only hope of safety was to get into the branches of a tree. Fortune he was, this hickory, easy of ascent on account of its stoopin' posture, stood within thirty yards. While preparin' to climb, the sight of the huge form in the darkness, within twenty yards, slippin' and crouchin' like a cat, as if preparin' to make the fatal bounce, nerved him for the effort. And up he went. Havin' made himself as comfortable as possible among the branches, he prepared for self-protection, and spent the slowly passin' hours of the 'tire night in sleepless, painful anxiety.

Jones: That was doubtless one night in Mr. Looney's history during which he did not become sleepy.

Old Gent: No sar, no sweet dreams that night for em. No sar. *(laughs a little)* Fortunate for Looney, having been thwarted in the first attempt, the panther never made the attack, but, like a faithful watch-dog, remained near the tree, sometimes within a few yards, until mornin.'

Jones: So morning came, and the panther left?

Old Gent: Wish it be so. Thar's more. At a late hour, perhaps eleven o'clock or midnight, while every thin' was as still and quiet as the grave, in the midst of a light mist of rain, and darkness which could almost be felt, the silence was disturbed by a keen, shrill scream.

Jones: Ah, the panther near the tree just wanted to let Looney know he was still there.

Old Gent: Oh, my, no. It was yet another panther in the distance which was answered by his mate near the tree in such a frightful tone that great drops of cold perspiration gathered on the prisoner's brow. The very hair rose on his head. His fears were by no means relieved when, an hour later, the clouds, to some extent, having passed away, he became conscious of the fact that the guard had been increased, and, instead of one, he saw two black slim forms, at least seven feet long, stealthy movin' 'round the tree, frequently raising their heads and sniffin' the air. For hours, with his eye steadily fixed upon those ferocious beasts as they slowly moved from place to place, he endured the most intense agony.

Jones: So what was Looney to do?

Old Gent: All earthly suffering has an end. To the anxious hunter, who had spent more than ten hours in the branches of that tree in waitin' and watchin,' now cold, tired, and hungry, the wheels of time seemed to have stopped, as no other night had been half so long. Finally the song of the birds and the gray dawn in the eastern sky proclaimed the coming day. Light had never seemed so lovely, was never hailed with greater joy than by the lost, imprisoned sportsman on that memorable mornin.' Before it was light enough to shoot, the panthers sought their dens in the cliffs, and Mr. Looney was free.

Jones: Tell me, sir, did he leave then?

Old Gent: Not quite yet. The sun was high in the heavens, and the earth filled with beauty and gold, before he ventured from his safe retreat. He reached his anxious family during the forenoon, and in answer to his wife's question, "Where did you stay last night?" He replied, "Oh, don't ask me no questions. I'm hungry. I spent the night at the tavern." Hence the hickory down yonder, to this day, is called "Looney's Tavern."

This restored turn-of-the-century Alabama house features a familiar "dog trot," running down the center of the home, front to back, dividing the kitchen from the bedrooms. Some might think of the "dog trot" as nothing more than a "breezeway."

VIII. The Remedy

Jones: It was a lovely day in early spring, 1878. The birds were happy, hopping from branch to branch, building their nests, and singing their cheerful songs. All nature—forests, fields, and gardens—rejoiced in their beautiful robes of green, so recently put on. As my horses, Molly and Jolly, drew up at the gate, the lady of the house—a woman of medium size, pretty face, neatly dressed, and near twenty-five years of age—was sitting in the door. In answer to my question if she wanted a Bible, she said,

Woman: Nope. Don't want none.

Jones: Have you a Bible?'

Woman: Nope. And if I had one it would do me no good. I can't read. But my husband can read, and is a member of the Church, and if you will go down to the mill he may git one. If he has any money.

Jones: Being both astonished and sad that woman of her appearance could not read, I said: "Madam, you are young. Why don' you learn to read? By a little effort you could do so in a very few months." At this she seemed to become excited, and rising to her feet, exclaimed:

Woman: What! Me larn to read at this age, and a married woman too! Did you ever? You must be crazy. No, now woun't I cut a nice figer settin' down here with a book, an' all these children cryin' round me? Why, I wud jist git mad an' run everybody off the place.

Jones: Do you get mad often?

Woman: When anybody troubles me I do. And they har from me, too.'

Jones: *(Aside to the audience)* It may have been rude and inexcusable in me, but the temptation was great, and I said, "Do you scold when you get mad?"

Woman: Scold!? I reckon I do when anybody troubles me.

Jones: Do you scold your husband?

Woman: When he needs it I do, an' that's often enough.

Jones: I expect he's gettin' very tired of bein' scolded.

Woman: Well, he needn't be; for he will get a many a one before he dies yit. (*As an after thought*) If he lives long enough.

Jones: *(Aside to the audience)* Just at this stage of the conversation, an old story, of which I had not thought in years, and which I never saw in print, though it may have been published, occurred to my mind.

Madam, I know a remedy for a scolding wife, and, if you wish me to do so, will relate it."

Woman: What is it, then?

(Lights up on a man and woman, stage right. The man sits at a table. He's finishing a bowl of meal. The woman is standing over him.)

Jones: I heard of an old man whose wife had been scolding him for more than thirty years, and though he tried various means to break her, yet she continued. *(The woman stands over him, shaking a finger at him.)* One morning, after giving him a severe round, just as he was leaving the table, she angrily said:

Wife: You have now got your fill again. Go and hunt that calf. That cow is in the pen to this time of day, starvin' to death.

(Husband holds his head between his hands, then stands up, leaves the room, followed by wife as Jones continues.)

Jones: A few weeks before a new doctor had established himself in the community, and already, by some remarkable cures, had created quite a sensation. For some days the old gentleman had been meditating the propriety of calling on him for a remedy for his wife's bad temper, and now resolved to do so without another hour's delay. Having passed through the gate, instead of going for the calf, as the old lady, in her rage, had so preemtively ordered, he turned toward the doctor's office, with a heavy heart.

(Lights up on a doctor seated at a desk as husband enters. On entering, and finding a doctor alone, he earnestly and hastily said,)
(Lights off Jones as he walks off stage)

Husband: I came down to see if you can fix the old woman up a little.

Doctor: Well, perhaps so. What is the matter with her?

Husband: *(Husband seats himself)* Matter!? I tell you that's matter enough. I have had no piece from her scolding for more than thirty years. An' this very mornin' she has bin scorin' it to me ever since daylight. I tell you I has bin mighty tired of it a long time, an' has tried to break her, but she always gits worse. I'll never try myself any more. They say you can cure everybody, an' I thought you might cure her too. Do you think you can fix her up?

Doctor: *(Rubbing his chin, in thought)* Yes, I think we can—very easily.

Husband: Now, doctor, you say "we." I tell you I don't want to have any thing to do with it, an' ef you tell her I told you this, an' told you to come thar, you'll never want to see her agin.

Doctor: I could very readily stop her scolding while there, but that would do you no good. After leaving, she would scold you still more. I can tell you, however, how you can stop her almost immediately, and within three days effect a permanent cure.

Husband: (*At this assertion the husband becomes excited, rises to his feet, and with animation exclaims*) Well, doctor, how? Will it hurt her? I tell you I wouldn't hurt that old woman for any thing. If she did not scold, she is just as good an' smart as anybody's wife.

Doctor: I assure you it will not hurt her in the least, though at first, and for a little while, she will try to scold worse than ever. Will you try it?

Husband: Yes, if thar's no danger. What is it?'

Doctor: Do you know what a bugle is?

Husband: Yes.

Doctor: Go to the tin-shop and have one made, eighteen or twenty inches long. Tell the tinner you want it to blow, and blow loud. When it is finished, attach a string to each end, put it around your neck after the fashion of a hunter's horn, and return to my office. I will then tell you what to do.

(Husband exits. Lights up on Jones as he has re-entered stage edge, briefly, leaning against stage proscenium.)

Jones: Equipped with the bugle, as directed, the old gentleman, eager for further instructions, was back a day or two later.

Husband re-enters with horn around his neck. The Doctor takes the bugle in his hand and gives it a loud, shrill blast or two.

Doctor: Ah, this is just perfect. You will now return to your home, and before getting in the house, no doubt, the old lady will begin to scold. When she does, without saying a word, you blow. If she scolds easy, you blow easy; if she scolds loud, you blow loud. As long as she scolds, you blow; when she stops, you stop, and when she begins again you do the same. Every time she speaks in a scolding tone you blow. Be firm. If she takes the broom or shovel to you, get out of the way, but by all means continue to blow.

(Husband and doctor exit. Doctor has arm around shoulder of husband, gesturing with other. Light on Jones as he re-enters, speaking from stage proscenium, as before. Rest of stage dark.)

Jones: Lingering between hope and fear, with grave doubts agitating his mind as to the propriety of his course, the old man slowly began to retrace his steps, and was soon at the gate. The wife within, being in a greater rage than usual, on account of the tardiness of her husband, hearing his footfalls, in a moment was at the door, and shrieked out:

Lights up on wife who is leaning over a table, arranging dishes.

Wife: Where in the world have you been all this time? Where is that calf? *(Husband enters, bugle hanging from around his neck)*

Jones: And then discovering the new tin glittering in the sunbeams,

Wife: What is that thing you've got on? Oh me! That poor cow is starvin' to death in the pen.

(As Jones begins, the Wife shakes her finger at husband, who then starts to place his mouth to bugle mouthpiece.)

Jones: The scene that followed is difficult to describe. As the contest was now upon him, the old man, having previously weighed all the dangers of the perilous step felt equal to the occasion, and, hastily placing the bugle to his lips, began,

Husband: *Toot, toot, to-o-o-t, toot, to-o-o-t.*

Jones: These terrible, piercing, grating, deafening blasts continued for some minutes, during which time the old lady raved, stamped her feet, and raved again, but all to no purpose. He would not stop. Finally, when well-nigh exhausted from loud talking, and almost blinded with rage, she became quiet, and the trumpet's hoarse voice was immediately hushed. Gazing at him for a moment, as if in doubt what to do next, and seeing he was ready at a word to blow again, she contemptuously turned away, saying,

Wife: You are a fool.

Jones: It was now time to look after dinner, and as she, not in the most amiable manner, continued her work at the table.

(The husband walks off stage right while Jones is speaking.)

The gentleman seated himself in the front room of the house. While kindling the fire, the cow, still in the pen, gave a long, pitiful, hungry low,

(Pitiful low from offstage)

which so vividly reminded her of the calf, and her husband's disobedience, that she arose, and in a moment confronted him again, with the exclamation:

Wife: *(Shouting at him off stage)* Put up that thing, and stop that noise. I will have no more of it. Git me some wood to get dinner, and go and hunt that calf. I tell you that poor cow is starvin' to death.'

Jones: *(Old gentlemen re-enters stage and interacts with wife behind Jones as he describes scene)* The old gentleman, having entered the warfare with the full determination to carry out the minute instructions of the doctor, entered the kitchen, adjusted the instrument, and again, in the most terrific, deafening strains, sent forth blast after blast, and peal after peal. She raved, smote with her hands, stamped with her feet, stood on tip-toe, and raved again; but, notwithstanding the orders, the offensive roar continued. Not hearing her own voice, and knowing every word was lost, in almost a breathless state, though convulsed with rage, she ceased to speak. The incensed and persecuted wife, in wonder and amazement, silently stood before him, then, while leaving the room, as the last note of the detestable music died away, amidst the awful stillness which ensued, she turned upon her husband and vehemently said,

Wife: You are an old fool.

Jones: The blowing and scolding had now been going on for fifteen or twenty minutes, and a dozen or more boys had been attracted to the house outside by the excitement to the scene of conflict. As the distressed and almost frantic old lady passed from the kitchen to the back-yard, *(wife exits stage left)*, she heard voices of merriment, *(chatter and laughter coming from offstage)* and saw boys peeping through the fence, and knew that they were laughing at her. As lightly and as rapidly as a lady of her age could walk she went to the wood-pile, thence to the well, all the time casting about in her mind for some way of relief. Finally, as if unable any longer to endure such an outrage, she made for the house, but on entering the hall, hesitated, and went on tip-toe to the door. Though so very softly, he had already heard her step, and was prepared to blow. Seeing this, and knowing that at the first word he would give another hateful blast, she stopped, and peeped in, as if in a doubt how to proceed. After a moment's excruciating suspense, though trembling from head to foot, she made a circle around him, and went to the mantel. After standing there in perfect silence for a moment or more, mechanically passing her hands over the board, as if searching for some article, her pent-up rage becoming too intense for longer suppression, she suddenly turned, and with a startling, piercing gaze looked upon him, but dared not speak.

There he was motionless, *(The husband is now seated)* with that frightful thing in his hand, ready to blow, with his eye steadily fixed upon her, eagerly watching every movement and motion. It would not do to speak in an angry tone. She knew he would blow. Already she was equally as tired of the blowing as he was of the scolding. This state of affairs was entirely new. It was all unexpected. She could not understand it. For the first time in her married life she was at a loss how to act, and felt forced to silence. Again the insinuating laugh of the incorrigible boys floated through the quiet atmosphere into the room, *(more laughter from offstage)* causing the violent, suppressed storm of rage, already heaving in her disturbed bosom, to break forth; and with her pointed finger gesticulating near his face, in rather a low, tremulous, squeaking voice, she said

Wife: Now, ain't you a nice-looking sight, settin' there with that thing in your hand makin' all this fuss. All the boys in town are here, round the yard, peepin' through the cracks, laughin' at us.'

Husband: *To-o-o-o-t, toot, toot, toot, to-o-o-o-t!*

Wife: You shall stop it, sir!

Jones: And she not very tenderly seized his arm, and gave him a jerk. The old man, fully appreciating his perilous condition, as if with renewed youth, actively sprung from his seat, quickly moved across the floor a time or two to keep out of her way, then backed up in the corner, never losing a note, but all the while sending forth most terrible peals of

Husband: *Toot, toot, to-o-o-o-t, to-o-o-o-t!*

Jones: Not being able to hear her own voice, nor endure any longer the hoarse, deafening music of the hideous bugle, she decided the best policy was to retreat, and while indignantly leaving his presence remarked,

Wife: You are the biggest old fool I ever saw. *(Wife walks off stage)*

Jones: The husband, having patiently endured the most heartless scolding for so many years, seeing that victory was now his, gave a long sigh of relief, and breathed easy.

(Lights go down behind Jones. Husband stays onstage, wife re-enters).

Other similar scenes may have occurred, but if so, the hero was firm, and within a few days had a quiet, amiable, lovely wife; none more happy and cheerful.

(Lights up as Husband and Wife, now appearing happy, walk arm in arm off stage)

Jones: *(Now speaking to the "Woman" who has just appeared on stage)* Madam, I will tell your husband to get a horn.

*(To audience)*While relating this story, which consumed more time than I expected, two beautiful little children, about three and five years of age, appeared outside, and, with their innocent faces turned up, were gazing at me through the door with the most intense interest.

(Turning to woman, pointing off stage) Are those your children?

Woman: Yes, sir.

Jones: They are beautiful and lovely. It is strange the good Lord permits such a wicked woman as you are to have them. It is a wonder he doesn't take them to heaven to live with the angels. You scold and curse, you chew tobacco, you don't belong to the Church, have no Bible in the house, and don't want one. You can't read, and won't try to learn how. I mean no harm, madam; but the time may come yet when you will weep tears of sorrow on account of your wickedness. *(Aside to audience)* The allusion to her children seemed to touch her deeply, and, as a tear came to her eye, she said,

Woman: I'm sorry I can't read, and do want a Bible to put my children's ages in.

Jones: I was almost sorry the remedy story had been told, and for everything else.

(To woman) "Well, madam, you shall have a Bible," *(Aside to audience)* intending, if her husband did not buy one, to make her a present.

Woman: We thank you kindly, sir. Thank you, indeed.

Jones walks to stage front as lights dim behind him. Woman walks off stage

Jones: *(Addressing audience)* While at Conference in Mobile, eight months afterward, a minister of the gospel from that part of the State stopped me in the aisle of the church, and told me that the lady to whom I had told the 'horn story' has been converted, joined the Church, and is now a shouting Methodist.

IX. Circus, Circus

(Lights up on Jones looking at a circus poster or two posted around him. He turns to audience,

Jones: *(Gesturing to the posters as he begins speaking)* There are 'blind guides which strain at a gnat and swallow a camel.' While at the seat of justice of one of the counties of North Alabama, I saw posted in a conspicuous place, large imposing, fancy, attractive pictures of a wonderful show soon to exhibit in the beautiful town. Through these pictures and the columns of the two weeklies the coming circus was extensively advertised, and the people aroused and excited for miles in every direction.

On the morning of the eventful day, knowing the old and the young, the white and the black, were going to turn out en masse, and that my canvassing from house to house would be in vain, I drove into the crowded town for the purpose, if possible, of placing in the hands of some of the thoughtless throng a few copies of the Holy Scriptures.

(As Jones speaks, men and women casually move onto stage They are looking at the posters and "silently" speaking and gesturing to one another.)

I passed near the place where the showmen were diligently putting up their canvas, and though not more than nine o'clock, there were already hundreds of men and boys, of both races, eagerly waiting the opening of the scene, while surging streams of animated humanity continued to pour in from every road and street.

With regret I confess that many long, long years ago I witnessed a degrading scene of this kind, and in the midst of the intoxication of the occasion, surrounded by beauty, refinement, and culture, my faced burned as much on account of the indelicate costumes of the actresses as at the vulgar insinuations of the clown. The next day my face and conscience both burned while listening to a sermon by the venerable Bishop Andrew …

(A clergyman, the Bishop Andrew, has entered stage right and is standing behind a podium, at an angle, to stage center. Jones turns toward the Bishop to listen to him. The circus crowd also turns to listen to him.)

Bishop: Dear friends. Do you know of this unchristian thing we see comin' to our dear town? Oh, beware, dearly beloved, of this depraved and vulgar mob which invades our peace. You shall know these folks by their unclean ways and the coarseness of their tastes and unchristian spirit. Do you not see that you are being tempted by the devil himself? Do you not know that the evil one and his minions offer themselves up in many such disguises to bring you into hell's fold? Verily I say to you, this day, that ye shall turn your faces from that which is evil and go to your homes and families—to be with your wives and husbands and children and to read diligently from the Holy Scripture. There shall ye find peace and sustenance, saith the Lord. Amen.

(The Bishop waves briefly at the crowd and leaves the stage.)

Jones: Amen. Since then I have felt no interest whatever in the grand farce—not even in the street procession. My only business on the crowded streets of that lovely town that day was by every appropriate means to circulate the Bible; and though the occasion of a show, the multitude wild and excited, I resolved to be true to the important trust committed to my hands.

(As members of the crowd file past Jones and off stage, he gives them individual testaments and Bibles, saying to the audience:)

By the assistance of Jim Malone, a colored preacher, sixty-seven books passed into the hands of the people. After the day's work was done, and a drive of ten miles, I rested at night with a thankful heart, believing that amidst so much wickedness at least some good had been accomplished. But imagine my surprise the next week, when the following editorial appeared in one of the county papers.

(Editor walks onstage and reads aloud from his newspaper. Jones turns to editor. Jones has copy of a newspaper in his hand)

Editor: DISGUSTING.—Passing down the east side of the square last Saturday, our attention was called to Jim Malone, a colored preacher, holding an auction, with several copies of the Bible as his only wares. This is the first time we ever saw such a sight, and it is sincerely hoped that it will be the last. Perhaps it is a necessary outgrowth of the 'revision,' and may be a less evil; yet it is disgusting to see that holy book hawked about in such style, and we, together with all who have a reverence for the sacred volume, justly condemn such sales.

(As editor walks off stage, Jones turns to audience, obviously agitated. As he speaks he gestures angrily to paper in his hand.)

Jones: If the editor had put himself to a little trouble, he might easily have learned both the nature and object of these 'sales,' and been informed that the American Bible Society has no connection whatever with the 'revision.' The books were not sold by 'auction'—not one copy to the highest bidder. The 'colored preacher' simply, in a loud tone of voice, with rather a nasal twang, called attention to the 'holy book,' and especially urged his own race to supply themselves with cheap Bibles.

While his language was such as is used by all uneducated colored people, yet there was not a word which could not have been uttered in the presence of the most fastidious and refined. It seems strange that an editor, after mingling with a promiscuous multitude of four thousand people, and witnessing all the scenes in the show, and doubtless many outside, could find nothing during the day worthy of his condemnation except a 'colored preacher' endeavoring to supply his poor, ignorant race with the Word of Life.

Suppose it was an evil—an offense against the common proprieties and decencies of life—why was it pointed out especially and held up in derision to the public gaze? Was there nothing 'disgusting' in four thousand white and colored people—men, women, and children—leaving their homes and business, and crowding around a grand fraud, a catch-penny, passing through the country in the name of a show?

(Becoming more angry by the moment.)

Was there nothin' 'disgusting' in those white men and negroes herding in and around those whisky dens, and staggering up and down the streets, swearing and in a state of drunkeness? Was there nothing 'disgusting' in three thousand people, many without the common comforts of life, and even destitute of the Bible, giving their hard-earned money to support a set of men and women who are not only a disgrace to humanity, but a curse to the world? Was there nothing 'disgusting' in five hundred, more or less, Church-members, who had vowed before God and man to 'renounce the devil and all his works,' being present at a scene where decency and modesty were put to the blush, and the name of the Savior blasphemed? No, nothing 'disgusting' in all this; but something exceedingly distasteful in 'a colored preacher' selling Bibles on the streets of a Christian town!

After seeing the above editorial, I prepared a communication, similar to my words just spoken, for publication in the other weekly . . .

(smiling cynically)

but it was declined as being 'a little too personal.' The distributing of the Holy Scriptures was denounced as 'disgusting,' yet I was a stranger in a strange community, without any public means to vindicate my cause. It may not be astonishing, however, that two editors, who had so completely swallowed one show, and already commenced on four others soon to pass through the county, should strain a little at the sight of the Bible, or the publishing of an article calling the attention of the people to the impropriety of support and encouraging such grand swindles and cheats.

(Shaking head)

Many men of weak minds. I was completely 'disgusted' with the show, the immense crowd, the drunkenness, and the swearing; but the editor passed by all these, patronized the circuses, and saw nothing offensive to his refined taste except the selling of the Holy Scriptures.

The five shows alluded to, cost the people of the county, at the lowest estimate, five thousand dollars.

Friends, give your influence in favor of that which is good, and always condemn the evil.

X. If It's Round, It Can't Be Square

(Standing stage center, Jones is wiping his face with a handkerchief. In background, 2-3 tree stumps, suitable for sitting upon, are spaced around. He speaks to the audience.)

Jones: It was a July day, 1881, and excessively warm. While Molly and Jolly, hot and tired from hours of severe travel over rocks and hills, and through small fertile valleys, stood in a beautiful limpid mountain-stream quenching their thirsts, faint, feeble strains of music were heard in the distance.

(Faint square dance music is heard, slowly rising in volume—but only as background, continues through Jones' following lines)

When I ascended the bank, making a turn in the road and passing a cluster of undergrowth, the enigma was explained, and a scene for an artist was spread out before me. Wagons, buggies, oxen, mules, horses, colts, dogs, and people, old and young, were arranged in the style of a modern picnic.

The first thing that attracted my attention was the dance, which seemed to be in full blast. The drive of a hundred yards gave me a little time for reflection, and I resolved, if not repulsed, to say something to the thoughtless multitude of the God whom I served, and exhibit before them a few copies of the Bible.

Stopping just before coming to the crowd, I asked a young man for the privilege of an introduction to the leaders of the occasion. Soon an old man of at least seventy summers approached my buggy.

(Man walks onto stage hailing Jones as he does so, holding out his hand to shake hands. Old Man is dressed in colored shirt and bib overalls.)

Old Man: Greetings, stranger. The youngin' says you asked for a meetin'?

Jones: I'm a man of the Bible, Sir. May I have a few minutes of your gatherin's time and show my books?

Old Man: Yes, you can set down with us for a bit. Follow me, but wait some 'til they done finished their dancing.

(Old man walks off. As Jones begins to speak he moves to one of the tree stumps and sits.)

Jones: I rested and waited for the set to close, but my mind and eyes were by no means unemployed. By considerable labor the plot of ground had been made smooth and level, freed from rocks and roots, but was destitute of both saw-dust and bran. The dancers danced upon the naked dirt, without anything to protect their delicate feet and snow-white skirts from the dust which, so very dry, rose at the least movement and mounted higher, and still higher, at every jump.

I supposed it was a square-dance, or at least the dancers, the men and women, danced square up to each other, face to face, joined hands, turned, backed, wheeled, and made for each other again. All these various movements, especially on the part of some, were accompanied by the most violent exertions.

(Music fades)

When the music ceased, and they began to apply both handkerchiefs and fans, their red faces, profusely covered with perspiration and dust, presented more of a sad than a laughable picture. What complete nonsense and folly!

(A few people, men and women, walk onto the stage, dressed as for a square dance and wiping their faces and fanning themselves with their handkerchiefs. They assemble informally in front of Jones, who is now standing off, at angle, in front of the group.)

Having been formally introduced, I began …

I have before me today the youth and beauty, the age and wisdom of this community engaged in a scene of revelry and mirth. The Bible, the Word of God, the Book of books, which I hold in my hand, will teach you a more excellent way. It will impart to you higher, holier, nobler, purer and more lasting pleasure than that of dancing between these two hills, in an atmosphere so still that there is not a leaf moving in the forest, and heat so intense that the thermometer at this hour is not less than ninety-nine degrees.

I am a Methodist preacher, and you never saw one who was not opposed to dancing. If you will dance, however, in this terrible heat, dance on; but in my opinion the young man who has no Bible is not even a fit dancing companion. If I were a marrying man, that lady who does not appreciate the Bible high enough to have a copy of her own would never be led to the sacred altar by me.

(Jones hands out a few Bibles to the assembled and waves to them as they depart. Jones turns to audience, speaking.)

Thus, concluding my speech and disposing of a half dozen or more Bibles, I bid them adieu.

(Music fades in again)

Before I was out of sight the music began again, and another set was on the dirt. Some good may have been accomplished by that day's work, after all. For I observed that the fiddler was a woman, and a young man made up a purse and had presented her a Bible worth thirty cents.

(As Jones moves stage right, a young man approaches him from off stage. Jones is speaking to audience as he meets up with him.)

Some weeks later, having related this before-mentioned adventure to a young gentleman, he said that he would not, under any circumstances, engage in an indecent scene like that. I immediately agreed with him, pleased that we were of a similar mind.

Young Man: It does not look well to dance in the woods, and the best class of young ladies won't do it. Besides that, the ground is not suitable for the round-dance, and I have but little use for the square-dance anyway.

Jones: Why is it that you do not like the square-dance?

Young Man: It is so tame and tasteless.

Jones: I have often heard of the round-dance, but never saw it performed. Will you explain the difference?

Young Man: In the square-dance you never touch the lady at all, except her hand occasionally; but in the round-dance you are in close contact with her all the time. A man having once danced the round-dance will never take pleasure in the square-dance again. I sometimes dance the square-dance now, but it is always dull and without animation. I would not give a cent for it.

Jones: Do you like the round-dance?

Young Man: Yes, I could dance it all night.

Jones: I mean no harm by the question, but will you be so kind as to tell me the position of the parties while engaged in this pleasant exercise?

Young Man: I have no objection to doing so; but I know what you will say. You preachers think all such as that a great sin. I place my arm around the lady's waist, she her around mine, and with her head or the side of her face against my bosom, we, keeping time to the music, go round and round.

(Young gentleman demonstrates the movement)

This is about the best description I can give.

Jones: It seems to me that is more of a hug than a dance.

Young Man: No, sir; there is no hug about it.

Jones: See here! Tell me the truth. When a young man has a lady in that position, is he not tempted to give her a slight pressure?

Young Man: That is altogether owing to his partner. If she is fully initiated, and an old hand at it, she will not object; but if she is just learning the round-dance, he had better be prudent. When the ladies become accustomed to the round-dance, they enjoy it as much as men do.

Jones: Honestly, do you think it proper for men and women to dance together in such style?

Young Man: I don't know as to that, but you will never break it up. Men will dance the round-dance as long as they can get ladies to dance with them.

(Jones turns to audience, obviously very agitated)

Jones: I was furious. I told him that this abominable dance ought to be stopped. It ought to be frowned upon by all good people, and discarded from every class of society. While human nature remains as it is now, if such dancing is practiced at all, it should be confined to married men and married women, and then every man should be strictly required to dance with his own wife.

XI. The Venerable Divine

Aged Minister: *(Looking over a couple Bibles)* Well, these are nice books, and the cheapest I ever saw. We have a Bible, but if I had the money I would take one of the larger size. A great many people in the community need Bibles, and I am glad to see you here supplying them. I am not like many of my bretherin, who oppose everything of the sort. Some people see this as God's work. God has no more to do with it than I have. It is only man's work. The Scripter teaches me that God is able to do his own work when he wants it done.

I hurd there was a Methodist preacher, who made out like he was might high-larnt, but I don't think he was much, who went all round on his circles and said he was doin' God's work. He said he would go anywhere his head-man—I believe he called him bishop—wanted him to go, even if he starved to death. All he wanted to do was to do God's work, and save souls. I knowed he couldn't save anybudy's soul. And he knowed it too; and when he was talking so big, I knowed he was a hypocrite.

The very next year his head-man; or bishop, told him to go to a circus and save souls, where he didn't want to go—or so I hurd—and he got mad and might have quit. I spose he might have up and joined the Missionary Baptist.

(At this comment, Jones looks at the audience, grimacing, recalling his experience with the circus and editor.)

Tho, I don't think he would've bettered it much. For the Missionary Baptist is as much of a bastard as the Methodist. Ha. Wharever he is I reckon he's still savin' souls.

(The minister, shades his eyes, then slowly moves to a chair next to a table that has been set, informally, for a meal. Jones remains standing, turning to the audience,)

Jones: After the conclusion of this speech, he shaded his eyes with his hand, and looking at the sun, told me to light, feed my horses, rest awhile, and take dinner with him.

The forgoing sentences were uttered by an aged minister of the gospel, who had the pastoral care of three or four large congregations. I was a stranger in a strange land, and notwithstanding his insinuation against my church—and me—yet the invitations to rest and dine was no small temptation. The horses were soon unharnessed and fed, and we were seated in the hall.

(Jones seats himself next to the minister)

Aged Minister: The Scripter teaches me that God knows everything, and predestined all things as they now exist from before the foundation of the world and man has nothing to do with his salvation.

Jones: *(Aside to audience)* In reply to this I quoted Isaiah. *(Jones raises a Bible to the minister)*

"Let the wicked man forsake his way, and the unrighteous man his thoughts; and let him return unto the Lord, and he will have mercy upon him; and to our God, for he will abundantly pardon."

Aged Minister: That does sound like Scripter. But I have never seed it in my Testament. If it is there at all it is Christ speaking to some of them edecated scribes and lawyers.

Jones: *(Aside)* In my astonishment, I said, a little impatiently, "Let me have your Bible, and I will read the passage."

Aged Minister: I stand by the New Testament, and hardly think you will find it there.

(Old Man goes off stage to speak to his son.)

Jones: Then he told his son, a sprightly, clever boy of about twelve years, to bring him that little Bible. The boy looked in all the rooms.

(Muffled sounds of drawers being opened, boxes being shuffled, dropped, come from off stage)

(To audience) From the noise, I suppose he searched every old trunk and box about the place. Finally he returned and timidly said that he couldn't find the Bible.

(Minister returns on stage, but speaks to son off stage.)

Aged Minister: Tell Sally to get it, then. She knows where it is; she is always readin' the Bible. *(Minister seats himself at the table)*

Jones: His wife came from the kitchen, and searched longer than his son did,

(More muffled sounds of boxes, drawers, perhaps a dropped pan or two)

but made the same report.—she could not find the Bible. At that, the aged minister left his seat to search for the missing Bible.

(Muffled conversations off stage)

I had almost forgotten the topic under consideration, when he returned and reported that the Bible could not be found,

(Minister returns, shrugs his shoulders, lifting his hands in apparent frustration.) at the same time giving it as his opinion that his son James had taken the Bible to Texas with him when he moved there last fall. This aged minister, of the only Church in the world, did not have a Bible from October to the following March, and what is worse still, did not even know that his house was destitute of the Holy Scriptures.

By this time, I thought it prudent not to press the Bible question further. While at the table, though, I innocently asked his mode of preparation for the pulpit.

Aged Minister: Preparation for the pulpit! What do you mean?

Jones: I mean, how do you prepare your sermons?

Aged Minister: Prepare my sermons! I never know what my text is until I go to the pulpit. Do you rec'on God would give me a text before he wants me to use it?

Jones: *(Speaking to the audience)* I expressed my astonishment at such a course and spoke at some length of the responsibility of preaching, and of the earnest prayer and profound thought which are necessary for a suitable preparation for the sacred desk.

Aged Minister: That will do for your educated men who preaches from book-larnin'; but God fills the mouths of his servants with jest sich things as he wants them to say.

Jones: *(Again, to audience)* I spoke of the danger of a preacher, without preparation, contracting the habit of using the same words in every sermon, and though he may take a different text, yet preach the same sermon all the time. As we rose from the table, he was saying,

Aged Minister: They accuse me of that, but I am doing what God directs, and do not care what edecated people say.

(Jones gets up, addressing the audience)

Jones: My horses were soon moving on, and I felt that my visit had not been in vain, as thereby the divine had discovered that he had no Bible.

XII. The Truth, the Light, the Directions

(We see Jones standing next to a rail fence with a gate, in front of a house that we cannot see off stage.)

Jones: Having been water-bound two days, in rather an unpropitious country, I felt impelled to make a long, laborious drive of twenty-five miles, in order to avoid a wild, dangerous mountain stream, which had become unusually violent by reason of the incessant spring rains. It was a dreary, dismal, threatening day, with dark, angry thunder clouds lingering in the west, and almost noon. From early morning I had been pressing forward, with as much rapidity as possible, over rocks, hills, and mountains, and now my buggy stood near a very small log-hut,

(Jones casually gestures offstage left)

enclosed by a rail fence, so close that it touched the wall on every side, except the front, and in four feet of the door.

This cabin, in the midst of a vast wilderness, was the only human habitation I had seen since leaving the kind family where I spent the previous night. Evidently I had missed the way and was lost. A horseman, who happened to cross my path only an hour before, gave me the best directions he could, and closed by saying: "You will not see another house on that road for the next ten miles."

As the mountaineer had been living there for years, and knew every path, rock, and bluff in the entire wilderness, I am of the opinion he could have conducted me safely through, but, for the life of me, I could not find the right road. Like many others, he was too wordy, too voluminous, too indefinite. When a man instructs another, he should use suitable words to convey his meaning, and no more.

(Instructing the audience, now, moving forward to stage front.) You know, there ought to be a book written, and a chapter in that book devoted to the teaching of men, women, and children, both white and black, the art of directing strangers in a strange country the way from one house to another. This chapter should be studied in all schools and colleges, and a copy placed in every office, place of business, dwelling, and cabin throughout the land. You may smile, but when one travels as many miles as I have, over every imaginable variety of roads, from the gulf to the mountains, and has been perplexed, annoyed, delayed, and lost as often as I have been on

account of the ignorant, bungling manner of directions given by kind people along the way, he will be of the same opinion. *(Jones returns back to the fence/gate)*

In answer to my call, the good housewife came to the door.

(A young woman, modestly dressed in an apron approaches the fence from offstage)

Housewife: My husband is gone to his daddy's today to take his horse home, and won't git back before dark; that's certain.

Jones: Madam, I am lost; can you tell me anything of the road leading east?

Housewife: No, I can't; for thar's none goin' that way.

Jones: A gentleman, only a few miles back, told me there was. You must be mistaken.

Housewife: No I ain't, nuther; becase I've lived right here, and at daddy's down thar under the hill, ever since I was ten year old, and I'll soon be thirty-one, an' I never he'rd of sich a thing before. Who told you that?

Jones: *(Aside to audience)* At that time I remembered the name, and gave it.

Housewife: Well, he jist told a lie; nor it's not the first, nuther. Do you think I don't know that ar feller? Why, he courted my sister three years one time, an' she wouldn't have him then. He's the biggest liar you ever seed. Why, I couldn't b'lieve him if he was gwine to die and doin' his prayin.'

You go over them bluffs and rocks in that ar thing?

(Pointing offstage to Jones' buggy)

You an' yer nice fat horses would both be kilt, an' that thing broke all to flinderations before you'd git a mile. I tell you, a bear itself couldn't got up some of them places, and I know you couldn't go whar a bear couldn't. You might go that way, but you couldn't git over Drew River; it would drownd an elephant. You might go the other way, but Buttiehachee is the wust crick you ever seed. It would wash you an' yer horses an' that little thing away before you could git in it. I tell you I wouldn't go in that crick in that thing for to save my ears. What made you make it so little? It's the quarest wagin I ver seed, anyhow. I think you had better go back the same you come, an' stay till the rain quits, if it ever does, an' you can cross without any trouble.

Jones: *(A bit impatiently)* Madam, is there not a road to the right of the one I came, which will lead me out on the dividing ridge between these two creeks?

Housewife: Oh, yes. If I'd knowed at first you wanted to go that way, I'd told you long ago. I 'spect that liar tried to tell you that way this mornin,' but you couldn't understand his bigity, lumberin' talk. Some folks can't tell nuthin,' nohow. Well, you'll understand me, beca'se when I tells anybody anything I tells it to 'em, an' don't tell a whole pack of stuff they don't want to hear about it. You take the road, out thata way …

(Motioning off in several different directions)

… an' the first right-hand you see take it, an' the next right-hand you see take it; witch fur a sharp bend to the left, cus thar it turns off at a spring whar an old house has bin. Not thar now, though—got washed away some time ago. Sad story, to say …

(She seems to go into deep thought, hesitating, then abruptly …)

Now, that there's all I knowd about it. I think you had better go fast when you start, and git to the place whar you wants to got to before it rains, beca'se its' gwine to come down like wild cats after dinner.

Jones: *(Aside)* I was truly glad when she ceased, and I said: "Don't you want a Bible?"

Housewife: A Bible? Yes, it's the very thing I told John last Sunday I wanted; but he won't get it, I know. He hardly knows what a Bible is, an' I don't know much. If I was a man, I think I'd try to know somethin' and have things. We's bein married more nor a year, an' ain't got narry one yit. But it's no use talkin.' I's got no money, an' John's got none, nuther; but I'll tell what I has got. I's got some of the best saft soap you ever seed, an' I'll give you jist as much of it as you want for the Testament.

Jones: *(To audience)* Her earnestness embarrassed me, while it was with difficulty that I suppressed a smile. On previous occasions, eggs, chickens, tallow, raw-hides, and almost every other article of farm produce, had been offered in exchange for Bibles; but this was the first time that soft soap had been tendered. While I was meditating how to decline as gently as possible, she continued:

Housewife: You can take it along and sell it; I'll give you a gourd, too.

Jones: No, madam, I cannot take the soap; sell it to someone else. I will give you this Testament. *(Jones hands her a Bible and then says to audience)*

At that, she opened her eyes in amazement and after turning the leaves for a moment, as if to convince herself that it was a genuine Testament, replied:

Housewife: Well, you are a might curious man, givin' away your things that way for nothin,' an' me wantin' to pay you for it, too.

Jones: *(Jones moves forward away from fence and speaks to audience)* Soft soap was the only article this poor woman had in her house for sale, and in the simplicity of her heart she made this proposition.

Gentle friends, do not smile; but rather pity, aid, and educate the poor and ignorant, and supply them with the Holy Scriptures—the truth, the light, *(pause, with slight shake of the head)* and the directions.

Author Notes

While doing our research on A.M. Jones and his book-selling travels through Alabama, we uncovered several interesting historical points. Much of A.M.'s work was in the northern county of Winston, nicknamed "The Free State of Winston." Winston received the nickname when 3,000 of the county's residents showed up at a conference at Bill Looney's Tavern on July 4, 1861, voting in favor of a declaration reaffirming their loyalty to the American flag, not take up arms against it, and that both North and South should recognize their neutrality and autonomy in dealing with their own issues. "The declaration was approved by a loud and enthusiastic voice vote, it seems. And if no Free State of Winston ever did emerge, 'the hill people still proudly recall the day they took a strong stand in the face of great danger,' writes Drue Drake."[1]

According to witnesses, a Confederate sympathizer in the crowd upon hearing the resolution read, shouted "Oh, Oh, Winston secedes! The Free State of Winston!" (Alabama historian Martine G. Bates, "Incident at Looney's Tavern," Jan. 23, 1999).

What makes this incident all the more interesting as it relates to A.M. Jones is that Scene VII of this play describes a Looney's Tavern in Winston County, though this tavern is a much earlier version (50 years prior to the Civil War) to the Looney's mentioned above. And A.M.'s tavern wasn't really a tavern at all – it was a tree up which a hunter named Looney climbed to avoid a couple of threatening panthers. He remained in the tree until the next day, when he returned home. His excuse to his wife for being away was that he had stayed the night at a tavern.

The final point that makes this all very interesting is that there exists an outdoor theater in Winston called Looney's Tavern that up until recently had been performing regularly a play "Incident at Looney's Tavern," documenting the people's vote against secession.

One might ask how it was that Winston stood against secession. It turns out that Winston was the "poorest county in the state, populated by farmers who barely made a living from the rugged ground. They were," according to Bates, "fiercely independent – outside the mainstream politically, geographically, and economically." Another historian, Joel S. Mize, suggests that the Northern Warrior Mountains" people viewed the Civil War "as a rich-man's fight (Southern Aristocracy) and very few of these citizens lived above the level of bare necessities."[2] Their poverty worsened through the post-Civil War years as Confederate raiding parties ravished the County's land and people as reprisal for the vote against secession.

Several other northern Alabama counties were also against secession, and, in fact, along with Winston, contributed many volunteers to the Union military force.

To obtain "local color" pictures to support this play, I traveled hundreds of miles through the back roads of northern Alabama. Along the way local historians Darryal Jackson and David Burleson enhanced my understanding of the people and land of the area. Jackson, who heads up the Winston County Geneological Society, elaborated some on William Bauck "Bill" Looney who is something of a legend, even in his own time. Jackson wasn't familiar with the panther chase though he had heard another story where Looney, while hauling some cotton, was chased up a tree by a bear. Looney, known as the "The Old Black Fox" during his day, was a thorn in the side of the Confederates, being something of a rebel against the rebels.

Our gracious Hartselle, AL, bed and breakfast hosts Ann and Ray Hill were also very much steeped in the traditions and history of the area and helped point me in the right direction to get my pictures. It was serendipitous that we were made aware of a very famous 19th Century A.J. Showalter hymn "Leaning in the Everlasting Arms" that was written while residing with the original owners, the Odens. To honor the event, the Hills had displayed the work in an open hymnal on a pump organ. No doubt, it was probably a hymn with which A.M. would have been familiar. Therefore a picture of the setting appears with this play.

B.C. Kelly, *The Best Little Stories from the Civil War*, (Charlottesville, VA: Montpelier Publishing, 1994). 94.

Mize, Joel S., Unionists of the Warrior Mountains of Alabama, Vol. A, (Lakewood, CO: Dixie Historical Research and Education Publications, 2004). 10.

BIBLIOGRAPHY

"Adventures of a Woman Book Agent," University of Virginia, http//etext.Virginia.edu/railton/marketing/facts2.html. March, 2007.

"Advertising Mascots-People: Duncan Hines," TV Acres, http://www.tvacres.comadmascots_hines.htm. July 29, 2006.

"Agents Wanted: Subscription Publishing in America, A Brief History of Subscription Publishing," http://www.library.upenn.edu/exhibits/rbm/agents/case2.html. University of Pennsylvania. March, 2007.

Anderson, Sherwood, "Business Types: The Traveling Man." *Agricultural Advertising*. 11 April, 1904.

Anecdota Americana; Five Hundred Stories for the Amusement of the Five Hundred Nations that Comprise America. New York: Nesor Publishing Company. 1934.

"Ann Sophia Stephens," http://www.britannica.com. Chicago: *Encyclopaedia Britannica*. 2004.

Arbour, Keith, *Canvassing Books, Sample Books, and Subscription Publisher's Ephemera, 1833-1951*. Ardsley, NY: Hadyn Foundation for the Cultural Arts. 1996.

Armstrong, David and Elizabeth Metzger Armstrong, *The Great American Medicine Show*, New York: Prentice Hall. 1991.

Atherton, Lewis, "Predecessors of the Commercial Drummer in the Old South," *Bulletin of the Business Historical Society*, Boston, Vol. XXI, No. 1, February, 1947.

Bacon, Elizabeth M., "Marketing Sewing Machines in the Post-Civil War Years," *Bulletin of the Business Historical Society*, Boston, Vol XX, No. 3, June, 1946.

Baldwin, William H., "Travelling Salesmen: Opportunities and their Dangers" (an address before the Boston Young Men's Christian Union), Boston: Boston Young Men's

Christian Union. 1874.

"Barbed Wire-The True Story," http://www.barbed-wire.net/blue/truehistory.html. December, 2001.

Barbed Wire Pioneers: Inventing a Community. Produced by Dr. Jeffrey Chown. 52 minutes. DeKalb, IL: Northern Illinois University. 1998.

Barnum, P.T., *The Humbugs of the World: An Account of Humbugs, Delusions, Impositions, Quackeries, Deceits, and Deceivers, Generally, in All Ages*. New York: Carleton. 1866.

Bartelle, J.P., *Forty Years on the Road*. Cedar Rapids, IA: The Torch Press. 1925.

Barth, Steve, "Britannica on the Virtual Bookshelf," *Knowledge Management Magazine*, http://www.destinationkm.com. September, 2000.

Barton, Bruce, *The Man Nobody Knows*. New York: Grossett & Dunlap. 1924.

Baum, Frank Joslyn and Russell P. MacFail, *To Please a Child: A Biography of L. Frank Baum Royal Historian of Oz*. Chicago: Reilly & Lee Co. 1961.

Baum, L. Frank, *The Wonderful Wizard of Oz*. New York: Dover Publications, Inc. 1960.

Becher, Barry & Edward Valenti, *The Wisdom of Ginsu: Carve yourself a piece of the American dream*. Franklin Lakes, NJ: Career Press. 2005.

Bennett, Charles, *Scientific Salesmanship*. St. Louis, MO: American Efficiency Bureau. 1933.

Blair, Walter, *Tall Tale America: A Legendary History of our Humorous Heroes*. Chicago: The University of Chicago Press. 1944, 1987.

Blashfield, Jean F., *The Awesome Almanac: Illinois*. Fontana, WI: B & B Publishing. 1993.

Blunt, Roy, "Community Roots, "http://lcweb2.loc.gove/gov/cocoon/legacies. July 18, 2005, from *Seattle Post-Intelligencer*. 15 November, 1999.

"Book Matches," American Matchcover Collecting Club, http://www.matchcovers.com 2003.

Botkin, Benjamin A., *A Treasury of American Anecdotes*. Secaucus, NY: Castle Publishing. 1957.

Brady, Shelly, *Ten Things I Learned from Bill Porter*. Novato, CA: New World Library. 2002.

Breyfogle, L.C., *The Commercial Traveler Hotel Guide and Gazetteer*. Lockport, NY: The United States Hotel Register Publishing Company. 1881.

Brockett, L.P., *The Commercial Traveller's Guide Book*. New York: H. Dayton & Company. 1871.

Brower, Bill, *The Complete Traveling Salesman's Joke Book*. New York: Stravon Publishers. 1952.

Brown, Amy Belding, "Amos Bronson Alcott," *American Transcendentalism Web*, http://www.vcu.edu/engweb/transcendentalism/authors/alcott, Virginia Commonwealth University. 2006.

Bruce, Philip Alexander, *Economic History of Virginia*. New York: Peter Smith. 1935.

Burton, William E. (ed), *The Cyclopaedia of Wit and Humor*, Vol. I. New York: D. Appleton and Company. 1859.

Carr, William H.A., *Perils: Named and Unnamed*. New York: McGraw-Hill. 1967.

Carver, Richard, *A History of Marshall*, Virginia, Beach, VA: The Donning Company. 1993.

Carwardine, William H., *The Pullman Strike*. Chicago: Charles H. Kerr. 1994. (Originally published in 1894)

Casson, Herbert., *Tips for Traveling Salesmen*. New York: B.C. Forbes Publishing Co. 1927.

Chandler, Jr., Alfred D., *The Visible Hand: The Managerial Revolution in American Business*. Cambridge, Mass: Belknap Press of Harvard University Press. 1977.

Chapin, Charles, "Old Technology: Printed Words," presentation. Springfield, IL: Illinois State Historical Society Symposium. 4 December, 2004.

"John Chapman," *Encyclopaedia Britannica*, Vol II. Chicago: Encyclopaedia Britannica, Inc., 1974.

"Charles Ives, Composer," http://www.dsokids.com/2001/dso.asp. Dallas Symphony Orchestra. December, 2001.

Chesman, Andrea (ed.), *The Inventive Yankee*. Dublin, NH: Yankee Books. 1989.

"Clark: A Historical Perspective," http://www.clarkbar.com/history.html. December, 2001.

Cohen, Lizabeth, *Making a New Deal*. New York: Cambridge University Press. 1990.

Cole, Harry Ellsworth, *Stagecoach and Tavern Tales*, Carbondale & Edwardsville: Southern Illinois University Press. 1997.

"Collis Huntington," http://www.schoolnet.co.uk.USAhuntington.htm. Spartacus Educational. 15 August, 2006.

"Colportage and Book-Hawking," *Meliora: A Quarterly Review of Social Science in its Ethical, Economical, Political and Ameliorative Aspects*, Vol. III. London: S.W. Partridge, 9, Paternoster Row. 1891.

"Commercial Sales Between Residents of the Several States," *Reports of Committees of the House of Representatives*: First Session of 50th Congress. Washington, DC: Government Printing Office. 1887-88, Report No. 1310.

"Commercial Travellers," *Chambers' Journal of Popular Literature, Science and Arts*,

London: W. & R. Chambers. Vol 43, 1866.

"Commercial Travelers," *Reports of Committees of the House of Representatives*: First Session of 48th Congress, Washington DC: Government Printing Office. 1883-84, Report No. 1321.

Constable, Burt, "Salesman's Email Becomes a Fuller Brush with the Past," Des Plaines, IL: *Daily Herald*:. 12 June, 2004.

Cook, Bill J., *The Johnny Appleseed Pew*, Cincinnati: Gruber Printing Company. 1977.

Copeland, Lee, "Return of the Salesman." *Chicago Tribune*. Business/Technology Section. 5 August, 2002.

Coyle, William, "From Scatology to Social History: Captain Billy's Whiz Bang," *Studies in American Humor*. http://www.compedit.com. 2004.

Crist, Charlie, (Forida Attorney General) "How to Protect Yourself: Multilevel Marketing," http://myfloridalegal.com. State of Florida. 2003.

Crowther, Samuel, *John H. Patterson: Pioneer in Industrial Welfare*. Garden City, NY: Doubleday, Page & Company. 1923.

Cummings, Robert, "Zig Ziglar," http://www.olemiss.edu/mwp/dir/ziglar.zig/., Yazoo, MS: Yazoo County Convention and Visitors Bureau. 18 January, 2004.

"Davey Tree Expert Company," http://www.library.kent.edu/speccoll/reghist/history.html/. Kent State University. December, 2001.

de Coster, Charles, (translated by F. M. Atkinson). *The Legend of Ulenspiegel and Lamme Goedzak and their Adventures Heroical, Joyous, and Glorious in the Land of Flanders and Elsewhere*, Vol. 1. Garden City, NY: Doubleday, Page & Company. 1922.

Denove, Chris & James D. Power, IV, *Satisfaction: How Every Great Company Listens to the Voice of the Customer*. New York, NY: Penguin Group. 2006.

Dirks, Tim, "The Wizard of Oz-1939" (film review), http://www.filmsite.org/wiza5.html 25 July, 2005.

Dolan, J. R., *The Yankee Peddlers of Early America*. New York: Bramhall House. 1964.

Door to Door, TNT: Rosemont Productions in conjunction with Angel Brown Productions, (directed by Steven Schachter, written by and starring William H. Macy). 2002.

"Dr. Forest C. Shaklee," http://www.enfuselle.com/main/aboutinfo. Pleasanton, CA: Shaklee Corporaton. 2007.

Drummers's Yarns, Fun on the "Road." New York: Excelsior Publishing House. 1886.

"Dun & Bradstreet," *Wikipedia*, http://en..wikipedia.org/wiki/Dun_and_Bradstreet. July, 2006.

"Duncan Hines, History of," http://www.duncanhines.com. December, 2003.

Duncan, Todd, *Killing the Sale: The 10 Fatal Mistakes Salespeople Make & How to Avoid Them*. Nashville, TN: Thomas Nelson Publishers. 2004.

"Early History of the American Tract Society," http://www.atstracts.org. American Tract Society: New York. 27 March, 2005.

Emord, Dawn & David Bushong, "Collis Huntington," The Transcontinental Railroad, http://www.bushong.net/dawn/about/college/ids100/. 15 August, 2006.

Esar, Evan, *Easar's Comic Dictionary*. New York: Harvest Home Publishers. 1943.

Esar, Evan, *20,000 Quips & Quotes*. Barnes and Noble Books. 1968.

Evans, George G., *Book of Anecdotes and Budget of Fun: Containing a collection of over one thousand of the most laughable sayings and jokes of celebrated wits and humorists*. Philadelphia: Geo. G. Evans. 1859.

Evans, Harold, *They Made America*. New York: Little, Brown and Company. 2004.

Fawcett, W.H., (ed.), *Capt. Billy's Whiz Bang*, (Author Solberg's personal magazine collection of 12 issues), Minneapolis, MN: Fawcett Publications. Vol. III, No. 26, 1 October, 1921; Vol. III, No. 36, August, 1922; Vol. V, January, 1924; Vol. VII, No. 81, January, 1926; Vol. VII, No. 84, April, 1926; Vol. IX,, 1927, (cover date, number defaced); Vol. X, No. 110, March 1928; Vol. XI, No. 131, Winter Annual, 1930; No volume or number, 12th Edition, *Winter Annual*, 1933; Vol. IX, 190, August, 1934; Vol. X, No. 206, December, 1935; Reprint, *A Nostalgic Look* ... 1975.

Fisher's Comic Almanac. Philadelphia: Fisher and Brother. 1885.

Flory, William E.S., *Parson Weems-First Biographer of Washington*, an address presented at a meeting of Historic Dumfries, Virginia, Inc., at the Dumfries Town Hall, 6 February, 1975. Weems-Botts Museum Archives.

Flory, William E.S., *Parson Weems-Marketer*, an address presented at a meeting of Historic Dumfries, Virginia, Inc., at the Dumfries Town Hall, 3 February, 1977. Weems-Botts Museum Archives.

Forbes, B.C., *America's Twelve Master Salesmen*. New York: B.C. Forbes & Sons Publishing Co. 1952.

Friedman, Lee M., "The Drummer in Early American Merchandise Distribution," *Bulletin of the Business Historical Society.* Boston, Vol. XXI, No. 2, April, 1947.

Friedman, Walter A. , *Birth of a Salesman: The Transformation of Selling in America*. Cambridge, MA: Harvard University Books. 2004.

Fuller, Alfred C., *A Foot in the Door.* New York: McGraw-Hill. 1960.

Furnas, J.C., *The Americans: A Social History of the United States 1587-1914*. New York: G.P. Putnam's & Sons. 1969.

Galaxy of Wit or Laughing Philosopher, The, (collection from the *Literary Emporium*). No specific author referenced. Boston: J. Reed Publisher, Volumes 1 & 2. 1830.

"Gallaudet University- Thomas Hopkins Gallaudet: The Legacy Begins," http://pr.gallaudet.edu/VisitorsCenter/GallaudetHistory/index.html. December, 2001.

Gaston, Jim, "Jim's Fountain Pen Site," http://jimgaston.com/parker.htm.1996.

Gerler, William R., *Executive's Treasury of Humor for Every Occasion*. West Nyack, NY: Parker Publishing, Inc. 1965.

"Gideon Bible, History of the," http://ky.essortment.com/gideonbible_rcwz.htm. December, 2001.

"Gimbel," http://www.infoplease.com. *Infoplease*, 2004.

Gitomer, Jeffrey, *Little Red Book of Selling*. Austin: Bard Press. 2004.

Goddu, Jenn Q., "C.J. Walker's Rise from Rags to Riches, Power," *Chicago Tribune*, Section 7, 16 June, 2006.

Green, James N. (edited by Michael Hackenberg) "From Printer to Publisher: Mathew Carey and the Origins of Nineteenth Century Book Publishing," *Getting the Books Out: Papers of the Chicago Conference on the Book in 19th-Century America*. Washington: The Center for the Book. 1987.

Green, Mel, *The Greatest Joke Book Ever*. New York: Avon Books. 1999.

Hannaford, E. *Success in Canvassing: A Manual of Practical Hints and Instructions, Specially Adapted to the Use of Book Canvassers of the Better Class*. New York: E. Hannaford. 1884 (rev).

Harris, Robert C. (ed.), *Johnny Appleseed Source Book*. (originally appeared in the *Old Fort News*, Vol. IX, Nos. 1-2, March-June, 1945).

Hawkins, Norval, *The Selling Process: A Handbook of Salesmanship Principles*. Detroit: Norval Hawkins. 1919.

Hendrickson, Robert, *QPB Encyclopedia of Word and Phrase Origins*. New York: Facts on File. 1997.

"Henry J. Heinz," *Pennsylvania People, Wikipedia*. Wikimedia Foundation, Inc. 2006.

"History of Chewing Gum." http://www.gum-mints.com/conaffairs/historyofgum.html. Warner-Lambert Consumer Group Home. December. 2001.

"History of the Great American MoonPie, The ," http://www.moonpie.com. Chattanooga Bakery. 2005.

Hoagland, Edward and Daniel P. Mannix, et al, *A Sense of History: The Best Writings from the Pages of American Heritage.* New York: American Heritage Press. 1985.

Holliday, Carl, *Woman's Life in Colonial Days.* Mineola, NY: Dover Publications. 1999.

Hosley, William, *Colt: The Making of an American Legend.* Amherst: University of Massachusetts Press. 1996.

Hoster, Mabel (A Hotel Stenographer), *The Traveling Man As I Found Him.* Indianapolis: W.D. Hord Company. 1904.

"Hotel de Paris: Salesman's Room," Hotel de Paris Museum. http:/www.hoteldeparismuseum.org. National Society of Colonial Dames of American in Colorado. 2005.

Hoyt, Edwin P., *The Supersalesmen.* Cleveland: The World Publishing Company. 1962.

Hunt, Francis, *American Anecdotes: Original and Select,* Vol. II. Boston: Putnam & Hunt. 1830.

Hunt, Mabel Leigh, *Better Known as Johnny Appleseed.* Philadelphia: J.B. Lippincott Company. 1950.

Illustrated Railway Anecdote Book, The (selected for the reading of railway passengers). London: Ward and Lock. 1870s.

"John Chapman," *Encyclopaedia Britannica,* Vol. II. Chicago: Encyclopaedia Britannica, Inc. 1974.

Johnny Appleseed Society Educational Center and Museum. Urbana University, Urbana, OH.

Johnson, Doug, Associated Press, http://missourifolkloresociety.truman.edu/hunter. 2005.

Johnson, Eric W., *A Treasury of Humor II.* New York: Ivy Books. 1994.

Johnston, J.P., *Twenty Years of Hus'ling,* Chicago: Donohue Brothers. 1900.

Jones, Chris, "Sarah Breedlove reflects lives of 2 strong women," Tempo Section, *The Chicago Tribune.* 19 June, 2006.

Jones, A.M.,, *Quaint Characters or Colportage Sketches.* Nashville, TN: M.E. Church. 1891.

Jones, Edgar R., *Those Were the Good Old Days—A Happy Look at American Advertising, 1880-1930.* New York: Simon and Schuster. 1959.

Jones, William Ellery (ed.), *Johnny Appleseed: A Voice in the Wilderness.* West Chester, PA: Chrysalis Books. 2000.

"Joyce C. Hall," http://www.emotionscards.com/museum/joycehall.htm. 2005.

"Julius Schmid," *Who Made America?* http://www.pbs.org/wgbh/theymadeamerica.

Keir, Malcolm, *The Pageant of America: The Epic of Industry.* New Haven, CT: Yale University Press. 1926.

Keller, Morton, *The Life Insurance Enterprise, 1885-1910.* Cambridge, MA: Harvard University Press. 1963.

Kellock, Harold, *Parson Weems of the Cherry-Tree.* New York: The Century Co. 1928. (cites Albert Bushnell Hart, "Historical Liars"). Weems-Botts Museum Archives.

King, Chris, "The Mountain Minstrel," *Spectator Magazine.* Raleigh, NC. 10 October, 1996.

Koehn, Nancy F., *Brand New: How Entrepreneurs Earned Consumers' Trust From Wedgwood to Dell.* Boston, MA: *Harvard Business School Press.* 2001.

Koehn, Nancy F., "Henry Heinz and Brand Creation in the Late Nineteenth-Century: Making Markets for Processed Food," *Business History Review.* Winter. 1999.

Kruesi, Margaret, "Herbs! Roots! Barks! Leaves!," *Folklife Center News*, Washington, DC: Library of Congress American Folklife Center. Fall, 2004.

Kunitz, Stanley J. & Howard Haycraft,, *American Authors 1600-1900*. New York: H.W. Wilson Company. 1966.

Lang, H. Jack, *Lincoln's Fireside Reading*. Cleveland: The World Publishing Co. 1965.

Leach, William, *Land of Desire*. New York: Pantheon Books. 1993.

Leary, Lewis, *The Book-Peddling Parson*. Chapel Hill, NC: Algonquin Books. 1984.

Lee, Harper, *To Kill a Mockingbird*. Philadelphia: J.B. Lippincott Company. 1960.

Levy, Joel, *Really Useful: The Origin of Everyday Things*. Buffalo, NY: Firefly Books. 2002.

Lichtenstein, Nelson, Susan Strasser, Roy Rosenzweig, *Who Built America? Volume 2: Since 1877*. New York: Worth Publishers. 2000.

Lienhard, John H., "Engines of our Ingenuity." http://www.uh.edu. University of Houston. 1988-1998.

Lindbergh, Reeve, (daughter of Chas. & Anne Morrow Lindbergh), *Johnny Appleseed*, New York: Little, Brown and Company. 1990.

"Madame C.J. Walker," *The Faces of Science: African Americans in the Sciences*, http://www.princeton.edu/~mcbrown/display/walker.html. Princeton University. 2005.

Madsen, Axel, *The Deal Maker: How William C. Durant Made General Motors*. Hoboken, NJ: John Wiley & Sons, 1999.

Maher, Wm. H., *A Man of Samples*. Toledo, OH: The Toledo Book Company. 1887.

Mandino, Og, *The Greatest Salesman in the World*. New York: Bantam Books. 1968.

Marburg, Theodore F.," Manufacturer's Drummer," 1832, *Bulletin of the Business Historical Society*. Vol. XXII, No. 2. Boston, April, 1948.

Marburg, Theodore F., "Manufacturer's Drummer," 1832, *Bulletin of the Business Historical Society*. Vol. XXII, No. 3. Boston, June, 1948.

Marshall, George L., *O'er Rail and Cross-Ties with Grip Sack*. New York: G. W. Dillingham. 1891.

"Mary Kay Ash," http://www.infoplease.com/ipa/A0880005.html. Infoplease, January, 2004.

Masson, Thomas L., *Little Masterpieces of American Wit and Humor*, Volume II. New York: Doubleday, Page and Company. 1904.

Mastony, Colleen, "Gave Puppy that Saved Nixon," (obituary). *The Chicago Tribune*. 17 May, 2006.

Mayhew, Henry, *Mayhew's London*. London: The Pilot Press. 1949.

Maysles, Albert, David Maysles & Charlotte Zwerin, *Salesman*. New York: Maysles Films. 1968.

McClary, Ben Harris (ed.), *The Lovingood Papers*. Athens, TN: The Sut Society, 1962.

McDonald, Archie P., "Bet-A-Million Gates," http:www.texasescapes.com/AllThingsHistorical/Bet-a-Million-Gates. Texas Escapes-Blueprint for Travel, East Texas Historical Association. 16 February, 2005.

McDonald, Maureen, "World-record salesman earns spot in Automotive Hall of Fame." http://www.detnews.com. *The Detroit News*, 7 August, 2001.

"McDonald's History," http://www.mcdonalds.com/corp/about/mcd_history_pg1.html. January, 2004.

McFarlan, Donald, (ed), *The Guinness Book of Records 1990*, United Kingdom: Guinness Publishing. 1989.

McNamara, Brooks, *Step Right Up*. Garden City, NY: Doubleday & Company. 1976.

McNeal, Violet, *Four White Horses and a Brass Band*. Garden City, NY: Doubleday and Co. 1947.

"MDRT History," http://www.mdrt.org/history.html. Park Ridge, IL: The Million Dollar Round Table. January, 2004.

Miles, Alfred H. (ed*), One Thousand & One Anecdotes*. New York: Thomas Whittaker. 1895.

Miller, C.L, "Skiff & Ross, The Jewel Tea Company," Hall China Collectors' Home Page, http://www.inter-services.com/HallChina/jhistory.html. East Liverpool, OH: Marty Kennedy. 1998.

Moody, Walter D., *Men Who Sell Things*. A.C. McClurg & Co. 1907.

Moore, Truman E., *The Traveling Man*. Garden City, NY: Doubleday & Company. 1972.

Moving Journey, A (plus update), "20/20" television report, New York: ABC News Productions. 24 December, 1999. (short documentary on Watkins Salesman Bill Porter, (#T991224-02).

"Mr. Charles William Post," http://www.posttexas.com/CWPostHHisstory.htm. Maxine Durrett Earl Charitable Foundation, Inc. 28 March, 2005.

"Mr. Kroutsmeyer on 'Drummers'," *Furniture Trade Journal*, Vol, 3, No. 8, August, 1876 and Vol. 6, No. 4, April, 1879.

"Mrs. Stewart's Bluing, The History of," http://www.mrsstewart.com.pages/msbhistory.htm. Luther Ford & Company. December, 2001.

Murphy, Sharon, "Life Insurance in the United States through World War I," (edited by Robert Whaples), http://eh.net/encyclopedia/article/murphy.life.insurance.us. *E.H. Net Encyclopedia*. 15 August, 2002.

"Napoleon Hill," *TheFree Dictionary*. http://www.encyclopedia.thefreedictionary.com/Napoleon+Hill. Farlex. 15 August, 2006.

"Og Mandino: The Greatest Salesman Home Page," http://www.ogmandiono.com. The Greatest Salesman. 2005.

Oliver, Dr. N.T., "Alacazam6The Story of Pitchmen High and Low," *Saturday Evening Post*. 19 October, 1929.

Olnslow, G., *Der Hausirer, Le Colporteur*. Berlin: Schlesingerschen Buch und Musikhandlung. 1879.

Orecklin, Michele, "Notebook Milestones: Estee Lauder," *Time Magazine*. 10 May, 2004.

Palmer, Edward E., *Forty Years of Hustling*. Wooster, OH: Edward E. Palmer. 1942.

Panati, Charles, *Extraordinary Origins of Everyday Things*. New York: Harper & Row. 1987.

Pattison, W. I., *How 'Tis Done*. Syracuse, NY. 1890.

Perret, Gene & Linda Perret, *Gene Perret's Funny Business*. Englewood Cliffs, NJ: Prentice Hall. 1960.

Pollan, Michael, *The Botany of Desire*. New York: Random House. 2001.

Popeil, Ron, *Salesman of the Century*, New York: Delacorte Press. 1995.

"Popular Medicine," http://iberia.vassar.edu/1896/medicine.html. Vassar College. December, 2001.

Price, Robert, *Johnny Appleseed: Man & Myth*, Urbana, OH: Urbana University Press. 2001.

Pungent, Pierce, *Chit-chat of Humor, Wit and Anecdote*. New York: Stringer & Townsend. 1857.

Putnam, Robert D., *Bowling Alone*. New York: Simon & Schuster. 2000.

Raynor, Richard, *Drake's Fortune: The Fabulous True Story of the World's Greatest Confidence Artist*. New York: Doubleday. 2002.

"Richard Martin takes out 1st life insurance policy," http://www.brainyhistory.com. BrainyMedia. 2006.

"Ron Popeil," http//www.ideafinder.com/history/inventors/popeil.htm. 27 July, 2005.

"Ron Popeil," *Chicago Stories*, narrated by John Callaway. Chicago: WTTW-TV. 2004.

Roth, Philip, *American Pastoral.* New York: Vintage International. 1977.

Russell, Francis, "Bubble, bubble6no toil, no trouble, "*American Heritage*, Vol. XXIV, Number 2, 1973.

"Sales of Goods and Merchandise by Samples,"*Reports of Committees of the House of Representatives*: First Session of 49th Congress, Washington, DC: Government Printing Office. 1885-86, Report No. 1762.

Samuelson, Timothy, *But, Wait! There's More!* New York: Rizzoli International Publications, Inc. 2002.

Samuelson, Tim, (curator) *Isn't That Amazing: The Irresistible Appeal and Spiel of Ronco and Popeil.* Chicago Cultural Center Exhibition. March-May, 2004.

Saxon, A.H., *P.T Barnum: The Legend and the Man.* New York: Columbia University Press. 1989.

Schlesinger, Arthur M. & Dixon Ryan Fox, *A History of American Life: The Completion of Independence, 1790-1830.* New York: The Macmillan Company. 1944.

Schneirov, Richard, Shelton Stromquist & Nick Salvatore, *The Pullman Strike and the Crisis of the 1890s: Essays on Labor and Politics,* Chicago: University of Illinois Press. 1999.

Science Museum, "A Century of Sucking: Did you Know?" (history of vacuum cleaners), http://www.sciencemuseum.org.uk/on-line/vacuums/index.asp. United Kingdom Science Museum. 2005.

Scott, Walter Dill, *Influencing Men in Business.* New York: The Ronald Press. 1911.

"70 Years of Tradition and Value," Stanley Home Products, http://www.shponline.com. 31 July, 2006.

Shaw, William Water, *Reveries of a Drummer.* Los Angeles: Sixth Avenue Publishing Company. 1926.

Shorris, Earl, *A Nation of Salesmen.* New York: W.W. Norton & Company. 1994.

Silver, A. David, *Entrepreneurial Megabucks: the 100 Greatest Entrepreneurs of the Last Twenty-Five years.* New York: John Wiley & Sons, 1985.

Slobodkina, Esphyr, *Caps for Sale.* New York: Harper Collins. 1968.

Smalley, Eric, "Agents learn from traveling salesman," Boston, MA: *Technology Research News.* 14 February, 2001.

Smith, Jessie Carney, (ed.), *Notable Black American Women.* Detroit: Gale Research, Inc. 1992.

"Snake Oil," HdLighthouse, http://www.hdlighthouse.org. (excerpted from *Fats that Heal, Fats that Kill: The Complete Guide to Fats, Oils, Cholesterols and Human Health* by Udo Erasmus, Alive Books. 1993).

Solberg, Helen M., Personal Letter to Norma and Ron Solberg. 7 January 2002.

"Sold Only by Subscription," http://www.etext.virginia.edu/railton/marketing/soldxsub.html. University of Virginia. March, 2007.

Spears, Timothy B., *100 Years on the Road.* New Haven, CT: Yale University Press. 1995.

Spignesi, Stephen, *American Firsts: Innovations, Discovered, and Gadgets Born in the U.S.A.* Franklin Lakes, NJ: New Page Books. 2004.

Stevenson, John Alford, *Salesmanship: Reading with a Purpose.* Chicago: American Library Association. 1929.

Stimson, A.L., "Commercial Travellers," *Hunt's Merchant Magazine and Commercial Review*: New York, Vol. 1, 1839.

Streeter, N.R., *Gems from an Old Drummer's Grip.* Groton, NY: The Compiler. 1889.

Strong, Edward K., *Psychological Aspects of Business.* New York: McGraw-Hill. 1938.

Stryker, Perrin, *The Incomparable Salesmen*. New York: McGraw-Hill. 1967.

Sutherland, Daniel E., *The Expansion of Everyday Life*. New York: Harper & Row. 1989.

Swafford, Jan, *Charles Ives: A Life with Music*. New York: W.W. Norton & Company. 1996.

Tedlow, Richard, *New and Improved: The Story of Mass Marketing in America*. New York: Basic Books, 1990.

Thayer, Wm. M., *Onward to Fame and Fortune or Climbing Life's Ladder*. New York: The Christian Herald. 1897.

"Thomas Chandler Haliburton," *Encyclopaedia Britannica*, http://www.britannica.com. Chicago: Encylopaedia Britannica, Inc., 2004.

Thomas, Landon, "Jay Van Andel Dies at 80 ... " *The New York Times*, 8 December, 2004.

Thomson, Andrew H., *The Feldman Method*. Lexington, KY: Lexington House. 1999.

"Timeline of American Bible Society, A," http://www.americanbible.org. New York: American Bible Society. 27, March, 2005.

Trafidlo, Greg, "Blue Ridge Minstrel Man," *Blue Ridge Country Magazine*, Jan-Feb., 1989.

Traveling Salesman Homepage, http://www.tsp.gatech.edu/hismain.html. 5 May, 2004.

Twyman, Robert W., *History of Marshall Field and Company, 1852-1906*. Philadelphia: University of Pennsylvania, 1954.

Untermeyer, Louis, (ed.) *A Treasury of Laughter*. New York: Simon and Schuster. 1946.

"Vacuum Cleaner," *Idea Finder*. http://www.ideafinder.com. 2005.

Vitale, Joe, *There's a Customer Born Every Minute*. Hoboken, NJ: John Wiley & Sons, Inc. 2006.

Vossler, Bill, "Salesman's Samples: Once a Sales Tool, Now a Window on the Past," *Farm Collector*. Topeka, KS: Ogden Publications. August, 2000.

Wadlington, Warwick, *The Confidence Game in American Literature*. Princeton, NJ: Princeton University Press, 1975.

Walden, William, "Birth of a Myth," http://www.pencollectors.com. Pen Collectors of America. 2002.

"Watkins Online," http://www.watkinsonline.com/history/timeline.cfm. January, 2004.

"W. Clement Stone," http://www.encyclopedia.thefreedictionary.com/W.%20Clement%20Stone. *Free Dictionary* by Farlex. 2006.

Weems-Botts Museum archives. *Bertrand Family Records, Virginia Genealogies* by The Rev. Horace Edwin Hayden; *Americans of Royal Descent* by Chas H. Browning; *An Encyclopedia of World History* by William L. Langer; *The Columbia Encyclopedia* by Columbia University Press; *The Encyclopedia Britannica*.

Wendt, Lloyd & Herman Kogan, *Give the Lady What She Wants: The Story of Marshall Field & Company*. South Bend, IN: And Books. 1952.

"William Wrigley, Jr.," http://en.wikipedia.org/wiki/William_Wrigley_Jr. May, 2007.

Williams, Anthony L., "Annie Turnbo Malone," http://www.isomedia.com. 23 January, 1905.

Wilson, R.L., *Colt: An American Legend*, New York: Abbeville Press. 1985.

Willson, Meredith, *The Music Man*, (Musical). Frank Music Corp and Meredith Willson Music. 1957.

Wisby, J.J., "The Commercial Traveler's Work of Civilization, *Arena Magazine*. New York: Alliance Publishing. Vol. 23, March, 1900.

Wright, Richardson, *Hawkers & Walkers in Early America*. Philadelphia: J.B. Lippincott Company. 1927.

"Yankee Pedler and Peddling in America," *The Penny Magazine*, London: Charles Knight & Company. Vol. 6, 1837.

Young, James Harvey, *The Toadstool Millionaires.* Princeton, NJ: Princeton University Press. 1961.

ENDNOTES

Foreword

1. Lee Copland, "A Return of the Salesman," *Chicago Tribune*. Business Technology, section 5. (August, 2002).
2. Truman Moore, *The Traveling Man*, (Garden City, NY: Doubleday & Company, 1972), 5
3. Timothy Spears, *100 Years on the Road*, (New Haven, CT: Yale University Press, 1995), Page ix.
4. Richardson Wright, *Hawkers and Walkers in America*, (Philadelphia, PA: JB Lippincott, 1927), 18-19.
5. Moore, 1.
6. A. L. Stimson, "Commercial Travellers," *Hunt's Merchant Magazine and Commercial Review* (New York, Vol. 1, 1939), 37-38.
7. Robert Hendrickson, *QPB Encyclopedia of Word and Phrase Origins*, (New York: Facts on File, 1997), 555.
8. Hendrickson, 733.
9. Lloyd Wendt and Herman Kogan, *Give the Lady What She Wants: The Story of Marshall Field & Company*, (South Bend, IN: And Books, 1952), 193.
10. Harper Lee, *To Kill a Mockingbird*, (Philadelphia, PA: J.B. Lippincott Company, 1960) 22-23.

Chapter 1

1. Solberg, personal recollection.
2. American Bible Society, "A Timeline of American Bible Society History," New York.http://www.americanbible.org (27 March, 2005).
3. American Tract Society, "Early History of the American Tract Society," http://www.atstracts.org New York, (27 March, 2005).
4. American Bible Society.
5. Walter A. Friedman, *Birth of a Salesman: The Transformation of Selling in America*, (Cambridge, MA: Harvard University Books, 2004), 103.
6. Friedman, 14.
7. Truman Moore, *The Traveling Man*, (Garden City, NY: Doubleday & Company, 1972), 53.
8. Robert Hendrickson, *QPB Encyclopedia of Word and Phrase Origins*, (New York: Facts on File, 1997), 38.
9. Richardson Wright, *Hawkers and Walkers in America*, (Philadelphia, PA: JB Lippincott, 1927), 232.
10. "Barbed Wire- The True Story," http://www.barbed-wire.net/blue/truehistory.html (December, 2001) and Jean F. Blashfield, *The Awesome Almanac*: Illinois. (Fontana, WI: B & B Publishing, 1993), 158-159.
11. *Barbed Wire Pioneers: Inventing a Community*. Produced by Dr. Jeffrey Chown. 52 minutes. (DeKalb, IL: Northern Illinois University, 1998).
12. Hendrickson, 98-99.
13. Timothy Spears, *100 Years on the Road*, (New Haven, CT: Yale University Press, 1995), 68.
14. Joel Levy, *Really Useful: The Origin of Everyday Things*. (Buffalo, NY: Firefly Books, 2002), 154-155.
15. Hendrickson, 139.
16. "Colportage and Book-Hawking," *Meliora: A Quarterly Review of Social Science in its Ethical, Economical, Political and Ameliorative Aspects* (London: S.W. Partridge, 1891, Vol. III), 311, 314.
17. L.P. Brockett, *The Commercial Traveller's Guide Book*, (New York: H. Dayton & Company, 1871), 27.
18. Friedman, 30.
19. Friedman, 160.
20. Perrin Stryker, *The Incomparable Salesmen*. (New York: McGraw-Hill, 1967), 36.
21. Harold Evans, *They Made America*, (New York: Little, Brown and Company, 2004), 468.
22. Moore, 27.
23. Friedman, 57.

24. Friedman, 86-87.
25. Hendrickson, 220.
26. "Dun & Bradstreet," *Wikipedia*, http://en.wikipedia.org/wiki/Dun_and_Bradstreet (July, 2006).
27. Stephen Spignesi, *American Firsts: Innovations Discovered, and Gadgets Born in the U.S.A.*, (Franklin Lakes, NJ: New Page Books, 2004), 107.
28. Hendrickson, 268.
29. Andrea Chesman (ed.), *The Inventive Yankee*, (New Hampshire: Yankee Books, 1989). 130-132.
30. "History of the Gideon Bible," *eSSORTMENT*, http://ky.essortment.com/gideonbible_rcwz.htm (29 July, 2006)
31. N.R. Streeter, *Gems from an Old Drummer's Grip*, (Groton, NY: The Compiler, 1889), 14-17.
32. Spears, 84.
33. L.C. Breyfogle, *The Commercial Traveler Hotel Guide and Gazetteer*, (Lockport, NY: The United States Hotel Register Publishing Company, 1881). In-book advertisement.
34. "Advertising Mascots-People: Duncan Hines," *TV Acres*, http://www.tvacres.com/admascots_hines.htm (29 July, 2006).
35. Hendrickson, 311.
36. Wright, 18-19.
37. Hendrickson, 343.
38. L. Frank Baum, *The Wonderful Wizard of Oz*, (New York: Dover Publications, Inc., 1960), 183, 186-187.
39. Hendrickson, 352.
40. Margaret Kruesi, "Herbs! Roots! Barks! Leaves!" *Folklife Center News*, Washington D.C.: Library of Congress American Folklife Center, (Fall, 2004), 6.
41. Evans, 108.
42. Friedman, 56-57.
43. Hendrickson, 383.
44. James Harvey Young, *The Toadstool Millionaires*, (Princeton, NJ: Princeton University Press, 1961). 192-193.
45. Brockett, 19-20.
46. Friedman, 145-147.
47. Stryker, 19-21.
48. Wendt, 192.
49. Richard Carver, A History of Marshall (Virginia Beach, VA: The Donning Company, 1993). 439
50. Carver, 441.
51. "Book Matches," *American Matchcover Collecting Club*, http://www.matchcovers.com (2003).
52. "MDRT History," *Million Dollar Round Table*, http://www.mdrt.org/history.html (January, 2007). And personal recollections.
53. "News & Events," National Association of Insurance and Financial Advisors, http://www.naifa.org/newsevents/factsheet.cfm (April, 2007)
54. David and Elizabeth Metzger Armstrong, *The Great American Medicine Show*, (New York: Prentice Hall, 1991), 174-175.
55. Ibid.
56. Brooks McNamara, *Step Right Up*, (Garden City, NY: Doubleday & Company, 1976). 195-196. These and many more pitchmen's terms are listed here.
57. Hendrickson. 708.
58. "The History of the Great American MoonPie," *Chattanooga Bakery*, http://www.moonpie.com (2005).
59. Hendrickson. 463.
60. *The Illustrated Railway Anecdote Book*, (selected for the reading of railway passengers), (London: Ward and Lock, 1870s). 111.
61. Charlie Crist, (Florida Attorney General) *State of Florida*,"How to Protect Yourself: Multilevel Marketing," http://myfloridalegal.com (2003).
62. "NAR Overview: History." *National Association of REALTORS*, http://www.realtor.org/realtororg.nsf/pages/NAROverview (April, 2007)
63. Armstrong. 159-160.
64. J.C. Furnas. *The Americans: A Social History of the United States 1587-1914*, (New York: G.P. Putnam & Sons, 1969). 907.

65. "Popular Medicine," *Vassar College*, http://iberia.vassar.edu/1896/medicine.html (December, 2001)
66. Friedman, 51.
67. Spears, 32.
68. Friedman, 19.
69. Armstrong, 175.
70. Tim Samuelson, (curator), *Isn't That Amazing: The Irresistible Appeal and Spiel of Ronco and Popeil*, (Chicago Cultural Center Exhibition, March-May, 2004).
71. Francis Russell, "Bubble, bubble — no toil, no trouble," *American Heritage* (Vol. XXIV, Number 2, 1973), 74-80.
72. Spegnesi, 188.
73. Hendrickson. 554.
74. Sharon Murphy, "Life Insurance in the United States through World War I," *EH.Net Encyclopedia*, (edited by Robert Whaples), http://eh.net/encyclopedia/article/murphy.life.insurance.us (August 15, 2002).
75. Bill Vossler, "Salesman's Samples: Once a Sales Tool, Now a Window on the Past," *Farm Collector*, (Topeka, KS: Ogden Publications, August, 2000), 6-9.
76. Hendrickson, 608.
77. Armstrong, 179.
78. "Snake Oil," *Hdlighthouse*, http://www.hdlighthouse.org, (excerpted from *Fats that Heal, Fats that Kill: The Complete Guide to Fats, Oils, Cholesterols and Human Health* by Udo Erasmus, Alive Books: 1993).
79. Friedman, 70.
80. Hendrickson, 633.
81. "70 Years of Tradition and Value," *Stanley Home Products*, http://www.shponline.com (July, 2006).
82. "Agents Wanted: Subscription Publishing in America, A Brief History of Subscription Publishing," *University of Pennsylvania*, http://www.library.upenn.edu/exhibits/rbm/agents/case2.html (March, 2007) and "Sold Only by Subscription," *University of Virginia*, http://etext.virginia.edu/railton/marketing/soldxsub.html (March 2007).
83. Stryker, 32.
84. Traveling Salesman Homepage, *Georgia Institute of Technology*, http://www.tsp.gatech.edu/hismain.html. (May, 2004).
85. Eric Smalley, "Agents learn from traveling salesman," *Technology Research News* (Boston, MA: 14 February, 2001).
86. Tim Samuelson, Presentation, "Isn't That Amazing: The Irresistible Appeal and Spiel of Ronco and Popeil," *Chicago Cultural Center* (8 April, 2004).
87. Personal recollection from professional involvement in insurance industry.
88. "Vacuum Cleaner," *IdeaFinder*, http:www.ideafinder.com (2005)
89. Spignesi, 241.
90. Hendrickson, 698.
91. Wendt, 193.
92. William Coyle, "From Scatology to Social History: Captain Billy's WhizBang," *Studies in American Humor*, http://www.compedit.com (2004)
93. Hendrickson, 213.
94. Francis Hunt, *American Anecdotes: Original and Select*, Vol. II, (Boston: Putnam & Hunt, 1830), 137-138.
95. J.R. Dolan, *The Yankee Peddlers of Early America*, (New York: Bramhall House, 1964), 10-11. and Hendrickson, 733-734.

Chapter 2

1. "History of Chewing gum," *Warner-Lambert Consumer Group Home*, http://www.gum-mints.com/conaffairs/historyofgum.html (December, 2001). And, Charles Panati, *Extraordinary Origins of Everyday Things*. (New York: Harper & Row, 1987). 417.
2. Richardson Wright, *Hawkers and Walkers in Early America*, (Philadelphia: J.B. Lippincott Company, 1927). 17. And, Amy Belding Brown, "Amos Bronson Alcott," *American Transcendentalism Web*, http://www.vcu.edu/engweb/transcendentalism/authors/alcott/ (Virginia Commonwealth University, 2006).

3. Sherwood Anderson, "Business Types — The Traveling Man," *Agricultural Advertising*, (11 April, 1904). 39-40.
4. Alfred. C. Fuller, *A Foot in the Door*, (New York: McGraw-Hill, 1960). 65-67.
5. "Mary Kay Ash," *Infoplease*, http://www.infoplease.com/ipa/A0880005.html (January, 2004).
6. Andrea Chesman (ed.), *The Inventive Yankee*, (Dublin, NH: Yankee Books, 1989). 122-123.
7. William Leach, *Land of Desire*, (New York: Pantheon Books, 1993). 57-61.
8. Frank Joslyn Baum and Russell P. MacFail, *To Please a Child; A Biography of L. Frank Baum Royal Historian of Oz*, (Chicago: Reilly & Lee Co., 1961). 23.
9. Edwin P. Hoyt, *The Supersalesmen*, (Cleveland: The World Publishing Company, 1962). 140-155.
10. Chesman, 123-124.
11. Richard Tedlow, *New and Improved: The Story of Mass Marketing in America*, (New York: Basic Books, 1990) 22, 112.
12. James N. Green, (edited by Michael Hackenberg) "From Printer to Publisher: Mathew Carey and the Origins of Nineteenth Century Book Publishing," *Getting the Books Out: Papers of the Chicago Conference on the Book in 19th-Century America*, (Washington: The Center for the Book, 1987). 36+.
13. Wright. 84-85.
14. Charles Panati, *Extraordinary Origins of Everyday Things*, (New York: Harper & Row, 1987). 247-248.
15. P.T. Barnum, *The Humbugs of the World: An Account of Humbugs, Delusions, Impositions, Quackeries, Deceits, and Deceivers, Generally in All Ages.* (New York: Carleton, 1866)
16. "Clark: A Historical Perspective," http://www.clarkbar.com/history.html (December, 2001).
17. R.L. Wilson, *Colt: An American Legend*, (New York: Abbeville Press, 1985). 4; andWilliam Hosley, *Colt: The Making of an American Legend*, (Amherst: University of Massachusetts Press, 1996). 15-16, 19.
18. Panati. 102.
19. "Davey Tree Expert Company," Kent State University. http://www.library.kent.edu/speccoll/reghist/history.html/.(December, 2001).
20. Axel Madsen, *The Deal Maker: How William C. Durant Made General Motors*. (Hoboken, NJ: John Wiley & Sons, 1999). 123.
21. Madsen. 28-29.
22. Walter A. Friedman, *Birth of a Salesman: The Transformation of Selling in America*. (Cambridge, MA: Harvard University Books, 2004). 190, 193.
23. Andrew H. Thomson, *The Feldman Method*, (Lexington, KY: Lexington House, 1999). 3-4.
24. Author Solberg's personal recollections: "In the mid-1970s, as the director of communications for the Million Dollar Round Table, I became familiar with many stories about Ben Feldman. One of the most intriguing is related to the filming of *The Man From East Liverpool.* The story goes, following the filming, several members of the production crew were so impressed with the "Feldman Method" that they were moved to buy life insurance policies from Ben.
25. Lloyd Wendt and Herman Kogan, *Give the Lady What She Wants: The Story of Marshall Field & Company.* (South Bend, IN: And Books, 1952). 53, 144.
26. Robert W. Twyman, *History of Marshall Field and Company*, 1852-1906. (Philadelphia: University of Pennsylvania, 1954). 94.
27. Nancy Koehn, *Brand New: How Entrepreneurs Earned Consumers' Trust From Wedgwood to Dell.* (Boston: Harvard Business School Press, 2001). 102.
28. Author Solberg's personal recollections: "During summer breaks from college I sold Fuller Brushes in Southern Minnesota for my father who was a field manager for the company."
29. Ibid.
30. "Gallaudet University-Thomas Hopkins Gallaudet: The Legacy Begins," http://www.pr.gallaudet.edu/VisitorsCenter/GallaudetHistory/index.html. (December, 2001).
31. Archie P. McDonald, "Bet-A-Million-Gates," East Texas Historical Association http://www.texasescapes.com/AllThingsHistorical/Bet-A-Million-Gates/ (Texas Escapes – Blueprints for Travel, February 16, 2005)
32. Truman E. Moore, *The Traveling Man*. (Garden City, NY: Doubleday & Company, 1972). 28.
33. Joel Levy, *Really Useful: The Origin of Everyday Things*. (Buffalo, NY: Firefly Books, 2002). 67.
34. "Gimbel," *Infoplease*, http://www.infoplease.com. 2004.

35. Maureen McDonald, "World-record salesman earns spot in Automotive Hall of Fame," *The Detroit News*, http://www.detroitnews.com.. (7 August, 2001).
36. Friedman. 100.
37. "Henry J. Heinz," *People of Pennsylvania*, Wikipedia. (Wikimedia Foundation, Inc: 29 July, 2006).
38. Alfred D. Chandler, Jr., *The Visible Hand: The Managerial Revolution in American Business.* (Cambridge, MA: Belknap Press of Harvard University Press, 1977). 505, 510.
39. Nancy F. Koehn, "Henry Heinz and Brand Creation in the Late Nineteenth-Century: Making Markets for Processed Food," *Business History Review.* (Winter, 2004). 73-75.
40. "Napoleon Hill," *TheFreeDictionary*, http://www.encyclopedia.thefreedictionary.com/ Napoleon+Hill.. (Farlex: 15 August, 2006).
41. "Duncan Hines, The History of," Duncan Hines Desserts, http://www.duncanhines.com/ DHAbout/default.asp. (15 August, 2006).
42. Doug Johnson (AP), http://missourifolkloresociety.Truman.edu, (19 July, 2005). And Ray Blunt, "Community Roots," http://www.lcweb2.loc.gov/cocoon/legacies(18 July, 2005) Seattle Post-Intelligencer, (11/15/99)
43. "Collis" Huntington," Spartacus Educational, http:// www.schoolnet.co.uk.USAhuntington.htm (15 August, 2006). And Dawn Emord and David Bushong, "Collis Huntington," The Transcontinental Railroad, http://www.bushong.net/ dawn/about/college/ids100/(15 August, 2006).
44. Friedman. 50
45. Perrin Stryker, *The Incomparable Salesmen.* (New York: McGraw-Hill, 1967). 28-41.
46. Jan Swafford, *Charles Ives: A Life with Music.* (New York: W.W. Norton & Company, 1996). 198.
47. "Charles Ives, Composer," Dallas Symphony Orchestra, http://www.dsokids.com/2001/dso/ asp. (December, 2001).
48. "John Chapman," *Encylopaedia Britannica*, Vol. II. (Chicago: Encyclopaedia Britannica, Inc., 1974). 746.
49. J.P. Johnson, *Twenty Years of Hus'ling.* (Chicago: Donohue Brothers, 1900). 82-88.
50. Walter Blair, *Tall Tale America: A Legendary History of our Humorous Heroes.* (Chicago: The University of Chicago Press, 1944, 1987). 23-25.
51. "Ann Sophia Stephens," *Encyclopaedia Britannica*, http://www.britannica.com. (Chicago: Encyclopaedia Britannica, Inc., 2004).
52. "McDonald's History," http://www.mcdonalds.com/corp/about/mcd_history.pg1.html. (McDonald's Corporation: January, 2004). And, Jean F. Blashfield, *The Awesome Almanac: Illinois.* (Fontana, WI: B & B Publishing. 1993). 161.
53. Michele Orecklin, "Notebook Milestones: Estee Lauder," *Time Magazine.* (10 May, 2004). 26.
54. Panati. 388-389.
55. Chris King, "The Mountain Minstrel," *Spectator Magazine*, (Raleigh, NC, 10 October, 1996). 9-10.
56. Greg Trafidlo, "Blue Ridge Minstrel Man," *Blue Ridge Country Magazine.* (Jan-Feb, 1989) 32-33, 42.
57. Harold Evans, *They Made Americ*a, (New York: Little, Brown, and Company, 2004) 255.
58. Jessie Carney Smith (ed.), *Notable Black American Women.* (Detroit: Gale Research, Inc., 1992). 724-726. And, Anthony L. Williams, "Annie Turnbo Malone," http:// www.isommedia.com. (23 January, 1905
59. "Og Mandino: Greatest Salesman Home Page," http://www.ogmandino.com. (The Greatest Salesman, 2005).
60. "Richard Martin takes out 1st life insurance policy." http://www.brainyhistory.com. (BrainyMedia, 2006).
61. Hoyt. 160.
62. Truman E. Moore, *The Traveling Man.* (Garden City, NY: Doubleday & Company, 1972). 161; and, Panati. 243-244.
63. David Armstrong and Elizabeth Metzger Armstrong, *The Great American Medicine Show.* (New York: Prentice Hall, 1991). 175.
64. Ibid., 180.
65. James Harvey Young, *The Toadstool Millionaires.* (Princeton, NJ: Princeton University Press, 1961). 191.
66. Edward E. Palmer, *Forty Years of Hustling.* (Wooster, OH: Edward E. Palmer, 1942). 352-356.

67. Moore. 28.
68. Evans. 359.
69. Friedman. 148-150.
70. Evans. 359.
71. "Mr. Charles William Post," http://www.postexas.com/CWPostHHistory.htm. (Maxine Durrett Earl Charitable Foundation, Inc.: 16 August, 2006)
72. Steve Barth, "Britannica on the Virtual Bookshelf," *Knowledge Management Magazine*. http://www.destinationkm.com. (September, 2000)
73. "Hotel de Paris: Salesman Room," Hotel de Paris Museum, http://www.hoteldeparismuseum.org. (National Society of Colonial Dames of America in Colorado, 2005).
74. Armstrong. 175.
75. Robert Hendrickson, *QPB Encyclopedia of Word and Phrase Origins*, (New York: Facts on File, 1997). 555.
76. John H. Lienhard, "Engines of our Ingenuity," http://www.uh.edu. (University of Houston: 1988-1990); and, "Thomas Chandler Halliburton," Encyclopaedia Britannica. http://www.britannica.com . (Chicago: Encyclopaedia Britannica, Inc. 2004)
77. Panati. 262-263.
78. Friedman. 173-186.
79. "Dr. Forrest C. Shaklee," http:www.enfuselle.com/main/aboutinfo (Pleasanton, CA: Shaklee Corporation 2007)
80. Elizabeth M. Bacon, "Marketing Sewing Machines in the Post-Civil War Years." *Bulletin of the Business Historical Society*. (Boston: Vol. XX, No. 3, June 1946). 92-93.
81. C.L. Miller, "Skiff & Ross, The Jewel Tea Company," Hall China Collectors' Home Page, http://www.inter-services.com/HallChina/jhistory.html. (East Liverpool, OH: Marty Kennedy, 1998).
82. Moore. 27-28.
83. Ibid. 33.
84. Evans. 108-113.
85. "The History of Mrs. Stewart's Bluing," http://www.mrsstewart.com.pages/msbhistory.htm. (Luther Ford & Company, 2001).
86. "W. Clement Stone," http://www.encyclopedia, thefreedictionary.com/W.%20Clement%20Stone .(The Free Dictionary by Farlex, 2006).
87. Ben Harris McClary, (ed.), *The Lovingood Papers*, (Athens, TN:The Sut Society, 1962). 19.
88. Ibid. 21.
89. Wright. 78-79.
90. Moore. 16.
91. Charles de Coster, *The Legend of Ulenspiegel and Lamme Goedzak and Their Adventures Heroical, Joyous and Glorious in the Land of Flanders and Elsewhere*, Vol. 1, translated by F.M. Atkinson. (Garden City, NY: Doubleday, Page & Company, 1922). 39.
92. Ibid. 41.
93. Chesman. 133-135.
94. Landon Thomas, "Jay Van Andel Dies at 80 . . ." *The New York Times*, (NY: Times Publishing Co, 8 December, 2004). A29.
95. Doron Levin, "Fate, patience bring DeVos a new heart; Amway cofounder back after journey for life," (Detroit, MI: Detroit Free Press, 8 October, 1997).
96. Traveling Salesman Homepage, *Georgia Institute of Technology*, http://www.tsp.gatech.edu/hismain.html. (5 May, 2004).
97. "Madame C.J. Walker," *The Faces of Science: African Americans in the Sciences*, http://www.princeton.edu/~mcbrown/display/walker.html,Princeton University, 2005.
98. "Adventures of a Woman Book Agent," *University of Virginia*, http://etext.virginia.edu/railton/marketin/facts2.html (March, 2007).
99. "Watkins Online," http://www.watkinsonline.com/history/timeline.cfm. (January, 2004)
100. *A Moving Journey*, (plus update), "20/20," television report, (New York: ABC News Productions, 24 December, 1999) T991224-02.
101. Hoyt. 194-197.
102. Ibid. 205-207.
103. Wright. 53-54.
104. Moore. 26.

105. Theodore F. Marburg, "Manufacturers Drummer," *Bulletin of the Business Historical Society*, vol. 22, No. 2, (April, 1948). 40-56.
106. Jean F. Blashfield, *The Awesome Almanac*: Illinois. (Fontana, WI: B & B Publishing, 1993).126, 156.
107. "William Wrigley Jr.," http:en.wikipedia.org/wiki/William_Wrigley_Jr.(May, 2007)
108. Robert Cummings, "Zig Ziglar," http://www.olemiss.edu/mwp/dir/ziglar.zig/.(Yazoo, MS: Yazoo County Convention and Visitors Bureau, 18 January, 2004).

Chapter 3

1. Truman E. Moore, *The Traveling Man*. (Garden City, NY: Doubleday & Company, 1972). 161; and Charles Panati, *Extraordinary Origins of Everyday Things*. (New York: Harper & Row, 1987). 243-244.
2. Moore. 161. Panati. 243-244.
3. "Mary Kay Ash," InfoPlease
4. Michele Orecklin, "Notebook Milestones: Esteé Lauder," *Time Magazine*. (10 May, 2004). 26.
5. Harold Evans, *They Made America*, (New York: Little, Brown, and Company, 2004) 255.
6. Jessie Carney Smith (ed.), *Notable Black American Women*. (Detroit: Gale Research, Inc., 1992). 724-726. And, Anthony L. Williams, "Annie Turnbo Malone," http://www.isommedia.com. (23 January, 1905
7. "Madame C.J. Walker," *The Faces of Science: African Americans in the Sciences*, http://www.princeton.edu/~mcbrown/display/walker.html, Princeton University, 2005.
8. Ibid.
9. Evans. 256.
10. Ibid. 257.
11. Chris Jones, "'Sarah Breedlove' reflects lives of 2 strong women," (Chicago Tribune, June 29, 2006) Temp Section, 1-2, and Jenn Q Goddu, "C. J. Walker's Rise from Rags to Riches, Power," *Chicago Tribune,* Section 7. (June 16, 2007).
12. Robert Price, *Johnny Appleseed: Man & Myth*, (Urbana, OH: Urbana University Press, 2001). 42.
13. Richardson Wright, *Hawkers and Walkers in Early America*, (Philadelphia: J.B. Lippincott Company, 1927). 215.
14. Robert C. Harris (ed.) *Johnny Appleseed Source Book* (n.d.) (originally appeared in the *Old Fort News*, Vol. IX, Nos. 1-2, March-June, 1945). Johnny Appleseed Museum Archives.
15. Bill J. Cook, *The Johnny Appleseed Pew* , (Cincinnati, OH: Gruber Printing Company, 1977). 3.
16. Price. 224.
17. Ibid. 38-40.
18. Michael Pollan, *The Botany of Desire*, (New York: Random House, 2001) 27-28.
19. Price. 34.
20. Pollan. 27.
21. Philip Roth, *American Pastoral*. (New York: Vintage International, 1977). 316.
22. Pollan. 56.
23. Reeve Lindbergh, (daughter of Chas. & Anne Morrow Lindbergh), *Johnny Appleseed*, (New York: Little, Brown and Company, 1990). 13.
24. Philip Alexander Bruce, *Economic History of Virginia in the Seventeenth Century*, (New York: Peter Smith, 1935). 377.
25. Ron Popeil, *Salesman of the Century*, (New York: Delacorte Press, 1995). Dust jacket blurb.
26. Ibid. 12-13.
27. Ibid. 18-19.
28. Ibid. 26-27.
29. "Ron Popeil," http://www.ideafinder.com/history/inventors/popeil.htm. (27 July, 2005)
30. Tim Samuelson, *But, Wait! There's More!* (New York: Rizzoli International Publications, Inc. 2002). 9.
31. Popeil. 63.
32. Ibid. 288.
33. Wright. 53.
34. Lewis Leary, *The Book-Peddling Parson*, (Chapel Hill, NC: Algonquin Books, 1984). 1
35. Ibid. 3,7.

36. Wright. 54.
37. Lewis Leary, *The Book-Peddling Parson,* (Chapel Hill, NC: Algonquin Books, 1984). 1.
38. Ibid.. 3
39. Ibid. 35-36.
40. Ibid. 79.
41. Stanley J. Kunitz and Howard Haycraft, *American Authors 1600-1900.* (New York: H.W. Wilson Company, 1966). 794.
42. Leary. 101.
43. Ibid. 97-98.
44. Harold Kellock, *Parson Weems of the Cherry-Tree* . citing Albert Bushnell Hart, "Historical Liars." (New York: The Century Co., 1928), 88. (Weems-Botts Museum Archives)
45. H. Jack Lang, *Lincoln's Fireside Reading* (Cleveland: The World Publishing Co., 1965). 9-10. (Weems-Botts Museum Archives)
46. Ibid. 9-10.
47. William E. S. Flory, *Parson Weems – First Biographer of Washington,* —an address presented at a meeting of the Historic Dumfries, Virginia, Inc., at the Dumfries Town Hall, February 6, 1975. (Weems-Botts Museum Archives)
48. Charles Chapin, "Old Technology – Printed Words," presentation, Springfield, IL: Illinois State Historical Society Symposium. (4 December, 2004).
49. William E. S. Flory, "Parson Weems- Marketer," presentation at a meeting of Historic Dumfries, Virginia, Inc. at the Dumfries Town Hall, 3 February, 1977. (Weems-Botts Museum Archives)
50. Hendrickson. 549.
51. Flory, "Parson Weems-Marketer."
52. Wright. 53-54.

Chapter 4

1. Truman Moore, *The Traveling Man,* (Garden City, NY: Doubleday & Company, 1972), 7.
2. Timothy Spears, *100 Years on the Road,* (New Haven, CT: Yale University Press, 1995), 109.
3. "This was Whiz Bang," *Captain Billy's Whiz Bang,* (Greenwich, CT: Fawcett Publications, Inc., 1972), Inside front cover.
4. Moore, 51.
5. No credit is provided for this and other material in this chapter because it was discovered that (except for several longer poems) these jokes and stories are rarely original. Repeated examples were found of the same story (with only minor alterations) which appeared again and again in a variety of sources over many decades (sometimes going back more than 100 years). However, when a book or publication occasionally references an author or source, we do provide credit. See Bibliography for important books and other sources concerning this topic.

Chapter 5

1. Francis Hunt, *American Anecdotes: Original and Select, Vol II,* (Boston: Putnam & Hunt, 1830). 254-255.
2. Hunt. 203-204.
3. Hunt. Vol. I. 59-60.
4. Pierce Pungent, *Chit-chat of Humor, Wit and Anecdote,* (New York: Stringer & Townsend, 1857). 340-342.
5. Hunt. Vol. I. 137-138.
6. N. R. Streeter, N.R., (ed.) *Gems from an Old Drummer's Grip,* (Groton, NY: The Compiler. 1889). 18-19.
7. Alfred H. Miles, (ed.), *One Thousand & One Anecdotes,* (New York: Thomas Whittaker. 1895). 260.
8. W. I. Pattison, W. I., *How 'Tis Done.* (Syracuse, NY, 1890). 186-190.
9. Pattison. 5.
10. Harry Ellsworth Cole, *Stagecoach and Tavern Tales,* (Carbondale & Edwardsville, IL: Southern Illinois University Press. 1997). 228.
11. Miles. 262-263.

12. Johnston, J.P., *Twenty Years of Hus'ling*, (Chicago: Donohue Brothers. 1900). 82-88.
13. Miles. 260.
14. Thomas Masson, Thomas L., *Little Masterpieces of American Wit and Humor*. Volume II, (New York: Doubleday, Page and Company. 1904). 144.
15. Bruce Barton, *The Man Nobody Knows*, (New York: Grossett & Dunlap. 1924). Foreword.
16. Barton. 5.
17. Barton. Foreword.
18. A much decorated hero of France's WWII Resistance, Gilbert Renault who, under the *nom de guerre* Colonel Remy, organized for Charles de Gaulle the Free French intelligence service.
19. Alfred C. Fuller, *A Foot in the Door*. (New York: McGraw-Hill. 1960). 224-226.
20. Colleen Mastony, "Gave Puppy that Saved Nixon," (Chicago, IL: *The Chicago Tribune*: 17 May, 2006). obituary.
21. Author's personal recollection. While working for the Million Dollar Round Table. Solberg heard the story of the MDRT member making the sale(s).
22. Burt Constable, "Salesman's email becomes a Fuller brush with the Past," (Des Plaines, IL: *Daily Herald*:. 12 June, 2004).
23. Barry Becher & Edward Valenti, *The Wisdom of Ginsu*, (Franklin Lakes, NJ: Career Press, 2005). 208.

INDEX

See also Quotations Section following Index, page 331.

FAMOUS QUOTATIONS

Arranged alphabetically by first line. See Index for individual author listings.